LIFE AND LETTERS

OF

WASHINGTON IRVING.

Washington Irving

Sunnyside Decr 15th 1851

The Gale Library of Lives and Letters
American Writers Series

THE

LIFE AND LETTERS

OF

WASHINGTON IRVING.

BY HIS NEPHEW

PIERRE M. IRVING.

VOLUME IV.

NEW YORK:
G. P. PUTNAM, 441 BROADWAY.
1864.

THE copious INDEX to these volumes has been kindly prepared, as a labor of love, by S. AUSTIN ALLIBONE, LL. D., of Philadelphia. The value of this service will be readily appreciated by many readers. It has been tendered in the midst of laborious application on his own great work, the "Dictionary of Authors." The article in the first volume of that work on the Life and Works of Irving, was remarkable for its comprehensive collection of facts and opinions.

Among the many letters of Mr. Irving to authors, which the editor has been unable to quote in the limits of these volumes, is one to Dr. Allibone, expressing a warm appreciation of the important contribution to literary history which Dr. Allibone is now engaged in completing.

CONTENTS.

CHAPTER V.

CHAPTER VI.

CHAPTER VII.

CHAPTER VIII.

CHAPTER IX.

APPENDIX.

(A.)

CHAPTER XXIII.

CHAPTER XXIV.

(B.)

(C.)

LIFE AND LETTERS

OF

WASHINGTON IRVING.

CHAPTER I.

M R. IRVING had for some time had it in contemplation to publish a revised and uniform
edition of his works, to which he had been strongly
urged. He was apt to be dilatory, however, in the
execution of his literary purposes ; and the intimation
thrown out to me in his late letter, quoted in the last
chapter, of the "rubbish" he had been working up to
pay for his new building, had awakened some concern
lest he should be losing sight of this object. I replied
to it therefore, that, though glad to learn he had been

at work with his pen in any way, I was chiefly anxious at present to have him commence with the uniform edition of his works, for which there was an expectation and demand. " You lost the Conquest of Mexico," I remark in the letter now before me, " by not acting upon the motto of *Carpe diem ;* and I am a little afraid you may let slip the present opportunity for a favorable sale of a uniform edition of your works, by suffering your pen to be diverted in a new direction. A literary harvest is before you from this source, on which you could reckon with confidence *now*, but which might turn to barrenness under a future pressure in the money market, of which many are not without misgivings at this moment. Therefore

    ' Now's the day and now's the hour.' "

He writes, in reply, April 14 :

Don't snub me about my late literary freak. I am not letting my pen be diverted in a new direction. I am, by a little agreeable exertion, turning to account a mass of matter that has been lying like lumber in my trunks for years. When I was in Madrid, in 1826–'27, just after I had finished Columbus, I commenced a series of Chronicles illustrative of the wars between the Spaniards and the Moors; to be given as the productions of a monk, Fray Antonio Agapida. The Conquest of Granada was the only one I finished, though I roughly sketched out parts of some others. Your uncle Peter was always anxious for me to carry out my plan, but, somehow or other, I let it grow cool. The Chronicle of the Conquest of

Granada was not so immediately successful as I had anticipated, though it has held its way better than many other of
my works which were more taking at first.   I am apt to get
out of conceit of anything I do ; and I suffered the manuscript
of these Chronicles to lie in my trunks like waste paper.   About
four or five weeks since, I was tired, one day, of muddling
over my printed works, and yet wanted occupation.   I don't
know how the idea of one of these Chronicles came into my
head.   It was the Chronicle of Count Fernan Gonzalez, one
of the early Counts of Castile.   It makes about sixty or eighty
pages of my writing.   I took it up, was amused with it, and
found I had hit the right vein in my management of it.   I
went to work and rewrote it, and got so in the spirit of the
thing, that I went to work, *con amore*, at two or three fragmentary Chronicles, filling up the chasms, rewriting parts.   In
a word, I have now complete, though not thoroughly finished
off, The Chronicle of Pelayo ; The Chronicle of Count Fernan
Gonzalez ; the Chronicle of the Dynasty of the Ommiades in
Spain, giving the succession of those brilliant sovereigns, from
the time that the Moslem empire in Spain was united under the
first, and fell to pieces at the death of the last of them ; also
the Chronicle of Fernando the Saint, with the reconquest of
Seville.   I may add others to the series; but if I do not,
these, with additions, illustrations, &c., will make a couple of
volumes ; and I feel confident that I can make the work a
taking one—giving a picture of Spain at various periods of the
Moorish domination, and giving illustrations of the places of
noted events, from what I myself have seen in my rambles
about Spain.   Some parts of these Chronicles run into a quiet,
drolling vein, especially in treating of miracles and miraculous
events ; on which occasion Fray Antonio Agapida comes to

my assistance, with his zeal for the faith, and his pious hatred of the infidels. You see, all this has cost me but a very few weeks of amusing occupation, and has put me quite in heart again, as well as in literary vein. The poring over my published works was rather muddling me, and making me feel as if the true literary vein was extinct. I think, therefore, you will agree with me that my time for the last five weeks has been well employed. I have secured the frame and part of the finish of an entire new work, and can now put it by to be dressed off at leisure.

Before I received this letter, having heard from a relative who was staying with him that he had been busy with some of his old Moorish Chronicles, I wrote him that I had a very agreeable through indistinct recollection of the manuscripts, and had no doubt of his working them up with effect, but still suggested a suspension of the publication, adding that the reading world might not be content with these literary " skimmings," while waiting with impatience the appearance of a uniform edition of his works now out of print. I added : " Make all despatch with the preparation of your uniform edition, and then to work to complete your Life of Washington, and take your ease forever after."

In reading the reply which I give below, the reader will bear in mind that my ill-starred epistle was despatched in *advance* of the receipt of the author's interesting letter of the 14th, giving me an insight into the character of his new labors, dwelling with such evident satisfaction on his "literary freak," and showing the attraction he felt in the theme.

[*To Pierre M. Irving.*]

SUNNYSIDE, April 15, 1847.

MY DEAR PIERRE:

I am glad I did not receive your note of this morning before my new work was beyond the danger of being chilled by a damper. You can know nothing of the work, excepting what you may recollect of an extract of one of the Chronicles which I once published in the Knickerbocker.* The whole may be mere "skimmings," but they pleased me in the preparation; they were written when I was in the vein, and that is the only guide I go by in my writings, or which has led me to success. Besides, I write for pleasure as well as profit; and the pleasure I have recently enjoyed in the recurrence, after so long an interval, of my old literary vein, has been so great, that I am content to forego any loss of profit it may occasion me by a slight postponement of the republication of my old works.

These old Morisco Spanish subjects have a charm that makes me content to write about them at half price. They have so much that is highminded and chivalrous and quaint and picturesque and adventurous, and at times half comic about them.

However, I'll say no more on the subject, but another time will ride my hobby privately, without saying a word about it to anybody. I have generally found that the best way. I am too easily dismounted, if any one jostles against me.

* Pelayo and the Merchant's Daughter.

VOL. IV.—(2)

The letter of the 14th, which, had it been received earlier, would have prevented my second unlucky epistle, like a thing "born out of due time," came straggling in on the 17th, two days *after* the letter just cited had been received by me. I was sufficiently annoyed at the consequences of the untimely potion I had so unwittingly administered, especially with the insight now afforded of the character of the work; and I wrote him immediately, explaining and recanting as far as I could, but in vain. He had been disconcerted, and would not resume the theme.

In the following letter, however, written a fortnight later, he returns to the subject in his characteristically playful vein, his annoyance having passed off almost with the letter that gave expression to it.

[*To Mrs. Pierre M. Irving.*]

SUNNYSIDE, April 30, 1847.

* * * The girls say you can come up to Sunnyside as soon as you please. * * * To-day my "women kind" of the kitchen remove bag and baggage into the new *tower*, which is getting its outside coat of white; so that, when you come up, you will find it, like the trees, in full blossom. The country is beginning to look lovely; the buds and blossoms are just putting forth; the birds are in full song; so that, unless you come up soon, you will miss the overture of the season—the first sweet notes of the year.

You tell me Pierre was quite distressed lest any "thoughtless word of his should have marred my happy literary mood."

Tell him not to be uneasy. Authors are not so easily put out of conceit of their offspring. Like the good archbishop of Granada, that model and mirror of authorship, I knew "the homily in question to be the very best I had ever composed;" so, like my great prototype, I remained fixed in my self-complacency, wishing Pierre "toda felicidad con un poco de mas gusto."

When I once get you up to Sunnyside, I shall feel sure of an occasional Sunday visit from Pierre. I long extremely to have a sight of him; and as there seems to be no likelihood of my getting to New York much before next autumn, I do not know how a meeting is to be brought about unless he comes up here. I shall see him with the more ease and confidence now, as, my improvements being pretty nigh completed, he cannot check me, nor cut off the supplies.

Tell him I promise not to bore him about literary matters when he comes up. I have as great a contempt for these things as anybody, though I have to stoop to them occasionally for the sake of a livelihood; but I want to have a little talk with him about stocks, and railroads, and some mode of screwing and jewing the world out of more interest than one's money is entitled to.

God bless you and him, prays your affectionate uncle,

WASHINGTON IRVING.

Late in the winter, Mr. Irving had commissioned his brother-in-law, Mr. Henry Van Wart, then on a visit to this country, to purchase a saddle horse for him. He had not mounted a horse since he went to Spain, but began to feel the necessity of this sort of exercise.   March 5th, Mr. Van Wart writes him: "I have at last succeeded in finding a horse which I think will suit you, and purchased him for $110.   He is handsome, and the best-tempered, gentle creature I ever saw ; and I think you will take much pleasure in riding him."   The horse, after being kept in a stable in New York for several weeks, and used and trained by Mr. Van Wart and his son Irving, was brought to Sunnyside toward the close of April.   Here is the first report of his qualifications by the long-dismounted equestrian :

SUNNYSIDE, April 26, 1847.

MY DEAR PIERRE:

    *   *   *   The horse purchased by Mr. Van Wart is a very fine animal, and very gentle, but he does not suit me.   I have ridden him once, and find him, as I apprehended, awkward and uncomfortable on the trot, which is the gait I most like.   He is rather skittish also, and has laid my coachman in the dust by one of his pirouettes.   This, however, might be the effect of being shut up in the stable of late, and without sufficient exercise ; but he is quite a different horse from the easy, steady, quiet "parson's" nag that I wanted.   I shall give him one more good trial, but rather apprehend I shall have to send him to town, to be sold for what he will fetch.

April 28th, he writes me :

In my letter, the other day, I spoke rather disparagingly of my new horse.   Justice to an injured animal induces me to leave the enclosed letter open for your perusal, after which you will hand it to I. V. W.

Here follows the letter enclosed :

SUNNYSIDE, April 28, 1847.

MY DEAR IRVING :

In a letter to Pierre M. Irving, the other day, I gave an unfavorable opinion of the horse, as it regarded my peculiar notions and wishes. That opinion was founded on a slight trial. I yesterday took a long ride on him among the hills, and put him through all his paces, and found him fully answering the accounts given of him by your father and yourself. His trot is not what I could wish ; but that will improve, or will be less disagreeable as we become accustomed to each other, and get into each other's ways. He shies a little now and then, but that is probably the result of having him kept in the stable of late, without use. Daily exercise will in a great measure cure him of it. He canters well, and walks splendidly. His temper appears to be perfect. He is lively and cheerful, without the least heat or fidgetiness, and is as docile as a lamb. I tried him also in harness in a light wagon, and found him just as gentle and tractable as under the saddle. He looks well and moves well in single harness, and a child might drive him. However, I mean to keep him entirely for the saddle. To conclude : when you write to your father, tell him I consider the horse a prize ; and if he only continues to behave as well as he did yesterday, I hardly know the sum of money would tempt me to part with him.

I now look forward to a great deal of pleasant and healthy exercise on horseback—a recreation I have not enjoyed for years for want of a good saddle horse. It is like having a new sense.

And he did enjoy his first rides wonderfully. " Instead," he says, " of being pinned down to one place, or forced to be trundled about on wheels, I went lounging and cantering about the country, in all holes and corners, and over the roughest roads."

In less than a month, however, the same horse was conducted to the city by the nephew to whom the preceding letter was addressed, and sold at Tattersall's; and here is the closing chapter of his equestrian experience with the animal whom he had hoped to find such a prize:

You are pleased to hear (he writes to his niece in Paris, Mrs. Storrow, June 6) that I have a saddle horse. Unfortunately, I have him no longer. Your uncle Van Wart purchased one for me, which appeared to be all that I could wish —handsome, young, gentle, and of excellent movement. I rode him two or three times, and was delighted with him, when, one day, the lurking fault came out. As I was taking a sauntering ride over the Sawmill River, and had gone a couple of miles, he all at once stopped, and declined to go any farther. I tried all manner of means, but in vain; he would do nothing but return home. On my way homeward, I tried him by different roads, but all to no purpose; home he would go. He was not restive, but calmly stubborn, and, when I endeavored to force him round, would quietly back against the fence, or get on two legs. So, as I did not care to waste time or temper on a sullen beast, home I did go—got off his back, and never mounted him again. He balked twice in like manner, but not so bad, with my coachman; so I gave him over to I. V. W., to be sold at auction, and was glad to get rid of him with the loss of twenty or thirty dollars. I shall not indulge in another saddle horse at present.

The new building being finished and inhabited, and the alterations and additions having turned out beyond his hopes, both as to appearance and convenience, Mr. Irving, in felicitating himself upon his internal improvements, writes to the same correspondent, June 6:

The north end of my study has been shelved like the other parts; the books which so long were exiled to the garret, have been brought down and arranged, and my library now makes a very respectable appearance.

Then passing from the internal to the external improvements:

As to my grounds, I have cut down and transplanted enough trees to furnish two ordinary places, and still there are, if anything, too many; but I have opened beautiful views, and have given room for the air to circulate. The season is now in all its beauty; the trees in full leaf, but the leaves fresh and tender; the honeysuckles are in flower, and I think I never saw the place look so well.

August 13, 1847, he writes to Mrs. Charlotte I. Grinnell, a niece recently severed from his household by marriage, in her new home on Cayuga Lake:

* * * For a month past I have been busy and bothered in an unexampled manner, in the improvement of my

farmyard, building of outhouses, &c., which has been altogether the most fatiguing and irksome job I have had in the whole course of my additions and improvements. I have now nearly got through, but it has almost made me fit to lie by again on the sofa. However, this job finished, I shall have my place in tolerable order, and will have little more to do than to see that my men keep it so.

Ten days later, he writes to Mrs. Storrow, at Paris:

* * * This has been a toilful year to me; for, after I had completed the additions to my house, I proceeded to bring my place into complete order, to enclose a kitchen yard, to enclose the stable, and make a large farmyard, poultry yard, outhouses, &c.; and working as much as possible with my own people, and planning and superintending everything my-self, it has kept me continually on my legs in the heat of the summer, fagged me excessively, and kept up and increased the inflammation of my unlucky ankles. I have now got through with all the essential improvements, and shall be able to give myself repose. * * * I have the satisfaction to have brought my place into order, and to have put it in a condition to be comfortably and conveniently managed hereafter. It is a snug establishment both within doors and without.

Four days later, he writes, after alluding to the improved beauty of the country in that neighborhood:

My own place has never been so beautiful as at present. I have made more openings by pruning and cutting down trees, so that from the piazza I have several charming views of the

Tappan Zee and the hills beyond, all set, as it were, in verdant frames; and I am never tired of sitting there in my old Voltaire chair, of a long summer morning, with a book in my hand, sometimes reading, sometimes musing, and sometimes dozing, and mixing all up in a pleasant dream.

To his sister, at Birmingham, Mrs. Van Wart, who had not seen her native city in forty years, he writes, August 29, 1847:

I often think what a strange world you would find yourself in, if you could revisit your native place, and mingle among your relatives. New York, as you knew it, was a mere corner of the present huge city; and that corner is all changed, pulled to pieces, burnt down and rebuilt—all but our little native nest in William street, which still retains some of its old features, though those are daily altering.* I can hardly realize that, within my term of life, this great crowded metropolis, so full of life, bustle, noise, show, and splendor, was a quiet little city of some fifty or sixty thousand inhabitants. It is really now one of the most racketing cities in the world, and reminds me of one of the great European cities (Frankfort, for instance) in the time of an annual fair. Here it is a fair almost all the year round. For my part, I dread the noise and turmoil of it, and visit it but now and then, preferring the quiet of my country retreat; which shows that the bustling time of life is over with me, and that I am settling down into a sober, quiet, good-for-nothing old gentleman. * * *

* This dwelling—No. 128 William street—the first home of which Washington or the sister to whom he was writing had any recollection, was pulled down in May, 1849, and a large edifice built on its site.

I am scribbling this letter while the family are all at church. I hear the carriage at a distance, and shall soon have all hands at home. Oh! my dear sister, what would I give if you and yours could this day be with us, and join the family gathering round my board. Every day I regret more and more this severance of the different branches of the family which casts us so widely asunder, with an ocean between us.

Eleven days later (September 9), he writes to Mrs. Paris:

I have just finished my last job, making a new ice pond in a colder and deeper place, in the glen just opposite our entrance gate; and now I would not undertake another job, even so much as to build a wren coop, for the slightest job seems to swell into a toilsome and expensive operation.

The following letter is addressed to a favorite little grandniece at Paris, daughter of Mrs. Storrow, who had sent him an offering of one of her first efforts at sewing—the same of whom he says, in another letter: "Kate, who was my idol when I was in Paris, and used to take such possession of me, and oblige me to *put away my spectacles*, and give up my book, and entertain her for the hundredth time with the story of little Miss Muss and Hempen House."

[*To Miss Kate Storrow.*]

SUNNYSIDE, August 27, 1847.

MY DEAR KATE;

I thank you very much for the beautiful handkerchief which you have sent me. I am very proud of it, and show it to everybody, to let them see how capitally my dear little Kate can sew. I hope you will teach Tutu to handle her needle as well as you do, and then you and she will be able to do all your mamma's sewing, which will be a great saving to her, and a great help to Henriette.

I am happy to hear that you have a nice little new sister. I trust, as you are a big girl now, you will take great care of her; and, above all things, set her a good example, by being a very good girl yourself, and very obedient to your mamma. As soon as she is old enough, you must take her with you and Tutu to the garden of the Tuileries, and show her to the little fish that used to give good little Betsey Posy a silver dish, and tell him that this is the new little sister of Betsey Posy and Jenny Posy, and that her name is Julie Posy, and then perhaps he will give her a silver dish also.

Give my love to Tutu, and remember me kindly to Nanna and Aya.   Your affectionate uncle,

WASHINGTON IRVING.

Though not in the order of time, I give in this place two other letters to the same little favorite, as specimens of the happy playfulness with which he adapted himself to the minds of children:

[*To the same.*]

SUNNYSIDE, July 15, 1852.

MY DEAR KATE:

I thank you for your charming little letter. It is very well expressed and very nicely written, and, what pleases me most of all, it is written to me. You must have had a pleasant time at Compeigne with such an agreeable party. I recollect the place well, and the beautiful palace, with the pretty boudoir which you all liked so much because there was a glass there in which you saw yourselves four times. I did not notice that glass, and therefore was not so much struck with the boudoir. I recollect Pierrefond also, and was all over the ruins and the surrounding forest, which put me in mind of what I had read about old castles in fairy tales. If I could only have seen you driving through the forest in your open carriage with four white horses, I should have thought you one of the enchanted princesses. You should take care how you venture out of your carriage in such a place to gather lilies of the valley and other wild flowers. Don't you know what happened once to a young lady (I think her name was Proserpine), who was carried off by a wicked king in sight of her mamma, as she was gathering flowers in the same way you were? Your mamma will tell you the story, if you have not heard it.

You say you would like to live at Compeigne always, it is so pretty, and you passed your time so pleasantly in the park, "sitting on the grass, making beautiful wreaths of buttercups and daisies." I think one might pass one's life very pleasantly and profitably in that manner. I recollect trying my hand at buttercups and daisies once, and finding it very agreeable, though I have got out of the way of it of late years, excepting that Dick, my horse, now and then cuts daisies with me when I am on his back; but that's to please himself, not me.

To-morrow I am going to set out on a journey with a large party, including your cousins Julia, Fanny, and Irving Grinnell. We shall see no castles, but will voyage on great lakes and rivers, and through wild forests. I wish you were going with us, but I suppose I must wish in vain; that must be for some future day. And now, my dear Kate, give my love to

Susie and Julie, and my kind remembrances to Henriette [the nurse].   Your affectionate uncle,

WASHINGTON IRVING.

Two years later, he writes to the same little correspondent as follows :

SUNNYSIDE, Feb. 21, 1854.

MY DEAR KATE:

I have just received the slippers which you have been so very good as to work for me, and which have been a long time in the shoemaker's hands.   Having put them on, I sit down to tell you how well they fit me ; how much I admire the colors you have chosen; how much I am astonished and delighted with the needlework ; and how very sensibly I feel this proof of affectionate remembrance.   I assure you I take great pride in exhibiting this specimen of the taste and skill of my Parisian niece, and, if I were in Paris, should be very much tempted to go to Court in them, even at the risk of causing a question of costume.

I dined, a few days since, in company with your father's partner, Mr. B.   *   *   *   He told me that it was very possible you might all pay a visit to America this year.   That, however, I put about as much faith in as in the return of the fairies.   I hope, however, you still keep up a recollection of your home on this side of the water, and of your young cousins who were your playmates.   They and their intimates make a very happy circle, and it grieves me much that you and your sisters are not with them, all growing up together in delightful companionship.   If you remain much longer separated, you will all forget each other.   *   *   *

Farewell, my dear Kate.   Give my love to my dear little

nieces Tutu and Gaga (who I fancy have completely forgotten me), and to your mother, to whom I wrote recently. Tell your father we should all give him a hearty welcome if he should really come out this summer; and a still heartier one should he bring you all with him.

Your affectionate uncle,

WASHINGTON IRVING.

The following is in reply to a youthful author, who sends him his "Summer in the Wilderness," of which he remarks: "It is an unpretending affair; but, though published only about three months ago, it has already passed through an edition of fifteen hundred. * * * If, after you have glanced over the pages of my little book, you will send me a brief letter of advice, I should consider myself your most grateful friend. Such a letter would be particularly acceptable at the present time, as I am preparing for the press no less than three new books—one upon American Art, one upon the Fishes of America, and another to be entitled 'Adventures of an Angler.'"

[To Charles Lanman, New York.]

SUNNYSIDE, Oct. 15, 1847.

MY DEAR SIR:

I would not reply to your very obliging letter of September 10th, until I had time to read the volumes which accompanied it. This, from the pressure of various engagements, I have but just been able to do; and I now return you thanks for the delightful entertainment which your summer rambles have afforded me. I do not see that I have any literary advice to give you, excepting to keep on as you have begun. You seem to have the happy, enjoyable humor of old Izaak Walton. I anticipate great success, therefore, in your works on our American Fishes, and on Angling, which I trust will give us still further scenes and adventures on our great internal waters, depicted with the freshness and graphic skill of your present volumes. In fact, the adventurous life of the angler amidst our wild scenery on our vast lakes and rivers, must furnish a striking contrast to the quiet loiterings of the English angler along the Trent or Dove, with country milkmaids to sing madrigals to him, and a snug, decent country inn at night, where he may sleep in sheets that have been laid in lavender.

With best wishes for your success, I am, my dear sir, very truly your obliged,

WASHINGTON IRVING.

Meanwhile, overtures were multiplying from the booksellers for a republication of his works, but he still delayed to make any definite arrangement. Transmitting to me some proposals he had received from different publishers toward the close of September, he writes: "I am so much occupied, mind and pen, just now, on the History of Washington, that I have not time to turn these matters over in my mind."

He was now, and for several months hereafter, hard at work on this biography, making it a daily task.

At the date of the following letter, he is on a visit to the city, to be within reach of the libraries, but intending, as will be seen, to be at home to hold his Christmas gathering:

[*To Miss Catherine Irving.*]

New York, Dec. 20, 1847.

My dear Kate:

I had expected to return home before this, but am so entangled in engagements, that I shall not be able before Christmas eve (Friday next). I trust you will have the rooms decorated with greens, as usual.

I have been very busy and very dissipated during my sojourn in town—at work all the mornings in the libraries, and frolicking in the evenings. I have attended every opera. The house is beautiful, the troupe very fair, and the audience very fashionable. Such beautiful young ladies!—but the town is full of them; almost as beautiful as the young lady I saw in my dream at the cottage.

CHAPTER II.

DINNER AT JOHN JACOB ASTOR'S—CONVERSATION ABOUT GHOSTS—ENGAGED ON
HIS LIFE OF WASHINGTON—ANNOYED AT THE WANT OF FEATURE IN PARTS
OF THE WAR—THE OPERA HOUSE, ONE OF THE GREAT CHARMS OF NEW YORK
—THE PROJECTED RAILROAD ALONG THE BANKS OF THE HUDSON—IMPEND-
ING DESECRATION OF SUNNYSIDE—TESTIMONIAL OF THE LAND COMMITTEE—
ADJUSTMENT OF DAMAGES—LETTER TO HACKETT—ARRANGEMENT WITH MR.
PUTNAM FOR THE REPUBLICATION OF HIS WORKS—KNICKERBOCKER—AU-
THOR'S REMARKS ABOUT THE REVISED EDITION—NOTICE OF HENRY T. TUCK-
ERMAN—A GERMAN COMMENTATOR CITING KNICKERBOCKER—SCHAEFFER'S
CHRISTUS CONSOLATOR—NOTICES OF THE REPUBLICATION OF THE SKETCH
BOOK—LIBERAL RECEPTION OF THE REVISED SERIES.

THE opening of this year finds Mr. Irving on a
prolonged visit to New York. The following
letter is addressed to Mrs. Storrow from the residence
of his nephew, John T. Irving, where he was fixed for
the present :

NEW YORK, Feb. 27.

* * * After eleven months' seclusion in the country,
during which I made but three or four visits of business to
town, going down and returning the same day in the boat, I
came down on a visit early in the winter, having recovered
sufficiently from my old malady to go again into society. The
cordial, and I may say affectionate reception I met with everywhere, and the delight I felt on mingling once more among old

friends, had such an enlivening effect upon me, that I soon repeated my visit, and have ended by passing almost the whole
of the winter in town. I think it has had a good effect upon
me in every way. It has rejuvenated me, and given such a
healthful tone to my mind and spirits, that I have worked with
greater alacrity and success. I have my books and papers
with me, and generally confine myself to the house and to my
pen all the long morning, and then give up the evening to society and amusement.

One great charm of New York, at present, is a beautiful
opera house, and a very good troupe. We have a *prima
donna*, named Truffi, who delights me as much as Grisi did,
and in the same line of characters, though I will not say she is
equal to her excepting in occasional scenes. She is an admirable actress and an excellent singer. We have an excellent
tenor also—a young man who, when he gets more cultivation
and training, will be worthy of the Paris stage. The theatre
is well arranged, and so fashionable in every part that there is
no jealousy about places, as in the old opera house here. Ladies are seated everywhere, and, with their gay dresses, make
what is the parquette in other theatres look like a bed of flowers. It is filled every night. Everybody is well dressed, and
it is altogether one of the gayest, prettiest, and most polite-
looking theatres I have ever seen. * * * I have not
missed a single performance since I have been in town.

*   *   *   *   *   *

One meets all one's acquaintances at the opera, and there is
much visiting from box to box, and pleasant conversation, between the acts. The opera house is in fact the great feature in
polite society in New York, and I believe is the great attraction that keeps me in town. Music is to me the great sweet-

ener of existence, and I never enjoyed it more abundantly than
at present.

March 8, Mr. Irving refers to " a fancy ball recently given at the opera house, of which," he says,
" I, sorely against my will, was made one of the man-
agers." It was a distasteful position, but he had not
the faculty of resisting well-intended importunity in
trifles.

A portion of this period of his lengthened sojourn
in New York he was the guest of John Jacob Astor,
then eighty-four years of age, whom he had often
urged, he tells us, to commence his noble enterprise of
the Astor Library, and enjoy the reputation of it while
living. It was left, however, to be carried out under
the provisions of his will.

Calling on Mr. Irving one morning before breakfast at Mr. Astor's, I found him engaged on his Life of
Washington, but somewhat out of patience at the want
of feature in parts of the war. It was so barren of
interest—such a cursed sand flat; the two enemies, like
two drunken men, impotently striking at each other
without hurting. Sometimes, he said, he dragged
along ; at other times got a little breeze, and went forward briskly ; then adverting to the changes of mood
in his task, sometimes felt as if he could remove mountains ; at other times, the molehill was a mountain.

I was dining with him, at another time, at Mr.
Astor's, during this period, when, the conversation

turning upon ghosts, I mentioned the story of Wesley, and the sanction given to it by Southey in his life of that eminent divine. ———, who was also dining there, instanced the story of Major Blomberg, and expressed his surprise that neither Scott in his Demonology, nor Dendie in his Philosophy of Mystery, had included this most remarkable ghost story. Two officers were sitting up with a corpse in the West Indies ; one was in the room with the body, the other in an adjoining room which communicated. The corpse rose ; came to the person in same room ; told him he had a secret to communicate, to prevent a great wrong ; had been permitted to return to life to reveal it ; bade him summon (which he did) his companion in the adjoining room, to hear his disclosure ; told of a secret marriage to a girl in Ireland now with child ; stated the name of the clergyman who married them, and how they could get the evidence. ——— had seen the depositions. Mr. Irving suggested the solution that the man was not dead, and that this secret lay so heavily on his mind as to rouse him from his state of apparent death. He then proceeded to say that he had been hardly treated by the ghosts ; that he had invoked the presence of the dead more than once, but in vain ; and brought up especially the singular compact with Hall, and its barren result, narrated in a previous volume.

Mr. Irving had been much disturbed by a project which had been started, of running a railroad along

the eastern bank of the Hudson. Besides the utter
desecration which he considered it of that beautiful
shore, it threatened to make his little cottage almost
untenable, inasmuch as its situation on the immediate
margin of the river would bring the nuisance, with all
its noise and unsightliness, to his very door, and mar
forever, as he feared, the peculiar charms for which he
had chosen the spot—its quiet and retirement. For a
time he hoped the plan would not be carried out, and,
when it was actually decided, was quite in despair. It
was hopeless, however, to rebel; and, once settled, he
began, in his accustomed way, to try to make the best
of it. As it was carried a short distance out in the
river, he was spared the trial of having it cross his
very grounds; and the trees along the bank formed a
screen that he hoped, with a little care, would soon
shut it out from view. Though in the first paroxysm
of annoyance, therefore, he wished " he had been born
when the world was finished," and declared he believed, " if the garden of Eden were now on earth,
they would not hesitate to run a railroad through it,"
yet, when the committee came whose duty it was to
call on the owners of property, and arrange for the
terms of compensation, Mr. Irving submitted at once,
giving them permission to commence the work when
they chose; and, as the damage to him was such as
could not be paid by money, left it entirely with themselves to determine the amount of their award.

" The liberal and courteous spirit," say the committee, in a letter of April 4, 1848, from which I quote, " in which you, last summer, gave permission to enter on your lands to commence the construction of the road, and in which the committee have uniformly been met by you in the discharge of their unpleasant duties, has been quite a solace to them amidst the many cases of a contrary character which have occurred. It is the more worthy of remark, as, in their view, you are more seriously invaded by this necessary work, in respect to derangement of rural taste and retirement, than is any other proprietor on the whole line of the road below the Highlands."

In adjustment of these land damages, the railroad company paid him thirty-five hundred dollars. On the receipt of the first payment, he remarked wittily : " Why, I am harder on them than the wagoner was on Giles Gingerbread ; for he let him walk all the way to London alongside of his wagon without charging him anything, while I make them pay for only passing my door."

The Mr. Putnam mentioned in this further extract from the same letter of April 10, is the well-known publisher, George P. Putnam, who had dissolved with his partner, John Wiley, at the close of the preceding year. John Jacob Astor, to whose vast estate Mr. Irving was named in his will as one of the executors, had died on the 29th of March.

I am now negotiating an arrangement with Mr. Putnam for

the republication of my works, which promises to be a very satisfactory one; and I am attending preliminary meetings of the board of executors of Mr. Astor's estate. All these things detain me in town, and may oblige me hereafter to visit town frequently.

    *   *   *   *   *   *

I trust the men are widening and cleaning out the side-walks. I shall send or bring up some seed or young plants of running vines for the porch by the front of the house—yearly plants, to serve while the roses are growing.

The following letter, addressed to James H. Hackett, the popular comedian, and one of the best Falstaffs known to the stage, was written on returning to him a portion of his manuscript Notes and Criticisms on Shakspeare and Actors of Shakspeare, published entire many years afterward:

New York, April 17. 1848.

My dear Sir:

I have detained your manuscript notes an unconscionable time, but I could not help it. I wished to read them attentively, for they are remarkably suggestive, and not to be read in a hurry; but for the last two or three months, spent among my friends and relatives in my native city after an absence of several years, I have been kept in such a round of engagements, and such constant excitement, that I have only now and then been able to command a little leisure and quiet for reading and reflection. At such moments I have perused your manuscripts by piecemeal, and now return you my many thanks for the great pleasure they have afforded me. I will not pretend to enter at present into any discussion of the topics they embrace, for I have not sufficient faith in my critical acumen to commit my thoughts to paper ; but when I have the pleasure of meeting with you personally, we will talk over these matters as largely as you please.   I have seen all the leading characters of Shakspeare played by the best actors in America and England during the present century ; some of them, too, admirably performed in Germany.   I have heard some of them chanted in the Italian opera, and I have seen the ballet of " Hamlet " gravely danced at Vienna.   Yet, with all this experience, I feel that I am an amateur rather than a connoisseur ; prone to receive great pleasure without nicely analyzing the source, and sometimes apt to clap my hands when grave critics shake their heads.

Excuse this scrawl, written in a hurried moment, and believe me, with great respect and regard, your obliged friend and servant,

WASHINGTON IRVING.

The agreement with Mr. George P. Putnam, by which Mr. Irving was to prepare revised copies of all his works for publication, bears date July 26, 1848. By this arrangement, which was to continue for five years, Mr. Putnam was to have the exclusive right of publishing his already published works and writings in uniform duodecimo volumes, until the whole series was completed, at such intervals as the publisher might find most for the mutual interest of the parties.   He had the right also to publish one or more of the works in a larger size, and illustrated.·   Mr. Putnam was to be at the whole charge of publication, "including all the expenses thereto incident," and was to pay Mr. Irving twelve and a half per cent. on the retail price of all the copies sold. The accounts of sales were to be balanced at the end of every year, commencing with July, 1849 ; and the author was to receive, in notes at four months, the amount accruing to him at the above rate ; but, in anticipation of such general adjustment, Mr. Putnam agreed to pay him, in quarterly payments, one thousand dollars for the first year, fifteen hundred for the second, and two thousand for the third, fourth, and fifth years ; all of which payments were to be made on account of the percentage above specified, in the confident expectation of the publisher that the year's receipts would overrun the amount advanced, and that the author would have a surplus to receive at the stated period of settlement. In case of a disappointment in this particular, and that the percentage within the year should not amount to the sum or sums advanced, the author was not to be called upon to refund any part of the advance. In other words, by this agreement, Mr. Putnam was answerable for the payment of eight thousand five hundred dollars—the sum provided for in the several annual advances—whatever be the amount of the percentage ; but whenever this guarantee of eight thousand five hundred dollars should be covered by the gross amount of profits received by Mr. Irving, the advances were to cease ; or, if continued at the stipulated rate, and at the annual settlement it should appear that they had overrun the percentage, the author was to refund the difference.

The arrangement redounded to the advantage of both.

On the 18th of August, during a holiday visit I was making at Sunnyside, Mr. Irving brought to the cottage, from the city, a copy of the revised edition of Knickerbocker's History of New York, printed, and to be published on the 1st of September. I turned over the pages, and observed to him that there appeared to be considerable additions besides the Author's Apology, which he had written expressly for this new edition. He replied that he had made some changes, and, he hoped, improvements; thought that he had mellowed and softened a good deal that was overcharged; had chastened the exaggerated humor of some portions —the effect of age and improved taste combined; and tempered the rawness of other parts without losing any of the raciness. If he had the work to write anew, he thought he could have brought out many things in a finer and higher vein of humor; but some of the jokes had got so implanted, he was afraid to disturb them.

The undertaking of Mr. Putnam was greeted with a cordial welcome by many of our literary luminaries. "A new edition of Washington Irving's works," writes the polished essayist, H. T. Tuckerman, on the first putting forth of Knickerbocker, "has long been in contemplation; but perhaps it is not so generally known, that the writings of this elegant pioneer of American

literature have long been out of print in his own country.   A stray volume or two of the cheap Philadelphia
edition, wholly unfit to grace a library shelf, or the
bulky octavo published in Paris, may occasionally be
encountered ; but, strange as it may seem, a complete,
readable, and authorized edition of ' Geoffrey Crayon '
has long been a desideratum.   Since the dawn of his
popularity, thousands of a new generation have sprung
up in the far West, and along the Atlantic, who know
this ornament to their country's genius only by frag-
ments, and from the voice of renown.   Accordingly,
the enterprise of Mr. Putnam was not only required
as a convenience, but almost as a necessity.   *   *   *
The series is very appropriately commenced with
' Knickerbocker's New York '—one of the most original and elaborate pieces of humor to which our language has given birth."

Another unknown but evidently practised pen,
after descanting on the beauty of the volume in its
type and finish, remarks :

If any works of our language are worthy of such choice
embalming, and such an honored place in all libraries as these
volumes are destined to fill, it is those of Washington Irving.
Their quaint and exhaustless humor, rich, graceful, and exuber-
ant fancy, and the pure and natural vein of feeling, deepening
into pathos, which runs through them, make them, in an eminent sense, household works—works to be read by the winter
fireside, or in the calm of summer twilight, always cheering
and soothing in their influence, and conveying strengthening

and instructive lessons in a form which the mind is always ready to receive. To the writings of Diedrich Knickerbocker, especially, may be applied the words of Sir Philip Sidney : "He cometh to you with a tale that holdeth children from play, and old men from the chimney corner."

The volume before us has been thoroughly revised, and now wears the final form in which posterity will receive it. Its interest is increased by a curious history of the manner in which the work was first published. The adroitness with which the public was prepared for the appearance of the book, is very amusing, and we wonder not that foreigners should have been puzzled in what manner to understand it.

It is an amusing fact in connection with this allusion to the difficulty of foreigners in what manner to understand Knickerbocker, that a learned German commentator, in some notes to a German edition of Thucydides, has a grave reference to Knickerbocker's History of the old factions of the Long Pipes and Short Pipes, as an illustration of the profound remarks of Thucydides on the evils arising from the prevalence of factions throughout Greece. "Laughable as this undoubtedly is," writes Tuckerman, in noticing the fact, "it is probable that a more flattering testimony was never borne to the inimitable skill displayed in every page of *Knickerbocker's History of New York*. It is highly amusing, however, to think of the utter mystification and bewilderment in which Goeller must have been, while laboriously perusing the *soi-disant* history, and endeavoring to treasure up in his memory

the well-authenticated and instructive facts with which
it abounds." *

On the same day that Mr. Irving brought to the
cottage this first volume of the revised edition of his
works, his most humorous composition, he brought
home also a picture which had strongly touched his
religious sensibilities. This was Dupont's engraving
of Ary Schaeffer's Christus Consolator, which he had
recently bought, and left to be mounted and framed.
The engraving first caught his eye, as he told me, in
the window of a German shop in Broadway, and he
then gazed at it until the tears gathered in his eyes,
without knowing whose it was. Finding it was from
Schaeffer, he went in at once and bought it, and
ordered it to be framed. After tea he took mallet and
chisel, and proceeded to unbox it. It was indeed an
exquisite thing, full of the deepest sentiment; and as
Mr. Irving continued to look at it, the tears started
again to his eyes. He thought he had never seen anything so affecting—" there was nothing superior to it
in the world of art;" then he burst out into an expression of regret at not having seen more of Schaeffer.
He had met him at Paris on his last visit to Europe, at
a house where he used to meet Lamennais and others,
and had been urged to go to his studio, but never went.
" It was one of the negligences of my life."

* The instance occurs in Goeller's Thucydides, in a note on the 82d
chapter of the 3d book, and the reference is to Washington Irving's History of New York, lib. vii, cap. 5.

It was in the autumn of this year that he united himself to the Episcopal Church, of which he had never before been a member; and he was no doubt particularly susceptible at this period to the emotions such an engraving was calculated to excite.

I give a few specimens from the literary notices of the day, to show the unbroken charm of the Sketch Book, and the cordial welcome it received. It was the second volume of the new series, and was published about the 1st of October. I should add, that the interest of the volume was enhanced by a preface, which contained a narrative of the circumstances of the first publication of the work.

The second volume of Putnam's elegant edition of Irving is before us. The Sketch Book, purely classic and beautiful as is its language, seems to read even more refreshingly in the present choice getting up. It is needless to refer to the work itself; for who that reads at all has failed to make acquaintance with its pages? The exquisite sketches of "The Wife," the "Broken Heart," and "Rural Funerals," have been an *utterance* and a consolation to many a heart, and they will not soon cease their mission. "Rip Van Winkle" and the "Legend of Sleepy Hollow" have taken root in the soil which produced them; and the graphic papers on the Christmas Festivities of England have been adopted as part of the records of her homes. Few single works have attained a wider reach of influence, or a more enduring fame.

I find in Bryant's *Evening Post* of October 13, the following notice of its republication:

Washington Irving's name is uppermost in our thoughts when speaking the claims or recounting the successes of American authorship. He has had the homage of critics on both sides of the Atlantic; the cordial praise of men of letters, his contemporaries and colaborers; some share of those executive favors which are rarely accorded as tributes to literary eminence; and he enjoys a reputation dignified by the union of high personal character, and unmarred by any of those personal jealousies that so often discredit established reputations, or that latter-day mediocrity that threatens them with final bankruptcy. We are glad to find him devoting part of the leisure of Sunnyside to the revision of his works for their uniform publication. * * * The first purchasers of this volume will be, if we mistake not, those who have read it oftenest. Its familiar papers come to most readers with the charm of long acquaintance; they are amongst the old wine in their stores of pleasant book recollections. Rip Van Winkle and Ichabod Crane are universal heroes; the Widow and her Son have made their appeal to everybody's sympathies; and every American traveller in England divides the enjoyment and the reminiscences of his pilgrimage to Stratford-on-Avon between Shakspeare and Irving. * * *

Late in October I called on Mr. Irving, then in New York, and found him engaged on his Life of Mahomet, evidently somewhat fagged. I told him I saw Putnam had advertised its appearance for the 1st of January. Yes, he said; he was afraid it would hurry him to get ready; he gave him a negligent answer, and he fixed a day. Was a good deal bothered in his anxiety to finish this and the Life of Washington. Hoped he would not drop in harness. I told him the uniform edition was doing so well, he could afford to take his ease, and not to drudge. " Yes," said he ; " but I know my nature. I must get through with the work I have cut out for myself. I must weave my web, and then die."

A few days afterward, the third of the series of the new edition of his works, being the first volume of " The Life and Voyages of Columbus," made its appearance ; and in the preface the author took occasion to notice the accusation that he had not given sufficient credit to Don Martin Fernandez de Navarrete for the aid he had derived from his collection of documents ; quoting, in refutation, a letter of Navarrete himself, and that author's own words also, in the third volume of his Collection of Spanish Voyages.

The next volume of the revised series—Bracebridge Hall—was published on the 1st of December. " When we consider," says the *Evening Post*, in a notice of its appearance, " that in Bracebridge Hall are to be found Ready-Money Jack and the Stout Gentleman, as examples of Irving's comic power, and Annette Delarbre as an instance of his command over the gentler emotions, we are tempted to ask whether he has done anything better than his Bracebridge Hall."

Four volumes of the revised series were now published, and the sale, for books that were not new, was unprecedented. By many, the enterprise had been pronounced a rash one ; but the reception given to these volumes by the public, proved, in the language of another, " the solidity of the author's reputation, and seemed like a recognition of his works as an abiding part of his ' land's language.' "

Forty years had gone by since Knickerbocker was first introduced to the public ; and thirty years had wellnigh passed away since, in his original preface to the first number of the Sketch Book, he wrote :

The following writings are published on experiment. Should they please, they may be followed by others. * * * Should his exertions be well received, the author cannot conceal that it would be a source of the purest gratification ; for, though he does not aspire to those high honors which are the rewards of loftier intellects, yet it is the dearest wish of his heart to have a secure and cherished, though humble corner, in the good opinions and kind feelings of his countrymen.

" Little did he then anticipate," says an anonymous contemporary, in quoting this passage, " that the Gospel annunciation, ' He that humbleth himself shall be exalted,' would be so fully verified in his case ; that the ' high honors ' to which he did not aspire, would be accorded to him of right ; and that the ' humble corner ' he coveted in the affections of his countrymen, should prove to be the most favored spot."

VOL. IV.—3   (4)

CHAPTER III.

UNPRECEDENTED SALE OF REVISED EDITION OF THE SKETCH BOOK—ENGAGED
UPON A LIFE OF GOLDSMITH—ITS PUBLICATION—RIPLEY'S NOTICE—CRITIQUE
OF GEORGE W. GREENE—APPEARANCE OF MAHOMET AND HIS SUCCESSORS—
THE REVISED ALHAMBRA AND CONQUEST OF GRANADA—ANXIETY TO BEGIN
ANEW ON LIFE OF WASHINGTON.

THIS year opened most encouragingly. The issue of the seventh thousand of the Sketch Book was advertised on or about the 1st of February, less than four months after its republication, and Putnam gave the most flattering reports of the manner in which the illustrated edition had gone off during the holidays. The profits of this last named edition were mainly the publisher's, Mr. Irving being at no expense for the embellishments, receiving merely the twelve and a half per cent. on the retail price of so many ordinary copies. All the illustrated editions of his works were got up exclusively by his.publisher.

Bracebridge Hall, the author's last monthly publication, was followed in January by the second volume of the Life and Voyages of Columbus, and in February by volume third, including the Companions of Columbus. The Tales of a Traveller were brought out in

March, Astoria in April, and the Crayon Miscellany in May.

In noticing the appearance of this last, which comprised the Tour on the Prairies, Abbotsford, and Newstead Abbey, the editor of the *Literary World* remarks:

The author's "Astoria," the last monthly publication of the series, has, from its timely issue, when men's eyes are directed to the "California Trail," met with the most distinguished success. It is appropriately followed by the Tour to the Prairies, included in the present volume. The next, we understand, will be a republication of Captain Bonneville's Adventures, which will complete the volumes through which Irving has so happily connected his name with the History of the Great West. The charm of the Tour to the Prairies is its unique, finished character. It is a little episode of the author's life, in which he has condensed the sentiment and fresh spirit of adventure consequent on his return to American life, after long familiarity with the over-cultivation of Europe. It will probably be read as long as any of his writings. The Sketch of Abbotsford and its Master is one of the most graceful and truthful of the many reminiscences of Scott. How admirably the character of Sir Walter's conversation is conveyed in a line—"The conversation of Scott was frank, hearty, picturesque, and dramatic." The anecdotes and traits of the great Master, charmingly told in this narrative, are all to the point. The paper which concludes this volume of the Miscellany on Newstead Abbey, reminds us of the best of the Sketch Book or Bracebridge Hall.

Of The Adventures of Captain Bonneville, the next in the series of Mr. Irving's collected works, a cotemporary remarks :

This book loses none of its freshness or interest with the lapse of years. The contrast between the polished, luxuriant style of its composition, and the wild, daring adventures of forest life which it describes, gives it a peculiar charm, and leads many to prefer it to the more universally admired productions of its popular author.

On the 5th of July, soon after a return from a short visit to his niece on Cayuga Lake, Mr. Irving writes to Mrs. Storrow as follows :

For upward of a year past I have been very much from home, obliged to be for the most of the time in the city, super-intending the publication of a new and revised edition of my works, making researches for other works on which I am employed, and attending to the settlement of Mr. Astor's estate, and the organization of the Astor Library. Altogether, I have had more toil of head and fagging of the pen for the last eighteen months, than in any other period of my life, and have been once or twice fearful my health might become deranged, but it has held out marvellously ; and now I hope to be able to ease off in my toils, and to pass my time at home as usual.

In the succeeding month, he received from the Astor estate, here mentioned, his share of the commissions devolving upon the executors, amounting to ten thousand five hundred and ninety-two dollars and

sixty-six cents. It was shortly before this that he
called at my office, and, speaking of his fagging at the
Life of Goldsmith, two or three chapters of which he
had still to write, said it had taken more time than he
could afford—had plucked the heart out of his summer ; and after all he could only play with the subject.
He had no time to finish it off as he wished.

He had now published all but two of the revised
edition of his works—The Chronicles of Granada and
The Alhambra—and had intermitted the continuation
of the series and his Life of Washington, to take up
the Life of Goldsmith. It was a sudden literary freak,
similar to that which had induced him, when first in
Spain, to break off from Columbus to begin the
Chronicles of Granada, and had subsequently drawn
him aside to his Moorish Chronicles.

His publisher, Mr. Putnam, in his Recollections of
Irving, communicated to the *Atlantic Magazine* in
November, 1860, has the following glimpse at its
origin :

Sitting at my desk, one day, he was looking at Forster's
clever work, which I proposed to reprint. He remarked that
it was a favorite theme of his, and he had half a mind to pursue it, and extend into a volume a sketch he had once made for
an edition of Goldsmith's Works. I expressed a hope that he
would do so ; and within sixty days the first sheets of Irving's
" Goldsmith " were in the printer's hands. The press (as he
says) was " dogging at his heels," for in two or three weeks
the volume was published.

I was on a visit to the cottage when it came out,
and, reading it at once, expressed to him my satisfaction with the work. He replied that he had been
afraid to look at it since it was brought up, for he had
never written anything in such a hurry. He wanted
more time for it, and did not know but that his talents
might be flagging. "Are you sure it does not smell
of the apoplexy ? " he inquired, in playful allusion to
Gil Blas and the Archbishop of Granada.

A few days after, Mr. Irving received a note from
Mr. George Ripley, at the head of the literary department of the *New York Tribune,* and more widely
known of late years as one of the editors of the New
American Cyclopædia, enclosing the following cordial
and animated notice :

Everything combines to make this one of the most fascinating pieces of biography in the English language. Enough
is known of the personal history and character of Goldsmith,
to tempt us to recur to the subject with fresh interest ; but he
has not been so bandied about by life-writers and reviewers as
to satiate curiosity. The simplicity, and even the weaknesses
of his nature, call forth a feeling of affection ; and the charm
of his writings, so unaffected, so naïve, so transparent in their
crystal purity of expression, attracts us to a more intimate acquaintance with the author. Mr. Irving was in possession of
abundant materials to do justice to the subject. He had only
to insert his exquisite magnetic needle into the mass, to give a
choice and shapely form to all that was valuable in the labors
of previous biographers. He has done this in a manner which

leaves nothing to be desired. With a genial admiration of Goldsmith, with a cordial appreciation of the spirit of his writings, and with many similar intellectual tendencies, he has portrayed the varied picture of his life with a grace and elegance that make his narrative as charming a piece of composition as can be found in the whole range of his former works. He has added a new enchantment to the potent spell with which he always binds the hearts of his readers. * * * He has performed this task with a facile excellence peculiar to himself; and henceforth the two names of Irving and Goldsmith will be united in the recollection of the delightful hours which each has given to such a host of "happy human beings." There could not be a more admirable description of the influence of his own writings, than Mr. Irving has given in his opening paragraph on Goldsmith. We will not forego the pleasure of quoting it entire. "There are few writers for whom the reader feels such personal kindness as for Oliver Goldsmith, for few have so eminently possessed the magic gift of identifying themselves with their writings. We read his character in every page, and grow into familiar intimacy with him as we read. The artless benevolence that beams throughout his works; the whimsical, yet amiable views of human life and human nature; the unforced humor, blending so happily with good feeling and good sense, and singularly dashed, at times, with a pleasing melancholy; even the very nature of his mellow, and flowing, and softly-tinted style, all seem to bespeak his moral as well as his intellectual qualities, and make us love the man at the same time that we admire the author. While the productions of writers of loftier pretension and more sounding names are suffered to moulder on our shelves, those of Goldsmith are cherished, and laid in our bosoms. We do not quote them with ostentation, but they mingle with our minds, sweeten our tempers, and harmonize our thoughts; they put us in good humor with ourselves and with the world, and, in so doing they make us happier and better men."

In an elaborate critique of some of Mr. Irving's works, contributed to the *Christian Review* in April, 1850, a skilful writer and ripe scholar, Prof. George W. Greene, holds this language about the Life of Goldsmith:

If there is anybody of whom it could be said that it was his duty to write a Life of Goldsmith, it is Washington Irving; and, often as we have had occasion to thank him for happy hours, we do not know that we ever felt so grateful to him for anything as for this. We have always loved Goldsmith, his poetry and his prose, and everything about him. There is not a poem in the language that we can go back to with the same zest with which we open the Traveller or the Deserted Village for the five hundredth time; and we can never get through a ten minutes' speech without quoting the Vicar of Wakefield. And yet we must say frankly, that we never understood Goldsmith's character until now. We have been vexed at his weakness, and have blushed at his blunders. We had always wished he could have thrown off his brogue, and had never put on his bloom-colored coat. That he should not have known how to keep his money, was not very wonderful—it is a professional weakness; but he might at any rate have thrown it away in better company. We have been more than once sorely troubled, too, by sundry little slips that savored somewhat of moral obliquity, and never been able to reconcile the elevation of his intellect with acts that far less rigorous judges than we have characterized as mean and degrading.   In short, with all our contempt for Boswell, we have been fairly Boswellized, and, much as we loved Goldsmith, loved him somewhat in despite of what we thought our better judgment.

Thanks to Mr. Irving, our doubts have all been solved, and we can love the kind, simple-hearted, genial man with as much confidence as we admire his writings.   This overflowing of the heart, this true philosophy, so interwoven with his whole nature, that, whether he acts or speaks, you find it as strongly marked in his actions as in his language; that quick sensibility, which makes him so keenly alive to all the petty annoyances of his dependent position, and that buoyancy of spirit which raises him above them, and bears him up on the wave while many a stouter heart is sinking around him; those ready sympathies, that self-forgetfulness, that innate, unprompted, spontaneous philanthropy, which, in the days of his prosperity as well as in his days of trial, was never belied by word or by deed—all these we understand as we never understood them before, and feel how rare and beautiful they are.   He was not wise in his own concerns, and yet what treasures of wisdom has he not bequeathed to the world!   Artless as an infant, yet how deeply read in human nature; with all his feelings upon the surface, ruffled by every breeze and glowing in every sunbeam, and yet how skilled in all the secret windings of the heart.   None but a man of genial nature should ever attempt to write the Life of Goldsmith: one who knows how much wisdom can be extracted from folly; how much better for the heart it is to trust than to doubt; how much nobler is a generous impulse than a cautious reserve; how much truer a wisdom there is in benevolence, than in all the shrewd devices of worldly craft.

Now Mr. Irving is just the man to feel all this, and to make you feel it too. He sees how weak Goldsmith is in many things, how wise in others, and he sees how closely his wisdom and his weakness are allied. There is no condescension in his pity, none of that parade which often makes pity tenfold more bitter than the sufferings which call it forth. He tells you the story of his hero's errors as freely as he does that of his virtues, and in a way to make you feel that a man may have many a human weakness lie heavy at his door, and yet be worthy of our love and admiration still. He has no desire to conceal, makes no attempt to palliate. He understands his hero's character thoroughly, and feels that if he can only make you understand it, you will love him as much as he does. Therefore he draws him just as he is, lights and shadows, virtues and foibles—vices you cannot call them, be you never so unkind. At his blunders he laughs, just as Goldsmith himself used to laugh in recounting them; and he feels the secret of his virtues too justly to attempt to gild them over with useless embellishment.

Speaking to Mr. Irving of this biography of Goldsmith, soon after its appearance, I asked him if he had introduced any anecdotes not in Prior's or Forster's Life of him. "No," playfully; "I could not invent any new ones; but I have altered the setting, and have introduced—not in their biography—Madame Darblay's anecdote about Boswell and Johnson, which is capital. I have also made more of the Jessamy

Bride, by adverting to the dates in the tailor's bill, and fixing thereby the dates of certain visits to her."

Mr. Irving, it will be remembered, before either Prior or Forster entered the field, had sketched a Life of Goldsmith, to accompany a Paris edition of that author's works. This sketch was subsequently amplified from the materials brought to light by Prior, and prefixed to some American selections of Goldsmith for Harpers' Family Library. It was now expanded into its present form from the additions of Forster. Of this biography, while giving full credit to the previous labors of Prior and Forster, the *Literary World* remarks: "You may have read the story a hundred times, but you will read it again as a new thing in this Biography of Irving."

On the 19th of September, I stopped in at Putnam's, who told me he had already disposed of the first edition of Goldsmith of 2,500, and was now busy on a second of 2,000. I wrote to Mr. Irving to that effect, and added that it had increased his publisher's impatience for the appearance of Mahomet. In his reply of the 21st, he says:

I am getting on very well, but am not yet in a mood to take up my pen; so Mr. Putnam must stay his stomach with Goldsmith a little longer. I suppose, because I knocked off that work in such an offhand manner, he thinks it a very easy matter with me " to blow up a dog."

If the reader should not see the point of this quo-

tation, he is referred to the preface of the second part
of Don Quixote.

It was some months after this that I mentioned to
him an article I had been reading in a weekly periodical, in which the writer, evidently alluding to his preface in his biography of Goldsmith, styles him, in an
invidious spirit, " a self-acknowledged imitator of that
author." At the close of that preface, the reader may
remember he addresses Goldsmith in the language of
Dante's apostrophe to Virgil :

> " Tu se' lo mio maestro, e'l mio autore ;
> Tu se' solo colui da cui io tolsi
> Lo bello stile che m'a fatto onore."

Translated,

> Thou art my master, and my teacher thou ;
> It was from thee, and thee alone, I took
> That noble style for which men honor me.

He smiled ; said he meant only to express his affectionate admiration of Goldsmith, but it would never
do for an author to acknowledge anything. Was never
conscious of an attempt to write after any model. No
man of genius ever did. From his earliest attempts,
everything fell naturally from him. His style, he believed, was as much his own as though Goldsmith had
never written—as much his own as his voice.

This was not the language of self-eulogy, but of
quiet self-vindication. He had never meant to warrant

such perversion of his quotation, any more than Dante meant to confess himself an imitator of Virgil. There were undoubtedly qualities of style as well as mental and moral characteristics in which he resembled both Goldsmith and Addison, the two with whom he is most frequently compared, while in others it would be impossible to confound them.

The first volume of Mahomet and his Successors, which had been prematurely advertised for the beginning of the year, appeared at its close, December 15, with the following preface, which gives a succinct history of the origin and scope of the work, and its gradual and intermitted composition :

Some apology may seem necessary for presenting a Life of Mahomet at the present day, when no new fact can be added to those already known concerning him. Many years since, during a residence in Madrid, the author projected a series of writings illustrative of the domination of the Arabs in Spain. These were to be introduced by a sketch of the life of the founder of the Islam faith, and the first mover of Arabian conquest. Most of the particulars for this were drawn from Spanish sources, and from Gagnier's translation of the Arabian historian Abulfelda, a copy of which the author found in the Jesuits' Library of the Convent of St. Isidro, at Madrid.

Not having followed out, in its extent, the literary plan devised, the manuscript Life lay neglected among the author's papers until the year 1831, when he revised and enlarged it for the Family Library of Mr. John Murray. Circumstances prevented its publication at the time, and it again was thrown aside for years.

During his last residence in Spain, the author beguiled the tediousness of a lingering indisposition by again revising the manuscript, profiting, in so doing, by recent lights thrown on the subject by different writers, and particularly by Dr. Gustav Weil, the very intelligent and learned librarian of the University of Heidelberg, to whose industrious researches and able disquisitions he acknowledges himself greatly indebted.*

Such is the origin of the work now given to the public; in which the author lays no claim to novelty of fact, nor profundity of research. It still bears the type of a work intended for a Family Library; in constructing which, the whole aim of the writer has been to digest into an easy, perspicuous, and flowing narrative, the admitted facts concerning Mahomet, together with such legends and traditions as have been wrought into the whole system of oriental literature; and at the same time to give such a summary of his faith as might be sufficient for the more general reader.

In April, 1850, Mr. Irving gave to the world the second volume of Mahomet and his Successors, which was greeted with the following notice from the same pen which heralded the appearance of his Life of Goldsmith:

The progress of the Moslem dominion, from the death of Mahomet in the year 622, to the invasion of Spain in 710, forms the subject of the present elegant volume. During this period of less than a century, the Moslems extended their dominion over the wide regions of Asia and Africa, carried their

* Mohammed der Prophet, sein Leben und seine Lehre.   Stuttgart, 1843.

conquests in one direction to the walls of Constantinople, and in another to the farthest limits of Mauritania, and trampled down the dynasties which once held universal sway in the East. " The whole," says Mr. Irving, "presents a striking instance of the triumph of fanatic enthusiasm over disciplined valor, at a period when the invention of firearms had not reduced war to a matter of almost arithmetical calculation. There is also an air of wild romance about many of the events recorded in this narrative, owing to the character of the Arabs, and their fondness for stratagems, daring exploits, and individual achievements of an extravagant nature." Mr. Irving has not felt himself bound to follow the example of the most cautious historians in suppressing or softening down these romantic adventures, but has interwoven them with consummate skill into his narrative, and has thus given it a fresh and vigorous vitality, in unison with the exciting and triumphant career of the people whom he describes.

In deciding on the plan of his work, Mr. Irving disclaims all pretensions to being consulted as an authority, and has attempted only to present a digest of current knowledge adapted to popular use. He has accordingly adopted a form between biography and chronicle, admitting of personal anecdotes and a more familiar style of narrative than is compatible with the severe dignity of historical composition. We scarcely need say, that, in a department of literary effort so congenial to the studies and tastes of the admirable author, we find the same flowing beauty of expression and felicitous grouping of individuals and events, which give such a magic charm to every production of his honey-dropping pen. The only sentence which we regret in the volume, is the concluding one, which expresses a doubt of the continuation of the fascinating

narrative to its natural and legitimate close. "Whether it will
ever be our lot to resume this theme, to cross with the Moslem
hosts the Straits of Hercules, and narrate their memorable conquest of Gothic Spain, is one of those uncertainties of mortal
life and aspirations of literary zeal which beguile us with agreeable dreams, but too often end in disappointment."

The Biography of Goldsmith, and the two volumes
of Mahomet and his Successors, were added to the list
of Mr. Irving's collected works while the publication
of the revised edition was yet incomplete. The Alhambra followed the last volume of Mahomet and his
Successors, in May; and the Conquest of Granada,
which closed the series, and of which he had written
some new chapters from new lights, appeared in the
succeeding summer. The publication of this work in
a revised form, seemed to revive his anxiety to complete the two manuscript volumes of Moorish Chronicles, mentioned in a previous chapter; while at the
same time he expressed the most earnest desire to begin
anew upon his Life of Washington, which had been
made to give place to the Life of Goldsmith, and the
preparation of the two volumes of Mahomet and his
Successors. "All I fear," was once his language to me,
"is to fail in health, and fail in completing this work
at the same time. If I can only live to finish it, I
would be willing to die the next moment. I think I
can make it a most interesting book—can give interest
and strength to many points, without any prostration

of historic dignity. If I had only ten years more of
life!" he exclaimed. "I never felt more able to write.
I might not conceive as I did in earlier days, when I
had more romance of feeling, but I could execute with
more rapidity and freedom."

VOL. III.—(5)

CHAPTER IV.

THE following is a reply of Mr. Irving to his friend Kemble, who had requested him, when in town, to call at Durand's, the artist, and tell him what he thought of a landscape he had some idea of purchasing when it was finished :

NEW YORK, Feb. 7, 1850.

MY DEAR KEMBLE :

I have called with ——— to see Durand's picture, and we were both delighted with it. It is beautiful—beautiful. Such truth of detail with such breadth ; such atmosphere, such harmony, such repose, such coloring. The group of trees in the foreground is admirable ; the characters of the trees so diversified and accurate ; the texture and coloring of their barks ; the peculiarities of their foliage. The whole picture had the effect upon me of a delightful piece of music. I think it would be a charming addition to the *Kemble gallery.*

*   *   *   *   *   *

I shall avail myself of the railroad, one of these days, to

pay you the visit you suggest; but I must first get out of the clutches of the printers.

His friend had informed him that he could now at any time take the railroad at New York at four P. M., and dine with him at Cold Spring at six; from which it would appear that the cars were passing his door. We hear no complaint from him, however, until he became for the first subjected to the annoyance of the steam whistle, during a severe fit of illness from which he was just recovering, when he breaks forth as follows, in a letter to Gouverneur Kemble, one of the directors of the company:

SUNNYSIDE, Aug. 7, 1850.

My DEAR KEMBLE:

Excuse my not answering sooner your kind letter. It found me in a terrible state of shattered nerves; having been startled out of my first sleep at midnight, on Saturday night last, by the infernal alarum of your railroad steam trumpet. It left me in a deplorable state of nervous agitation for upward of an hour. I remained sleepless until daybreak, and miserable all the following day. It seemed to me almost as if done on purpose, for the trains had ceased for several days to make their diabolical blasts opposite my house. They have not molested me in this way since, and have clearly shown, by the cautious and tempered management of their whistle, that these unearthly yells and howls and screams, indulged in for a mile on a stretch, and destructive to the quiet of whole neighborhoods, are carried to an unnecessary and unwarrantable excess. They form one of the greatest nuisances attending railroads, and I am surprised that, in the present state of mechanical art, some signal less coarse and brutal could not be devised.

You will laugh at all this; but to have one's family disturbed all day, and startled from sleep at night by such horrific sounds, amounts to a constant calamity. I feel obliged to the company for the attention that has been paid to the complaints made in this instance, and I trust to their continuing to protect my homestead from the recurrence of such an evil.

It would give me great pleasure, my dear Kemble, to come at once to you; but I am advised, as soon as I have sufficient strength to leave home, to go where I may have the benefit of a complete change of air. I intend, therefore, to pay a visit to my niece, Mrs. Gabriel Irving, at her place at Oyster Bay, where I shall have the benefit of salt air and sea breezes. My visit to you I shall defer until I feel in more companionable trim.

Ever, my dear Kemble, yours, affectionately,

WASHINGTON IRVING.

The following letter is addressed to the eminent scholar, George Ticknor, who had sent him, a considerable time previous to its date, his History of Spanish Literature, a work in three octavo volumes, which he had early meditated, and upon which he had been long engaged. Mr. Ticknor, in the autumn of 1818, had come, from a residence of some months in Spain, to London, and here he formed the acquaintance of Mr. Irving, Leslie, and Newton, all of whom made the excursion together from London to Windsor, "which resulted," says Mr. Ticknor, in a letter to myself, " in the beautiful paper in the Sketch Book." "He read to me," he continues in the same letter, "some of the other papers, and I brought out for him the first number for publication, and delivered it to Mr. Brevoort."

[*To George Ticknor.*]

SUNNYSIDE, Feb. 15, 1850.

MY DEAR TICKNOR:

I ought long since to have thanked you for the copy of your work which you had the kindness to send me, but I thought it best to read it first. This the pressure of various affairs has permitted me to do only at intervals, so that I have not yet got farther than the threshold of the third volume; but I will delay an acknowledgment no longer. I have read enough to enable me to praise it heartily and honestly. It is capital—capital! It takes me back into dear old Spain; into its libraries, its theatres; among its chronicles, its plays; among all those scenes and characters and customs that for years were my study and delight. No one that has not been in Spain can feel half the merit of your work; but to those who have, it, is a perpetual banquet. I am glad you have brought it out during my lifetime, for it will be a *vade mecum* for the rest of my days. When I have once read it through, I shall keep it by me, like a Stilton cheese, to give a dig into whenever I want a relishing morsel. I began to fear it would never see the light in my day, or that it might fare with you as with that good lady who went thirteen years with child, and then brought forth a little old man, who died in the course of a month of extreme old age. But you have produced three strapping volumes, full of life and freshness and vigor, and that will live forever. You have laid the foundations of your work so deep that nothing can shake it; you have built it up with a care that renders it reliable in all its parts; and you have finished it off with a grace and beauty that leave nothing to be desired. It is well worth a lifetime to achieve such a work.

By the way, as you appear to have an extensive collection of the old Spanish plays, there is one which Captain Medwin mentioned to me, the story of which had made a great impression on Lord Byron. It was called *El Embozado de Cordova* (or perhaps *Encapotado*). I have sought for it in vain in all the libraries and collections in Spain. If you should have a copy of it, let me know; though I apprehend Captain Medwin has given me a wrong name, as I could find none of the dramatic antiquaries that knew anything about it.

I regret that you did not fall into the hands of my worthy publisher, Mr. Putnam, who is altogether the most satisfactory man in his line that I have ever had dealings with. But I trust you have made a good arrangement with the Harpers, who command a vast circulation.

When you see Prescott, give him my cordial remembrances. You two are shelved together for immortality.

Ever, my dear Ticknor, yours very faithfully,

WASHINGTON IRVING.

The "old Spanish play" here alluded to as having been mentioned to him by Captain Medwin, and which had eluded his researches in Spain, has been spoken of in a quotation from his diary, heretofore given, as a play by *Calderon*. In the following extract of a letter to his brother Peter, written from Paris in March, 1825, I furnish a glimpse of the curious plot, and all the light I can throw upon the subject of this mysterious drama, here, too, spoken of as a production of Calderon :

Medwin is in Paris, but returns almost immediately to his nest. * * * I find he is well acquainted with Calderon in the original, and has talked to me of a play of Calderon's which is rarely to be found in the edition of his works, but of which he once obtained a copy. It is called sometimes *El Embozado*, and sometimes *El Capitado* (*i. e.*, The man muffled or disguised). The story is of a young man who has been dogged through life by a mysterious masked man; who thwarts all his plans, and continually crosses his path, and blasts his hopes at the moment of fruition. At length he is in love with a lady, and on the point of entering her house to be made happy. The *Embozado* issues out of it. They fight. The mask of the unknown falls off, and he discovers the very counterpart of himself! He dies with horror at the sight. Such is Medwin's mere recollection of the plot. Lord Byron was so much struck with it, that he intended to make something of it, and repeatedly mentioned the way he thought of treating it. Medwin wrote a sketch of the subject and Lord Byron's ideas about it, which he had intended to append to a new edition of his Memoirs, but he has promised to hand it to me. It is certainly very striking, and something fine might be struck out from the mere idea. The *Embozado* is supposed to be a personification of the young man's passions. I mean to search for the play.

On the 4th of April, 1825, he writes again to Peter :

I have just purchased an edition of Calderon, the same with that in the King's Library. It is in seventeen volumes. I had to give one hundred and eighty francs for it. I do not find the *Embozado* in it. I mean to get my Spanish master to write to Spain for that and any other plays of Calderon that may not be in this edition.

In less than a year after this, Mr. Irving went to Spain, where, it seems, by his letter to Mr Ticknor, he sought in vain for The Embozado in all the libraries and collections of the country. It is singular that a play of Calderon, of which *Medwin had once obtained a copy*, the story of which came near engaging the pen of Byron, should have eluded research. It could hardly have been a production of Calderon, and Medwin probably erred in characterizing it as such.

The niece to whom the following is addressed, had returned to Paris in May, 1850, from a visit of some months in New York:

[*To Mrs. Storrow.*]

SUNNYSIDE, July 18, 1850.

MY DEAR SARAH:

Your letter could not have arrived at a more welcome moment, for it has found me in a state of languor and debility, and somewhat depressed in spirits, the effects of an intermittent fever, from which I am but imperfectly recovered. I find I do not rally from any attack of the kind so speedily as I used to do; and this one has pulled me down so much, that I think I shall make an excursion for change of air.

* * * * * *

Just as I had got out of the clutches of my fever, we had

a visit from Mr. James, the novelist, and his family. He had arrived in New York several days previous, but I had been too unwell to go down to visit him. As soon as I could crawl out, I went to New York, and called upon him. I found he had intended seeking me out the next day. I kept him to his intention. * * * The next morning, by one of the early trains, he came up with his wife, his daughter, a very pretty and intelligent girl about sixteen years of age, and his two sons, one of seventeen, the other of fourteen years of age. They passed the day with us. The weather was delightful and the visit went off charmingly. James is a worthy, amiable fellow, full of conversation, and most liberal in his feelings.

*   *   *   *   *   *

We have all been shocked and distressed by the death of our good old President, General Taylor, after a very brief illness. It is a great loss to the country, especially in our present perplexed state of affairs. He has left a name behind him that will remain one of the most popular ones in American history. He was really a good and an honest man, uniting the bravery of the soldier with the simplicity and benevolence of the quiet citizen. He had not been long enough in political life to have straightforward honesty and frankness falsified, nor his quick sense of right and wrong rendered obtuse. I deeply regret not to have seen him. I had always looked forward with confidence to taking him by the hand either in New York or Washington. Report speaks well of his successor, Mr. Fillmore ; but I am entirely unacquainted with him, and of course feel nothing of the personal interest that I felt for the good old General.

And now I must break off, my dear Sarah. I have writ-

ten a longer letter than I thought I should be able to write
when I undertook it.   I wish it were a more amusing or interesting one ; but you must take the will for the deed.   I'll write
a better one when I feel better.

Two days after the date of this letter, he was seized
with chills in the cars on his way to New York, which
proved the advance of a serious indisposition. Alarmed
at the progress of the fever, Dr. Delafield, an eminent
physician from New York, who chanced to be on the
opposite side of the river, was called in, and the same
day Mr. Irving made his will, to be prepared for the
worst.   The skilful treatment of his physician, however, soon produced a favorable change ; and in a few
days he dismissed his patient as out of danger, though
still feeble.

It was during this period of languid convalescence
that he lifted up his protest against the diabolic blasts
of the steam trumpet.

In the following extract we have a passing allusion
to the home of his early literary associate, James K.
Paulding, at Hyde Park on the Hudson, and also to
some of the compensating advantages of the railroad.
The visit to Kemble was made early in September.

During my visit to Kemble (he writes to Mrs. Storrow), I
set off with him, one day, by railroad, for James Paulding's
country residence, where I had never been. We went by railroad to Poughkeepsie, and then took a carriage to Paulding's.
He has a lovely situation, commanding one of the most beauti-

ful prospects of Hudson scenery, with the Kaatskill Mountains in the distance. * * * We had a very pleasant dinner there, and got back to Cold Spring in the evening. This railroad makes every place accessible on the easiest terms.

The letter, which is dated October 31, continues :

You will see, by the papers, that the world has all been music-mad here at the arrival of Jenny Lind. With all my love of music, I have not yet heard nor seen her, but expect to do so next week. I do not like any more to cope with crowds, and have become a little distrustful of these public paroxysms. Besides, I am not over-fond of concerts, and would prefer somewhat inferior talent, when aided by the action and scenic effect of the theatre. I anticipate more pleasure, therefore, from Parodi as *prima donna* of the opera, than from the passionless performances of Jenny Lind as a singer at a concert.

In the following letter we have a further allusion to the renowned songstress :

[*To Miss Mary M. Hamilton.*]

SUNNYSIDE, Nov. 12, 1850.

MY DEAR MISS HAMILTON :
* * * You wish to know what I think of the "Priestess of Nature." I have seen and heard her but once, but have at once enrolled myself among her admirers. I cannot say, however, how much of my admiration goes to her singing, how much to herself. As a singer, she appears to me of the very first order ; as a specimen of womankind, a little more. She is enough of herself to counterbalance all the evil that the

world is threatened with by the great convention of women. So God save Jenny Lind !

Parodi's Norma is the best I have seen, except Grisi's ; but Grisi's in some respects is much superior. Parodi has much dramatic talent, a good voice, a commanding person, and a countenance very expressive, *in spite of her teeth,* which are a little on the " Carker " order. I doubt, however, with all her tragic fire, I shall like her as much in Lucretia Borgia as the fair Truffi, for whom I still cherish a certain degree of *tendresse.* But I do not pretend to be critical, having had all conceit of that kind killed by Ford, the Gatherer in Spain. who, in one of his papers in the *Quarterly Review,* denominated me " the easily pleased Washington Irving."

I presume our social rides are all over for the season, and that you and A—— will abandon the rocks and woodlands and other scrambles on horseback, for Broadway and the opera.   I took a ride on Dick this morning, but he seemed to miss his companions, Ned and Dandy, and to have lost all spirit.

As we have a kind of intermittent Indian summer, which incessantly returns after very brief intervals, I still hope to have some more rides among the hills before winter sets in, and should be rejoiced to take them with the female chivalry of Tillietudlem.   Yours very truly,.

WASHINGTON IRVING.

The day after the date of this letter, Mr. Irving came to town to attend Jenny Lind's morning concert of that day, expecting seats to have been taken.   Finding that none had been procured, he returned home to make the attempt another day.   Meanwhile, a party was arranged for Friday evening, to include Mr. Irving and all his household, who were to come down for the occasion. On arriving in the city, however, finding that another lady had been added to the party, which would make up the number without him, and being withal a little out of mood, he suddenly decamped for home, to the great surprise and regret of his nieces, who had locked up the silver preparatory to leaving, and were fearful that he would not be able to make himself comfortable. The next morning one of the party wrote, expressing her regret and uneasiness at his sudden and unexpected departure, informing him of " a nice arrangement" she had made for lodging him for the night, and " fancying him sitting alone and desolate, and, worse than all, without teaspoon or fork." This is his characteristic reply :

SUNNYSIDE, Nov. 17, 1850.

MY DEAR HELEN :

I am sorry to find my hegira from town caused you so much regret and uneasiness. It was a sudden move, on find-ing that the party for the concert would be complete without me, and that, if I stayed, I should have to look about for quar-ters, and put others to inconvenience. Besides, I find myself growing more and more indisposed to cope with the bustle and confusion of the town, and more and more in love with the quiet of the country. While tossing about, therefore, on the troubled sea of the city, without a port at hand, I bethought myself of the snug, quiet little port I had left, and determined to " 'bout ship " and run back to it.

You seem to have pictured my move as a desperate one,

and my evening as solitary and forlorn ; but you are mistaken. I took a snug dinner at Frederick's, where I met A—— H——. He was bound to Staatsburg, to rejoin his wife. We went up in the four o'clock train together. I endeavored to persuade him to stop and pass the night at the cottage, when we would break open the storeroom and cellar, rummage out everything that the girls had locked up, and have "high jinks" together. He was strongly inclined to yield to my temptation, but the thought of his wife overawed him. He is evidently under petticoat government, like other married men, and dare not indulge in a spree, like we free and independent bachelders.

When I arrived at the cottage, all was dark. Toby barked at me as if I were a housebreaker. I rang at the front door. There was a stir and commotion within. A light gleamed through the fanlight. The door was cautiously opened by Bernard ; behind him was Sophia, and behind her Hannah, while Peter and the cook stood ready as a *corps de reserve* in the kitchen passage. I believe, for a moment, they doubted whether it was myself or my ghost.

My arrival caused no little perplexity, everything being locked up. However, by furbishing up the kitchen plate and china, the tea table was set out after a fashion by Sophia, and I made a very cosy though somewhat queer repast.

My evening passed very serenely, dozing over a book, and dreaming that the girls, as usual, were all silently sewing around me. I passed a comfortable night ; had a cosy bachelor breakfast the next morning, took a ride on gentleman Dick, and, in fact, led a life of single blessedness, until my womankind returned, about two o'clock, to put an end to my dream of sovereignty.

CHAPTER V.

APPLICATION FOR AN ORIGINAL THOUGHT—BORING LETTERS—LETTER TO JESSE
MERWIN, THE ORIGINAL OF ICHABOD CRANE—HIS LAST PORTRAIT—LETTER
TO MRS. STORROW—THE REVERIES OF A BACHELOR—THE SCARLET LETTER—
LETTER TO M. H. GRINNELL—BOHN'S INFRINGEMENT OF COPYRIGHT—LETTER
TO BENTLEY—LETTER OF JOHN MURRAY—LETTER TO JOHN BARNEY—LETTER
TO H. T. TUCKERMAN, ALLUDING TO ROGERS, AND TO ARTICLE IN HOMES OF
AMERICAN AUTHORS—LETTER TO WM. C. BRYANT ON THE SUBJECT OF THE
DIFFERENT PORTRAITS OF COLUMBUS.

THE following letter was written to a young-lady,
who proposed to come to him and ask his counsel
about the publication of some poems of a brother who
had graduated with distinction, and been cut off in the
bloom of his youth :

SUNNYSIDE, Feb. 8, 1851.

DEAR MADAM:

While I sincerely sympathize with you in the affliction
caused by your great bereavement, and have no doubt your
brother was worthy of the praise bestowed on his memory, I
must most respectfully excuse myself from the very delicate
and responsible task of giving an opinion of his poems. I
have no confidence in the coolness and correctness of my own
judgment in matters of the kind, and have repeatedly found
the exercise of it, in compliance with solicitations like the present, so productive of dissatisfaction to others, and poignant

regret to myself, that I have long since been driven to the necessity of declining it altogether.

Trusting you will receive this apology in the frank and friendly spirit in which it is made, I remain, with great respect, your obedient servant,

WASHINGTON IRVING.

Here is a reply to a modest application from an unknown admirer to "pen (him) just *one* original *thought*" :

DEAR SIR :

I would be happy to furnish you with the "original thought" you require ; but it is a coinage of the brain not always at my command, and certainly not at present. So I hope you will be content with my sincere thanks in return for the kind and complimentary expressions of your letter.

No man could be more bored than Mr. Irving, by, as he once expressed it, "all sorts of letters from all sorts of persons." I remember his once showing me a letter asking him to subscribe to some particular book. "Now," he said, turning to me, "this must be answered. Every letter to be answered is a trifle ; but your life in this way is exhausted in trifles. You are entangled in a network of cobwebs. Each letter is a cobweb across your nose. The bores of this world are endless."

The following letter is addressed to Jesse Merwin, a schoolmaster whom he had met long years before at

Judge Van Ness's, at Kinderhook.   Merwin had called on him at New York, but, not finding him, had afterward written to him, and, among various allusions to the olden time, had mentioned the death of Dominie Van Nest, a clergyman whom they had both known at that period.   To Mr. Irving's surprise, the letter appeared in print a few days after.   Jesse Merwin's letter is indorsed in Mr. Irving's own handwriting: "From Jesse Merwin, the original of Ichabod Crane."

SUNNYSIDE, Feb. 12, 1851.

You must excuse me, my good friend Merwin, for suffering your letter to remain so long unanswered.   You can have no idea how many letters I have to answer, besides fagging with my pen at my own literary tasks, so that it is impossible for me to avoid being behindhand in my correspondence.   Your letter was indeed most welcome—calling up, as it did, the recollection of pleasant scenes and pleasant days passed together in times long since at Judge Van Ness's, in Kinderhook.   Your mention of the death of good old Dominie Van Nest, recalls the apostolic zeal with which he took our little sinful community in hand, when he put up for a day or two at the Judge's; and the wholesome castigation he gave us all, one Sunday, beginning with the two country belles who came fluttering into the schoolhouse during the sermon, decked out in their city finery, and ending with the Judge himself, in the stronghold of his own mansion.   How soundly he gave it to us!   How he peeled off every rag of self-righteousness with which we tried to cover ourselves, and laid the rod on the bare backs of our consciences!   The good, plain-spoken, honest old man!   How I

honored him for his simple, straightforward earnestness, his
homely sincerity! He certainly handled us without mittens;
but I trust we are all the better for it. How different he was
from the brisk, dapper, self-sufficient little apostle who cantered
up to the Judge's door a day or two after; who was so full of
himself that he had no thought to bestow on our religious de-
linquencies; who did nothing but boast of his public trials of
skill in argument with rival preachers of other denominations,
and how he had driven them off the field, and crowed over
them. You must remember the bustling, self-confident little
man, with a tin trumpet in the handle of his riding whip, with
which I presume he blew the trumpet in Zion!

Do you remember our fishing expedition, in company with
Congressman Van Alen, to the little lake a few miles from
Kinderhook; and John Moore, the vagabond admiral of the
lake, who sat crouched in a heap in the middle of his canoe in
the centre of the lake, with fishing rods stretching out in every
direction like the long legs of a spider? And do you remember our piratical prank, when we made up for our bad luck in
fishing, by plundering his canoe of its fish when we found it
adrift? And do you remember how John Moore came splash-
ing along the marsh on the opposite border of the lake, roaring
at us; and how we finished our frolic by driving off and leaving the Congressman to John Moore's mercy, tickling ourselves
with the idea of his being scalped at least? Ah, well-a-day,
friend Merwin, those were the days of our youth and folly. I
trust we have grown wiser and better since then; we certainly
have grown older. I don't think we could rob John Moore's
fishing canoe now. By the way, that same John Moore, and
the anecdotes you told of him, gave me the idea of a vagabond

character, Dirck Schuyler, in my Knickerbocker History of New York, which I was then writing.

You tell me the old schoolhouse is torn down, and a new one built in its place. I am sorry for it. I should have liked to see the old schoolhouse once more, where, after my morning's literary task was over, I used to come and wait for you occasionally until school was dismissed, and you used to promise to keep back the punishment of some little, tough, broad-bottomed Dutch boy until I should come, for my amusement—but never kept your promise. I don't think I should look with a friendly eye on the new schoolhouse, however nice it might be.

Since I saw you in New York, I have had severe attacks of bilious intermittent fever, which shook me terribly; but they cleared out my system, and I have ever since been in my usual excellent health, able to mount my horse and gallop about the country almost as briskly as when I was a youngster. Wishing you the enjoyment of the same inestimable blessing, and begging you to remember me to your daughter, who penned your letter, and to your son, whom, out of old kindness and companionship, you have named after me,

I remain ever, my old friend, yours very truly and cordially,

WASHINGTON IRVING.

About this time, Mr. Irving was induced to sit to Martin, an English artist, for the last portrait ever taken of him. Though somewhat idealized, and too youthful for his age at that time, it had much of his character and expression about it, and received the following notice from the pen of the poet, N. P. Willis, in the *Home Journal :*

We spoke, the other day, of Geoffrey Crayon's having once more consented to sit for his picture. Mr. Martin has just finished it, and we fancy there has seldom been a more felicitous piece of work. It is not only like Irving, but like his books; and, though he looks as his books read (which is true of few authors), and looks like the name of his cottage—Sunnyside—and looks like what the world thinks of him, yet a painter might have missed this look, and still have made what many would consider a likeness. He sits leaning his head on his hand, with the genial, unconscious, courtly composure of expression that he habitually wears; and still there is visible the couchant humor and philosophic inevitableness of perception, which form the strong undercurrent of his genius. The happy temper and the strong intellect of Irving; the joyously indolent man and the arousably brilliant author, are both there. As a picture, it is a fine specimen of art. The flesh is most skilfully crayoned, the pose excellent, the drawing apparently effortless and yet nicely true, and the air altogether Irving-y and gentlemanlike. If well engraved, we have him —delightful and famous Geoffrey—as he lives, as he is thought to live, as he writes, as he talks, and as he ought to be remembered.

The letter which follows, was written soon after his return from a visit to Mr. William Swain, at New Bedford :

[*To Mrs. Storrow.*]

MY DEAR SARAH: SUNNYSIDE, May 6, 1851.

Your most delightful letter of March 5th has remained too long unanswered; but it found me crowded with occupation, getting out a revised edition of the Alhambra, in which I was making many alterations and additions, with the press close at my heels.

  *   *   *   *   *   *

I have been very little in town this winter. Indeed, I may say that I have lived almost exclusively in the country since your departure. My time has been very much occupied with my pen, preparing and printing my revised editions, &c. ; and it will continue to be so occupied until I finish the Life of Washington, on which I am now busy. I am always happiest when I have a considerable part of my time thus employed, and feel reason to be thankful that my intellectual powers continue capable of being so tasked. I shall endeavor, however, not to overtask myself; shall mount my horse often, and break off occasionally to make an excursion like that to New Bedford.

  *   *   *   *   *   *

You speak, in one of your letters to the family, of the pleasure you have had in reading the " Reveries of a Bachelor." It is indeed a very beautiful work. The author was kind enough to send me a copy, and to call on me. I am much pleased with him. He is quiet and gentlemanlike in manners and appearance, and I shall be very glad to cultivate his acquaintance. I understand he is engaged to be married; I hope to one worthy of being the subject of one of his reveries.

There are two very clever works which have made their appearance within a year or so, one quite recently—*The Scarlet Letter* and *The House with the Seven Gables.* They are by Hawthorne, and two of the best works of fiction that have issued from the American press.

Remember me affectionately to your husband, and kiss the dear little women for me.

Ever, my dear Sarah, your affectionate uncle,

WASHINGTON IRVING.

Of one of the works here mentioned—The Scarlet Letter—I inquired his opinion just after he had finished reading it, and the impression was fresh. "Masterly! masterly!! masterly!!!" was his emphatic reply.

The following amusing letter is addressed to M. H. Grinnell, the husband of his niece, who had invited him to dine with him in the city, and who had just completed a house in the neighborhood of Sunnyside, which he expected soon to occupy:

SUNNYSIDE, May 20, 1851.

MY DEAR GRINNELL:

I must beg you to excuse me from dining with you to-morrow. Sunnyside is possessed by seven devils, and I have to be continually on the watch to keep all from going to ruin. First, we have a legion of womenkind, cleaning and scouring the house from top to bottom; so that we are all reduced to eat and drink and have our being in my little library. In the midst of this, our water is cut off. An Irishman from your establishment undertook to shut up my spring, as he had yours, within brick walls; the spring showed proper spirit, and broke bounds, and all the water pipes ran dry in consequence. In the dearth of painters, I have employed a couple of country carpenters to paint my roofs, and it requires all my vigilance to keep them from painting them like Joseph's coat of divers

colors.   Your little man Westerfield is to plaster my chimneys
to-morrow, and your plumbers and bellhangers to attack the
vitals of the house.   I have a new coachman, to be inducted
into all the mysteries of the stable and coach house; so all
that part of the establishment is in what is called a halla baloo.
In a word, I never knew of such a tempest in a teapot as is
just now going on in little Sunnyside.   I trust, therefore, you
will excuse me for staying at home to sink or swim with the
concern.   Yours, affectionately,

WASHINGTON IRVING.

P. S.—Lee has not yet commenced the long-promised filling up, which was certainly to be begun yesterday.   I begin
more fully to understand what is meant by *Lee-way.*

This was the filling up of a space between the bank
and the railroad, in which the water was apt to rest,
and generate, as he believed, unwholesome miasma.
Lee was an agent of the railroad, and Mr. G. a
director.

The following is in reply to an application of Mr.
Richard Bentley, the London publisher, who was
meditating a suit against Mr. Bohn for an infringement of the copyrights of three of the author's works
purchased by him.   Murray had already gone to great
expense to defend his copyrights, the sale, on the republication of the works, being greater than ever in
both countries.   For fifteen years some of the volumes
had not been reprinted by him or his father.

[*To Richard Bentley.*]

SUNNYSIDE, July 7, 1851.

DEAR SIR:

I have received your two letters, dated June 3d and 4th, informing me of your intention to proceed against certain book-sellers for an infringement of the copyrights of the Alhambra, Astoria, and Bonneville; and, inasmuch as you had no formal deed of assignment from me, requesting me to authorize your solicitor, Frederick Nicholls Devey, Esq., to institute proceedings in my name.

As the whole proceeding is for your account and benefit, and at your expense, I cannot refuse to delegate this authority to the gentleman named; but I confess I give my consent most reluctantly to a measure by which I am made to appear as a litigant, and, though only nominally so, yet at the great hazard of misconception.

If your solicitor could prepare an assignment, or other instrument which might have a retroactive operation, and enable you to sue in your own name, I would greatly prefer it. If this be impracticable, then you may take this letter as a warrant to your solicitor to appear for me, with full power and authority to represent me in any suit you may deem necessary in regard to the beforementioned works, and before any court. I wish it to be publicly understood, however, in this contingency, that you have recourse to my name on your own behalf, and only from a technical necessity, and that I have no personal interest in the event of the proceeding.

Yours very truly,

WASHINGTON IRVING.

I presume no proceedings were ever instituted by Mr. Bentley, as it will be seen, by the following letter of Mr. Murray to Mr. Irving, that *he* had compromised his suit with Bohn in September, only two months after the date of the preceding letter:

ALBEMARLE STREET, Sept. 19.

MY DEAR SIR:

Having troubled you so often, and, I fear, seriously, on the subject of my lawsuit with Bohn, it is with peculiar satisfaction that I now write to tell you that it is at an end. Mr. Bohn has offered me terms which are satisfactory to me and not humiliating to him. He has destroyed for me all value in your works, and I make over to him the copyright.

I regret to part with them, but it seemed to me the only way to get out of the squabble, which was becoming very serious, *my* law expenses alone having run up to £850.

One good, at least, has been elicited out of the contest— it has settled the right of foreigners to hold copyright in this country; for I am assured by my counsel, Sir Fitzroy Kelly, one of the soundest heads at our bar, that the recent decision of our judges on that head is not likely to be reversed by the House of Lords, or any other tribunal. Sir F. K. has studied the subject minutely, and made an admirable speech in the Queen's Bench on my side. I hope, therefore, that the Life of Washington, and other works *to come* from your pen, may yet bring advantage to their author from this country; but *priority* of *publication* in *England* is an indispensable condition, and must in all cases be guaranteed and carefully attested at the time of appearance.

No one can desire more than I do an international copy-

right arrangement with the Americans. In my desire I am
not surpassed by Mr. Bohn, nor Sir E. L. Bulwer; but I differ
from them in the strong conviction which I feel that it is not
by pirating American books that the object is to be attained.

I remain, my dear sir, yours very sincerely,

JOHN MURRAY.

The following letter is addressed to John Barney,
better known to the world as " Beau Barney," one of
the patriarchs of the fashionable circles of Washington
City for many years, and is in reply to one from him
recalling their first meeting at Burr's trial at Richmond, forty-three years before, and mentioning the kind
recollections of his sister, whom he met at that time:

SUNNYSIDE, Oct. 30, 1851.
MY DEAR MR. BARNEY:

Your letter of the 25th has acted upon me like a charm,
calling up such pleasant scenes in times long past, when we
were both gay young fellows, that I cannot go to bed before
answering it. What you mention of kind recollections of me
that were cherished by your sister, flatters my old bachelor
heart even now; for she was one of my early admirations, and
her image dwells in my memory as she appeared to me at the
time, so amiable, graceful, and ladylike. I well remember seeing her also at Baltimore, after her marriage, with her first
child, a fine boy, and, though a mere infant, remarkably sensible to music, being easily moved by it either to tears or transports. I believe I have since met him a man grown.

You talk of children and grandchildren. I have nothing
but literary bantlings to boast of. I trust your progeny will

outlive mine, and increase and multiply, and continue your name from generation to generation; which is more than can be expected from the progeny of the Muse, however prolific she may be.

Wishing you many pleasant and prosperous days, I will now bid you "good night," and will endeavor to continue in my sleep the agreeable dreams you have awakened.

Yours ever, very truly,

WASHINGTON IRVING.

The letter which follows, from Mr. Henry T. Tuckerman, and Mr. Irving's reply, I introduce with the single remark, that the former had lately contributed to a publication of Mr. Putnam, entitled "Homes of American Authors," a graceful notice of Sunnyside and its proprietor:

[To Washington Irving.]

NEW YORK, Dec. 6, 1852.

MY DEAR SIR:

I expect to sail for England in the Baltic on Saturday next; and, although my stay will probably be quite brief, I am desirous of seeing Mr. Rogers. Will you give me a line to him, and any other friend in England whom it would be pleasant for me to see? and oblige,

Yours ever, truly and respectfully,

HENRY T. TUCKERMAN.

[*To Mr. H. T. Tuckerman.*]

SUNNYSIDE, Dec. 8, 1852.

MY DEAR SIR:

I send you three letters of introduction, which I hope may be of service to you. My poor friend Rogers, I fear, is growing too infirm to render those attentions he was formerly so prompt to show to Americans of worth. Sir Robert Harry Inglis is a man of the most genial character, full of intelligence, and in communion with the most intellectual society of England. He is a man *I love and honor.*

John Murray has succeeded to his father in the literary realm of Albemarle street, which I used to find a favorite haunt of notorieties.

Permit me to make my acknowledgments for the very kind and flattering notice you have taken of me and my little rural nest, in Putnam's late publication. I wish I could feel myself worthy of half that you have said of me.

Yours ever, very truly,

WASHINGTON IRVING.

The following letter to Mr. Bryant, respecting the different portraits of Columbus, embraces the result of Mr. Irving's researches on that subject, and will be found to contain many particulars of interest. Joseph E. Bloomfield, the gentleman alluded to in the first paragraph, had been for some years a resident of the south of Spain, and, having become familiar with the portraits purporting to be the likenesses of the great discoverer, a correspondence on the subject had taken place between him and Mr. Irving. In the letter to

Mr. Bryant, who had applied to Mr. Irving for leave to publish his hasty notes to Mr. Bloomfield, he has recast his replies to that gentleman, with some additions. I transfer the letter from the columns of the *Evening Post*, the journal edited by Mr. Bryant, in which it first appeared :

[*To William C. Bryant, Esq.*]

MY DEAR SIR :

In consequence of the interest expressed by you as to a recent correspondence with Mr. Joseph E. Bloomfield, of Mexico, New York, on some points relative to Columbus, I have thrown the purport of my replies to that gentleman into something of a connected form. Mr. Bloomfield was desirous of my opinion of a portrait of Columbus existing in the Lonja, or Royal Exchange, at Seville, and which he says was the only one acknowledged in Spain as a true likeness. In reply, I have stated, that I know of no portrait extant which is positively known to be authentic. The one in question, according to his account of it, is full length, and that of a person from thirty to thirty-five years of age, armed in mail, and wearing a full white ruff. Now Columbus, by the time his discoveries had made him a subject for such a painting, was quite advanced in years. The ruff, too, was not an article of dress in Spain until after his death. It was a Flemish fashion, brought, I believe, from Flanders to Spain in the time of Charles V, who did not arrive in the Peninsula until 1516, ten years after the death of Columbus. The portrait may have been one of Diego Columbus, the heir and successor of the discoverer, and who, like him, was denominated " the Admiral."

Various portraits of Columbus have appeared from time to time in Italy, not one resembling the others, and all differing essentially from the description given by Fernando of his father. Theodore de Bry, in his "America," published in the sixteenth century, gave an engraving of one in his possession, which he pretended had been stolen from a saloon of the Council of the Indias, and sold in the Netherlands, where it fell into his hands. The same has been copied in an eulogium of Columbus by the Marquis of Durazzo, printed .by Bodoni, and in a life of the discoverer published in Milan by the Chevalier Bossi. This pretended portrait also differs entirely from the graphic description given by Fernando Columbus of his father. According to this, his visage was long, and neither full nor meagre; the cheek bones rather high, his nose aquiline, his eyes light gray, his complexion fair and high colored (*acceso di vivo colore*). In his youth, his hair was blonde; but by the time he was thirty years of age it was *quite white*. This minute description I consider the touchstone by which all the pretended portraits of him should be tried. It agrees with accounts given of him by Las Casas and other contemporaries.

Peschiera, a sculptor, employed in Genoa to make a bust of him for a monument erected to his memory in that city in 1821, discarded all existing portraits as either spurious or doubtful, and guided himself by the descriptions I have cited.

While I was in Madrid, in 1826, Don Martin Fernandez de Navarrete, President of the Royal Academy of History, published a lithographed copy of an engraved portrait of Columbus, which he found in an old Italian work containing likenesses of distinguished persons. He and the Duke of Veraguas (the descendant of Columbus) placed confidence in it, because other portraits in the same work were known to be correct. I doubted its authenticity. It did not agree sufficiently with the description before mentioned; and the hair especially, in the notice which accompanied it in the Italian work, was said to be *black*. Still, I published a copy of the engraving, some years since, in an abridged edition of my Life of the discoverer.

While I was in Paris, in 1845, Mons. Jomard, the learned principal of the Royal (now National) Library, had the kindness to send me a lithographic copy of a portrait in oil, recently discovered. The original bore, in one corner of the canvas, the inscription, CHRISTOFORUS COLUMBUS. The countenance was venerable and dignified, and agreed, more than any I had seen, with the description given by Fernando Columbus. Around the neck, however, was the Flemish ruff, which I pointed out as an anachronism. M. Jomard endeavored to account for it by supposing the portrait to have been made up toward the year 1580 by some scholar of Titian, from some design or sketch taken during the lifetime of Columbus, and that the artist may have decked it out in the costume in vogue at the time he painted it. This is very possible. Such a custom of vamping up new portraits from old ones seems to have been adopted in the time of Charles V, when there were painters of merit about the court.

In 1519, Juan de Borgoña, a Spanish artist, executed a whole series of portraits of the primates of Spain for the chapter room of the Cathedral of Toledo; some of them from the life, some from rude originals, and some purely imaginary. Some degree of license of the kind may have been indulged in producing this alleged portrait of Columbus. As it is evidently a work of merit, and bears the stamp of his character,

I have published an engraving of it in one of the editions of his biography.

Painting had not attained much eminence in Spain during the lifetime of Columbus, though it was improving under the auspices of Ferdinand and Isabella. There were, as yet, no Italian painters in the peninsula; and the only Spanish painter of note was Antonio Rincon, who is said to have been the first who "left the stiff Gothic style, and attempted to give to his figures something of the graces and proportions of nature." He executed portraits of Ferdinand and Isabella, who made him their painter-in-ordinary.

The originals have disappeared in the war of the French intrusion; but copies of two of his full-length portraits of the sovereigns exist in one of the lower corridors of the Royal Gallery of Madrid. It is very probable that he painted a portrait of Columbus at the time when he was at the court, the object of universal attention on account of his discoveries; but if so, it likewise has disappeared, or may exist anonymously in some corner of Spain, or in the collection of some picture hunter.

So much for the portraits of Columbus. Another subject of inquiry with Mr. Bloomfield was the name of the discoverer. He asks why he should not call him by the name he signed to all his letters now in the Royal Exchange of Seville, *Christoval Colon;* and he wishes to know "how did or could *Colon* be changed to *Columbus?*"

In regard to the name there is some petty mystery. That of the family in Genoa was *Colombo,* and his original Italian designation was Cristoforo Colombo. When he first came into Spain from Portugal, he seems to have retained his Italian family name, with a slight variation; for, in the records of Francisco Gonzalez, of Seville, the royal treasurer, there are still extant three several entries of money paid, in 1487 and 1488, by order of the Catholic sovereigns, to him, by the name of *Cristóbal Colomo.*

So also, in a royal cedula of May 12th, 1480, signed by the sovereigns, the public functionaries throughout the kingdom are ordered to furnish accommodations and facilities to Cristóval *Colomo.*

And the Duke of Medina Celi, his first patron in Spain, in a letter to the Grand Cardinal, dated 19th March, 1493, says: " I do not know whether your lordship knows that I had for much time in my house Cristóbal *Colomo,* who came from Portugal," &c.

In the capitulations entered into between him and the sovereigns, 17th April, 1492, by which he was constituted admiral, viceroy, and governor of any lands he might discover, we find him for the first time recorded as Don Cristóbal *Colon.* In adopting this appellation, he may have recurred to what his son Fernando intimates was the original patrician name of the family in old times, at Rome—*Colonus*—and may have abbreviated it to Colón, to adapt it to the Spanish tongue.

Columbus was a later version of his family name, adopted occasionally by himself and his brother Bartholomew, according to the pedantic usage of the day. His son Fernando says (chap. xi), that his father, before he was declared admiral, used to sign himself " Columbus de Terrarubra; " that is to say, Columbus of Terrarossa, a village or hamlet near Genoa. So also his brother Bartholomew, on a map of the world, which he presented to Henry VII, dated London, 13th February,

1488, inscribed on it some Latin verses, of which the following gave the name and country of the author:

> " Janua cui patria est; nomen cui Bartolomæus
> Columbus de Terrarubra opus adidit istud."

By this Latin version of his family name, he has always been known in English literature. If we change it, we ought to go back to the original Italian, Cristoforo Colombo. Long usage, however, like long occupancy, constitutes a kind of right, that cannot be disturbed without great inconvenience.

Yours, my dear sir, very truly,

WASHINGTON IRVING.

CHAPTER VI.

LETTER TO MRS. STORROW—COUP D'ÉTAT OF LOUIS NAPOLEON—KOSSUTH—LET-
TER TO GOUVERNEUR KEMBLE—THE COOPER COMMEMORATION—BRYANT'S
ALLUSION TO THE COOLNESS BETWEEN COOPER AND IRVING—WHAT THE LAT-
TER SAID ABOUT IT—A PROSPECTUS FOR A COURSE OF LECTURES SENT TO
HIM—LETTER THEREUPON—LETTERS FROM SARATOGA—ANECDOTES OF CHARLES
AUGUSTUS DAVIS—THE IRVING LITERARY UNION—A BREAKFAST WITH SON-
TAG—LETTER TO MISS HAMILTON—LETTER TO GEORGE P. PUTNAM.

THE following letter is addressed to Mrs. Storrow,
at Paris, just after the world had been astounded
by the *coup d'état* of Louis Napoleon. New York, in
addition, had been filled with excitement by the arrival of the graceful and eloquent Hungarian patriot,
Kossuth.

SUNNYSIDE, Jan. 13, 1852.

MY DEAR SARAH:

We have all been quite electrified by the *coup d'état* of our
friend Louis Napoleon. It is one of the most complete things
of the kind I have ever heard or read of, and quite Napoleonic.
His uncle could not have done the thing better in his most vigorous day. Who would have thought, "when his gracious
Majesty took his *disjeune* with us at Tillietudlem," he had so
much in him? You are in a fair way of becoming experienced in warfare, and seasoned to alarms, by your residence in a

capital where every political change is a military convulsion.
At present you are likely to have a great deal of the pomp
and parade of arms, without any more of the ragamuffin warfare of the barricades; for no doubt Louis Napoleon will keep
up such a military force in the capital as to render insurrection
hopeless. I should not be surprised if there were a long spell
of tranquillity in Paris under his absolute sway. Had his *coup
d'état* been imperfectly effected, or his election been but moder-
ately successful, France might have been thrown into a terrible
turmoil; but now he will hold her down with a strong hand,
until she has kicked out the last spasm and convulsion of
French liberty, and is quiet. You will then most probably
have all the splendors of the imperial court, with the spectacles
and public improvements by which Napoleon used to dazzle
the capital, and keep the Parisians in good humor. All this, I
presume, will be more to the taste of temporary residents like
yourself, than the stern simplicity of republicanism; and a
long interval of quiet would be a prosperous interval for the
commercial world; so both you and Storrow may find yourselves comfortable under the absolute sway of Napoleon the
Second.

It is a pity Van Wart had returned to England before this
event took place. He lost an opportunity of seeing that grand
spectacle, Paris in a tumult and under arms; though perhaps
he might have had a propensity to go about and see everything, as I should have done in like case, and have paid for the
spectacle by being shot down at a barricade. I never could
keep at home when Madrid was in a state of siege and under
arms, and the troops bivouacking in every street and square;
and I had always a strong hankering to get near the gates
when the fighting was going on.

We have had a great turmoil and excitement, though of a peaceful kind, here, on the arrival of Kossuth, the Hungarian patriot.   New York, you know, is always ready for a paroxysm of enthusiasm on the advent of any great novelty, whether a great singer, a great dancer, a great novelist, or a great patriot; and it is not often it has so worthy an object to run mad about.   I have heard and seen Kossuth both in public and private, and he is really a noble fellow, quite the beau ideal of a poetic hero.   There seems to be no base alloy in his nature.   All is elevated, generous, intellectual, and refined, and with his manly and daring spirit there is mingled a tenderness and sensibility of the gentlest kind.   He is a kind of man that you would idolize.   Yet, poor fellow! he has come here under a great mistake, and is doomed to be disappointed in the high-wrought expectations he had formed of coöperation on the part of our Government in the affairs of his unhappy country. Admiration and sympathy he has in abundance from individuals; but there is no romance in councils of state or deliberative assemblies.   There, cool judgment and cautious policy must restrain and regulate the warm impulses of feeling.   I trust we are never to be carried away, by the fascinating eloquence of this second Peter the Hermit, into schemes of foreign interference, that would rival the wild enterprises of the Crusades.

*   *   *   *   *   *

I can give you but little of New York news.   Indeed, I have not been much there since you were last here.   I draw more and more into the little world of my country home as the silver cord which binds me to life is gradually loosening; and, indeed, I am so surrounded here by kind and affectionate hearts, and have such frequent visits from one or other of the family, that I feel no need and but little inclination to look beyond for enjoyment. Even the opera does not draw me to town so often as formerly, although we have had a very excellent one, and New York, in fact, is inundated with musical talent.

*   *   *   *   *   *

It is now half-past twelve at night, and I am sitting here scribbling in my study, long after all the family are abed and asleep—a habit I have fallen much into of late. Indeed, I never fagged more steadily with my pen than I do at present. I have a long task in hand, which I am anxious to finish, that I may have a little leisure in the brief remnant of life that is left to me. However, I have a strong presentiment that I shall die in harness; and I am content to do so, provided I have the cheerful exercise of intellect to the last. * * *

The first paragraph of the letter which follows refers to a fortunate investment in Western lands, in which he had embarked with his friend Kemble years before, and from which the returns were steadily coming in:

[*To Gouverneur Kemble.*]

SUNNYSIDE, Feb. 5, 1852.

MY DEAR KEMBLE:

I have received with much satisfaction the intelligence of a further remittance from the enchanted purse of Godfrey, and have drawn upon William for my share.

You talk of having made a jovial tour among the gastronomes of Philadelphia, Baltimore, and Washington. So it is. Some men may steal a horse with impunity, while others are hanged for only looking over a hedge. I did but venture to town, about two weeks since, to eat a dinner or two, when I returned home with an attack of bile, and have been confined to the house ever since. I, this afternoon, for the first time, ventured out in my sleigh to breathe a little fresh air.

Any time that you will stop, on your way to or from town, I shall be happy to see you, and to give you the best my humble house affords; not pretending to rival the luxurious aristocrats with whom you have been jollifying.

Yours ever, my dear Kemble,

WASHINGTON IRVING.

February 17th, he had a visit from Clark, of the *Knickerbocker*, and Leutze, the painter, who came by appointment and dined with him. "We had a very pleasant dinner. I was much pleased with Leutze," he writes to me. In the same letter, which was written on Thursday, February 19th, though it is without date, he says: "I shall come to town in the beginning of next week—on Monday, if Webster's address to the Historical Society is on that night, though I rather think it is on Tuesday. The Cooper celebration is advertised for Wednesday."

James Fenimore Cooper, the distinguished novelist, had died on the 14th of the previous September. This meeting to honor his memory took place at Metropolitan Hall, February 25th, 1852, Mr. Webster presiding, supported by Bryant and Irving. In the fine address delivered by Mr. Bryant on the occasion, he quotes Irving's compliment to the *Pathfinder*, and

alludes incidentally to " an unhappy coolness that had
existed between them." Adverting afterward to this
passage to me, Mr. Irving remarked that the coolness
was all on Cooper's side ; that he had never been conscious of any cause of difference between them.

It was not long after this meeting, that the steamer
brought the tidings of the death of the poet Moore, which
had occurred on the day following the commemoration.
It was mournful news to Mr. Irving, whose attachment
to the Irish bard had been warm and sincere. The
circumstance, too, that his mind, like Scott's, had suffered eclipse during his life, he dwelt on with much
feeling. It had always been to him, in contemplation,
the saddest possible fate. After a time he went back
to many reminiscences of his pleasant intercourse with
Moore in Paris and London. Among other anecdotes,
he mentioned that Moore once told him of his hearing
an eager exclamation from a carriage as he was passing : " There's Moore ! there's Moore ! " and, looking
round, saw a lady with upraised hands and an expression of sad disappointment, as much as to say : " Good
heaven ! *can* that be Moore ? "

Moore once introduced him to a friend of his who
had the misfortune afterward to be thrown into King's
Bench for debt. Subsequent to his release, he offered
to show Mr. Irving the mysteries of the prison house,
and he accompanied him to spend the day there.
They took dinner within, and Mr. Irving was introduced to several who seemed to be enjoying themselves

very much.   In the evening, two or three women were
introduced, who were confined for debt.   They were
rung out at nine o'clock.   Before they were rung out,
one of them accosted Mr. Irving: " If you think of
coming here, let me give you a word of advice.   Don't
come empty handed.   With fifty pounds or so in the
pocket, one can make oneself very comfortable."
" From here," said Mr. Irving, " I went to Holland
House.   What a contrast ! "

To Mrs. Storrow he writes, May 29th :

*   *   *   My Life of Washington lags and drags latterly.
I have repeatedly been interrupted by turns of ill health—
bilious attacks—which have dogged me for the last two or
three years, and obliged me occasionally to throw by the pen
and take to horseback.   This spring I have been almost entirely idle, from my mind's absolutely refusing to be put in harness.   I no longer dare task it as I used to do.   When a man
is in his seventieth year, it is time to be cautious.   I thought I
should have been through this special undertaking by this
time ; but an unexpected turn of bilious fever in midwinter
put me all aback, and now I have renounced all further pressing myself in the matter.

*   *   *   *   *   *

I am glad to find the Prince President is getting on so
quietly, and that the 10th of May has passed off without ex-
plosions.   I hope Paris may be spared, for a time, all further
paroxysms either imperial or republican, and that the schemes
set on foot for its improvement and embellishment may be car-

ried out before everything is again thrown into chaos. Not that I expect ever to enjoy the result of them; but it is a city associated with too many happy scenes of my life not to be endeared to me; and, though I may never see it again, I carry so familiar a picture in my mind of all its localities, that I can fancy to myself every new modification that I read of. If Louis Napoleon continues in power, he will make Paris the centre of everything splendid and delightful, and will treat its *fête*-loving inhabitants to continual spectacle and pageant. He seems to understand the tastes and humors of the Parisians.

July 15th, he writes to the same correspondent:

I write a hasty line, in the midst of preparations for an excursion. To-morrow, Mr. G——, Julia, and the young folks, with S—— G——, P—— M., and H——, set off on a tour to Canada, and some of them to the White Mountains. I shall accompany them to Saratoga, Lake George, and Lake Champlain, but think it probable I shall then return to the Springs and take the Saratoga waters. It is a hot time of the season for such an excursion, and therefore I am dubious of following it out; but Mr. G—— could not conveniently time it better. I do not feel the same disposition to travel as I did in younger days. The quiet of home is becoming more and more delightful to me, and I find it difficult to tear myself away from it, even for a short absence. But I am sensible even too much quietude is to be resisted. A man, as he grows old, must take care not to grow rusty or fusty or crusty—an old bachelor especially; and for that reason it is good for him now and then to dislodge himself from the chimney corner. In this hot summer weather, however, how delicious it is to loll in the shade of the trees I have planted, and feel the sweet southern breeze stealing up the green banks, and look out with half-dreaming eye on the beautiful scenery of the Hudson, and build castles in the clouds, as I used to do, *hereabouts*, in my boyhood.

"Oh, blessed retirement! friend to life's decline." How fortunate has been my lot in being able so completely to enjoy it; so completely to realize what was once the mere picturing of my fancy. I wish you could see little Sunnyside this season. I think it more beautiful than ever. The trees and shrubs and clambering vines are uncommonly luxuriant. We never had so many singing birds about the place, and the humming-birds are about the windows continually, after the flowers of the honeysuckles and trumpet creepers which overhang them.

In the following letter, addressed to one of the inmates of Sunnyside, we have a glimpse of him on his tour:

[*To Miss Kate Irving.*]

SARATOGA SPRINGS, July 17, 1852.

MY DEAR KATE:

We had a glorious hurry-scurry drive along the railroad—left steamboats behind as if they had been at anchor. A flight of wild pigeons tried to keep up with us, but gave up in despair. We arrived here between eleven and twelve. The weather was pleasant, and there was but little dust. * * *

I have found some old friends here: Mr. and Mrs. Kennedy, of Baltimore; Mr. S——, President of the Bank of Commerce, and his family; our neighbor, Mr. B——, but without his pleasant little wife, who remains at home, castle building. By the by, they do not expect to get into their castle before October, if then.

We were all at a little *hop*, as they call it, last evening, in one of the saloons of the hotel. It was not very brilliant, but gratified the small folks, who, however, could not summon up resolution to dance. * * *

The Springs appear to be quiet and sociable, without any attempt at dashing and flashing, and therefore suit me better than they would at a gayer season. I should like very well to pass some days here, and take the waters; but we have marching orders for eleven o'clock for Lake George. I find it so easy to get here, and in such brief time, that I shall be apt to pay the Springs another visit. I have no idea of remaining mewed up at home until I grow to be an old fogy. * * *

To another of his nieces at home, he writes from the same place, July 21st :

MY DEAR MARY:

Having written to Kate and Sarah (who have my permission to show you my letters, though in great confidence), I now write a hasty line to you in turn. A letter which I forwarded from H—— to E—— has no doubt given you all an idea of our voyage across Lake George, and our visit to Ticonderoga, in all which we were favored with delightful weather, bright, yet temperate, and enjoyed to perfection the interesting and beautiful scenery. At Ticonderoga I made up my mind to give up the visit to Canada, and return here and take the waters. The party went off in splendid style yesterday morning, at eleven o'clock, in a fine steamer down the lake. At two o'clock I embarked on board of another one for Whitehall, and, after a fine run through lovely scenery, got into the rail-road cars at the latter place, and arrived here about six o'clock in the evening.

Here, to my great joy, I found Mr. Gouverneur Kemble, and Mr. Davis (Major Jack Downing), so that I am well provided with cronies. My friend Mr. Kennedy, however, leaves here to-morrow for Washington, being appointed Secretary of the Navy. His wife, however, and her father and sister, remain here; and I have promised Kennedy to pay some small attentions to Mrs. Kennedy during his absence, taking his seat beside her at table. I have, therefore, a little domestic party to attach myself to in place of the G—— party; but I see I shall be at no loss for acquaintances here. I began this morning to take the waters regularly, and mean to give them a fair trial.

This morning, after breakfast, I set off in a carriage, with Mr. Kemble and Mr. Stevens, to visit the scene of the battle of Saratoga, about twelve miles off. We had a fine drive through beautiful scenery, crossing Saratoga Lake in a scow. The day was very warm, but there was a pleasant breeze which tempered it.

After passing an hour or two at the battle ground, and acquainting ourselves with all its localities, we returned to a hotel on the banks of the lake, where we had an excellent dinner of black bass, lake trout, and game, and enjoyed ourselves in what little Fan would call "tip-top style." A pleasant drive home completed one of the most charming days I have had in the course of my charming tour.   *   *   *

[*To Miss Kate Irving.*]

MY DEAR KATE :

I really don't know when I shall get home ; for either the waters or the company agree so well with me in this place, that I find myself in first-rate health and spirits, and very much tempted to prolong my sojourn. It is really delightful to me to have this social outbreak after my long course of quiet life. I have found some old friends, and have made new acquaintances here, all very cordial and agreeable. * * * We have fine music, sometimes professional, sometimes by amateurs, and all of an excellent quality. This morning we had splendid performances on the piano, in the saloon, by Mr. Bull (or some such name), I believe a Norwegian, and one of the best performers on that instrument I have ever heard. Afterward we had charming singing by Miss L—— S——, who has cultivated her fine voice in a high degree since I heard her, two or three years since.

* * * * * *

Gouverneur Kemble returned yesterday to his old bachelor's nest in the Highlands. I did all I could to keep him here, but in vain. I wonder he should be so anxious to get home, when he has no womankind to welcome him, as I have. Yet even I, you see, can keep away.

There are some very agreeable talking ladies here, and a great number of very pretty-looking ones ; two or three with dark Spanish eyes, that I sit and talk to, and look under their dark eyelashes, and think of dear old Spain.

Mr. Frank Granger is here, and has joined the Kennedy set, with which I am in a manner domesticated. I am strong in the belief that Mr. Granger will have the situation of Postmaster offered to him, and that he will accept of it; though he shakes his head whenever it is mentioned. I regret extremely that A—— is not with him. She is on a visit to a friend at Niagara.

It is dinner time, and I must travel down stairs from my room, which is near the roof. Give my love to all the household.   Your affectionate uncle,

WASHINGTON IRVING.

To the same correspondent he writes, the day following:

* * * In my letter of yesterday, I told you I was going to a children's party at a gentleman's country seat in the neighborhood. * * * The house was of stone, spacious, and solid, built in the skirts of what had once been a forest, but which was now thinned out into groves and clumps and green lawns, until it had the air of British park scenery. A platform had been laid beneath some spreading trees, and here the little fairy people danced, while the grown-up people sat around in groups. It was one of the most charming little *fêtes* of the kind that I have ever seen. There were beautiful children, very beautifully dressed, from the age of two and three years upward. I felt like a patriarch among them; for among the spectators was Mrs. J——, an aunt of Mr. Finlay, whom I had danced with in my younger days, when she was a Miss B——, but who was now a venerable grandmother; and there was a maiden lady, Miss B—— L——, whom I had likewise danced with nearly fifty years ago. I sat by them, and talked of old times, and looked at the dancing group, in which we recognized the descendants (some two or three generations off) of some of our early contemporaries. To strike a balance, however, I paid some small attentions to two or three little belles from six to ten years of age, and was received with smiles that might have made me vain had I been fifty or sixty years younger.

  * * * * * *

I think it is the excitement of this cheerful society in which I am mingling, even more than the waters, which has had an effect of lifting me into a more elastic buoyancy of frame and spirits than I have experienced for a long time; and I am con-vinced, that if I had come up here for a few days when I felt so heavy and bilious, several weeks since, I should have swept all the clouds out of my system immediately.

Give my love to your father, and to such of the family as you have with you.

Your affectionate uncle,

WASHINGTON IRVING.

Two days later, he writes again to the same, from Saratoga:

I expected before this to have seen you face to face. Here, however, I linger, as it were, with one foot in the stirrup; and as I may continue to linger indefinitely, I have thought proper to scrawl you another line. The truth is, I am passing my time so agreeably, and find my sojourn here operating so admirably on health and spirits, that I am continually tempted to prolong it. I am linking up so many old friendships that had almost run out, and meeting, on the easiest of terms, so many pleasant and inter-esting people from all parts of the Union, that every day brings some new gratification and excitement. One sees society here without the trouble, formality, late hours, and crowded rooms of New York. This hotel in which I am quartered (the United States) is a little world of itself, with its spacious saloons, long galleries, broad piazzas, and shady walks; where there is a constant succession of polite society circulating, and you may throw yourself in the current, or remain aloof and look on, just as you please. I think I have never seen a watering place on either side of the Atlantic, where things were on a better footing, and better arranged, than in this, especially at the particular hotel in which I reside.

I take the waters every morning, and think they have a great effect on my system. I have entirely got rid of all bilious symptoms, and find my mental faculties refreshed, invigorated, and brightened up.. I have no doubt I derive some benefit from gossiping away part of the day in very agreeable female society, in which I experience such favorable treatment as inclines me to think old gentlemen are coming into fashion. They won't allow me for a moment to enrol myself in the respectable order of old fogies. My worthy coexecutor and cotrustee, Mr. Lord,* is here with his wife and daughter, and I am to take my afternoon's drive with them. Yesterday I had a beautiful drive among the hills with Mrs. R—— and a party in her carriage, and saw a succession of lovely landscapes, such as I had no idea were to be found in the neighborhood of Saratoga.

Early in August, Mr. Irving left Saratoga for

* Daniel Lord, an eminent counsellor of New York, one of the executors of John Jacob Astor, and a trustee of the Astor Library.

home, accompanied on his journey as far as Troy by
Charles Augustus Davis, the " Major Jack Downing "
and " old crony " mentioned in one of the preceding
letters as sojourning at the Springs with his family.
From some reminiscences of Mr. Irving at this period,
kindly furnished me by this gentleman, whose grotesque history of " The First Locomotive " the readers
of the *Knickerbocker Magazine* will not easily forget,
I select the following :

No one seemed more unconscious of the celebrity to which
he had attained.   In this there was not a particle of affecta-
tion.   Nothing he shrank from with greater earnestness and
sincerity and (I may add) pertinacity, than any attempt to
lionize him.   Although he was at once surrounded, at Saratoga, by a very gay and brilliant circle assembled there from near
and distant parts of our Union, he was sure to withdraw at
once from any circle that attempted to make a lion of him.
He much preferred sauntering out alone, or with some familiar
friend—trusting to any accidental event that might occur to indulge his own whim or fancy, or crack a joke, as occasion might
call.

In one of these rambles, I recollect his attention was arrested by the crying and sobbing of a poor little barefooted
and ragged boy, wearing an old " cone-shaped " hat that had
lost all its original form.   He had just been punished by an
elder sister, a thin, slatternly young vixen, who was following
him.   Mr. Irving at once, reading the whole story, turned
aside from our route, and commenced, in a most friendly and
affectionate tone, with, " I know what is the matter with my
little boy.   It is enough to make anybody cry, to wear a hat

that falls down over his eyes so he can't see, and stubbing his little toes.   I see the cause of all this trouble;" and, with that, he took off the old hat, and rolling its flabby brim inward, replaced it on the little boy's head.   "There," said he; "that is all right now."   Both the children, confounded by the event, stood for a time silent, and then moved off, chuckling together at its oddity; while Mr. Irving, resuming his walk, seemed not less gratified at his success in turning a scene of grief into one of gladness.

And in this connection I will venture to relate another simple incident, showing his interest in children.   On his return from Saratoga, I accompanied him a portion of his way homeward.   We were seated together, and directly in front of us sat an anxious mother with three children—one, an infant, in her arms, and the other two (a little boy and girl of some two and three years of age) giving the mother great trouble, and waking the infant by striving to clamber over her to look out at the window.   Mr. Irving at once interposed, and, lifting each alternately over to his lap, and looking at his watch, said : "Now, three minutes for each to look out of my window;" and began lifting them over and replacing them, each in turn, accordingly, till they were tired of it, though much gratified. "Ah, sir," said the relieved mother, "any one can see that you are a kind father of a big family."   This amused him greatly, and amply rewarded him for his interposition.   He would not spoil a good joke by refutation or controversy.

After his return home, we all missed him so much, I was induced (at the instance, also, of many friends) to renew the invitation, and ask his return; to which I received the following reply :

MY DEAR DAVIS:

Your letter found me lolling under the trees, and rumi-
nating, like one of my own cows, over the past pleasures of Saratoga. It was most welcome, smacking, as it did, of that eminently social resort, and bringing back the flavor of the happy
hours passed there. It will take me some time, however, to
get over the excitement of gay scenes, gay company, and the
continual stimulus of varied and animated conversation, and
bring myself down to the meek quiet of country life, and the
sober equanimity of Sunnyside. You who are always enjoying these gay chirpings of society, have no idea of what an
effect such a long draught has upon one of my present abste-
mious habits. I really think, for a part of the time, I was in a
state of mental intoxication. I trust, however, it will be bene-
ficial in the end; as I have heard it said by old-fashioned doctors, in the days of hard drinking, that "it was good for a
man's health now and then to get tipsy." Still it will not do
for me to repeat the revel very soon; so I am not to be
tempted by your suggestion of another visit to Saratoga
during the present season. That must be for next summer's
outbreak.

I envy those who have quiet conversations with Alboni
about her art. I delight in conversations of the kind with
eminent artists, whom I have always found very communica-
tive and interesting when properly drawn out. So I have
found Talma, Pasta, Mrs. Siddons, and Cooke, who were the
greatest in their respective lines that I ever was acquainted
with. I was much pleased with Alboni. She appears to be
of a frank, happy, joyous nature, and I think it is her rich,

mellow, genial temperament, which pours itself forth in her voice like liquid amber.

I thank you, my dear friend, for saying a kind word for me to such of my acquaintances and intimates at Saratoga as I came away without seeing. I made several delightful acquaintances there, whom it is probable, considering my time of life and my retired habits, I may never see again; yet I shall always retain them in choice recollection. Really, such an easy, social intercourse with the intelligent, the matured, the young, the gay, and the beautiful, rallies one back from the growing apathy of age, and reopens one's heart to the genial sunshine of society.

Farewell, my good friend. Give my kind remembrance to your wife, and that "discreet princess," your daughter; and tell Mrs. R—— I shall ever remember her as one of the most striking and interesting features of my visit to Saratoga.

Yours, very faithfully and affectionately,

WASHINGTON IRVING.

Two days after his return from Saratoga, he addressed the following letter, in response to an intimation that a club of young men of the city of New York had associated for literary improvement, and denominated themselves the "Irving Literary Union."

[*To Richard C. McCormick.*]

SUNNYSIDE, Aug. 9, 1852.

MY DEAR SIR :

Three weeks' absence from home has prevented an earlier reply to your letter of the 21st of July, and to the letter from your Society which accompanied it. I now thank you heartily for the kind expressions of your letter, and assure you that I appreciate most deeply the esteem and goodwill manifested by yourself and your associates in adopting my name as a designation for your literary union.

To inspire such sentiments in the bosoms of the young and ingenuous, is one of the purest and dearest rewards that an author can receive ; and as my long and desultory career is drawing to a close, I regard such demonstrations on the part of my youthful countrymen as a soothing assurance that, with all my shortcomings, and however imperfectly I may have performed my part, I have not lived entirely in vain.

With great respect, your obliged and humble servant,

WASHINGTON IRVING.

" When this club held its anniversary gatherings," says Mr. McCormick, " which were public, and occasions of peculiar interest to its members and their friends, an invitation to Mr. Irving to attend was always sent, and always promptly and courteously accepted ; but the modest author never managed to get to the city ! "

A breakfast with the delightful *prima donna*, Sontag, whose early appearance he had witnessed at Prague, some thirty years before, is thus alluded to in the following letter :

[*To Miss Mary M. Hamilton.*]

SUNNYSIDE, Sept. 20, 1852.

MY DEAR MISS HAMILTON :

When I engaged to join your party on the 28th, I was not

aware that the following day was the last Wednesday in the month, when I have to attend the stated meetings of the executors of the Astor estate, and the trustees of the Astor Library. I cannot be absent on this occasion, as it is the last meeting of the Library board previous to Mr. Cogswell's departure for Europe. Should you set off on Tuesday, I can join your party at any designated place on Thursday.

I set off this morning for Mr. Kemble's, in the Highlands, to be absent until the last of the week.

How the breakfast went off at Mr. King's, at Highwood; and how the Sontag looked and moved and conducted herself, and how I admired, but did not talk with her; and how I returned to town with the S——s, in their carriage; and how I went with Mrs. S—— to Niblo's theatre; and how Mr. S—— was to join us there, and how he did not join us there, but left me to be her cavalier for the whole evening; and how I wondered that he should trust such a charming wife with such a gay young fellow: all this, and more also, I will recount unto you when next we meet. Until then, farewell.

Yours truly,   WASHINGTON IRVING.

November 10th, 1852, he writes to Mrs. Storrow:

George Sumner has been twice up here: once on a visit to us, and another time at the H——s. He was, as usual, full of floating history about the men and the events of the day; having mingled in the most striking scenes and among the most striking people of the countries in which he has travelled and sojourned. I really was heartily glad to meet him again, for he is altogether one of the most curiously instructed American travellers that I have ever met with. Mr. Mitchell (Ike Marvel, author of Reveries of a Bachelor, Dream Life, &c.) came up from town and passed a day with us while Sumner was making his visit. * * * I have taken a great liking to him, both as an author and a man.

I close the year with the following letter to his publisher, who had sent him, the day before Christmas, a parcel of books for the acceptance of " the young ladies," with the remark that it would require a good many more if he were to *begin* even to suggest the obligations which had been incurred by the honorable and pleasant privilege of being associated with his name even in his " humble capacity."

[*To George P. Putnam, Esq.*]

SUNNYSIDE, Dec. 27, 1852.

MY DEAR SIR:

Your parcel of books reached me on Christmas morning. Your letter, not being addressed to Dearman, went to Tarrytown, and did not come to hand until to-day.

My nieces join with me in thanking you for the beautiful books you have sent us, and you and Mrs. Putnam for your wishes for a merry Christmas and a happy New Year.

For my own especial part, let me say how sensibly I appreciate the kind tone and expressions of your letter; but as to your talk of obligations to me, I am conscious of none that have not been fully counterbalanced on your part; and I take pleasure in expressing the great satisfaction I have derived, throughout all our intercourse, from your amiable, obliging, and honorable conduct. Indeed, I never had dealings with any man, whether in the way of business or friendship, more perfectly free from any alloy.

That those dealings have been profitable, is mainly owing to your own sagacity and enterprise. You had confidence in the continued vitality of my writings. * * * You called them again into active existence, and gave them a circulation that I believe has surprised even yourself. In rejoicing at their success, my satisfaction is doubly enhanced by the idea that you share in the benefits derived from it.

Wishing you that continued prosperity in business which your upright, enterprising, tasteful, and liberal mode of conducting it merits, and is calculated to insure; and again invoking on you and yours a happy New Year,

I remain, very truly and heartily, yours,

WASHINGTON IRVING.

CHAPTER VII.

IN the course of the preceding year, Mr. Irving had promised his friend Kennedy, the Secretary of the Navy, to pay him a visit at Washington; and "having occasion to rummage the public archives for historical information," he sets out on his journey in the beginning of January.

January 13th, he writes from New York on his way: "The day of my arrival in town I tried to get a ticket to hear Sontag, but, finding there was trickery in disposing of seats, I went off in a huff to the other house, and saw Alboni in the Somnambula, which she performed to admiration."

On another evening before his start, "feeling in want of city amusement," he writes, "I went to Wallack's, and saw the old play of the Road to Ruin, played in excellent style." He also went to a ball,

where, though after the opera, he found himself
" among the early ones." " I think it," he writes to
an unmarried niece, " one of the pleasantest balls I
have been at for a long time, inasmuch as I sat all the
evening on a sofa beside N——, in the front room up
stairs, where they received their guests, so as to leave
the rooms down stairs free for the dancers.   In this way
I saw a great part of the company in the course of the
evening, without fatigue, and without going into the
ballrooms to be crowded and cramped, and kicked into
a corner.   Besides," he adds, with a touch of fun,
" the dances that are the fashion put me out of countenance, and are not such as a gentleman of my years
ought to witness."

On the 17th, he had reached Baltimore, as will
appear by the following letter :

[*To Miss Catherine Irving, Sunnyside.*]

BALTIMORE, Jan. 17, 1853.

MY DEAR KATE :

In a letter to Sarah, I gave an account of my whereabouts
and whatabouts while in New York, last week, where I was
detained beyond my intended time by a snowstorm.   I was
rather in a humdrum mood during my sojourn, and, although I
had big dinners, gay balls, Italian operas, and Banvard's Dio-
rama to entertain me, I would willingly have stolen back to
" my native plains," and given up the " gay world " and all
terrestrial joys.   The last evening of my detention, however,
the weather and my dull humor cleared up ; the latter, doubt-
less, under the influence of Sontag's charms, who, in the

"Daughter of the Regiment," looked, played, and sang divinely.

The next morning proving bright and fair, I broke up my encampment, and got down to the foot of Cortlandt street, in time for the ferry boat which took over passengers for the express train. I looked forward to a dull, wintry journey, and laid in a stock of newspapers to while away time; but, in the gentlemen's cabin of the ferry boat, whom should I see but Thackeray. We greeted each other cordially. He was on his way to Philadelphia, to deliver a course of lectures. We took seats beside each other in the cars, and the morning passed off delightfully. He seems still to enjoy his visit to the United States exceedingly, and enters into our social life with great relish. He had made a pleasant visit to Boston; seen much of Prescott (whom he speaks highly of), Ticknor, Longfellow, &c. Said the Bostonians had published a *smashing* criticism on him; which, however, does not seem to have ruffled his temper, as I understand he cut it out of the newspaper, and enclosed it in a letter to a female friend in New York. * * * I arrived, after dark, at Baltimore.

I had to inquire my way to Mr. Kennedy's, or rather Mr. Gray's, as Mr. K. shares the house of his father-in-law in Baltimore. The door was opened by Mr. Gray's old factotum and valley-de-sham Phil, an old negro who formed a great friendship with me at Saratoga last summer, and, I am told, rather values himself on our intimacy. The moment he recognized me, he seized me by the hand with such exclamations of joy, that he brought out old Mr. Gray, and then Miss Gray, into the hall; and then a scene took place worthy of forming a companion piece to the return of the prodigal son. In a moment I felt myself in my paternal home, and have ever since

been a favored child of the house. To be sure, there was no
fatted calf killed ; but there was a glorious tea table spread,
with broiled oysters and other substantial accessories worthy of
a traveller's appetite.

Here, then, I am delightfully fixed, in this most hospitable,
spacious, comfortable mansion, with Kennedy's library and
study at my command, where I am scribbling this letter, and
with my friend Phil ever at hand to take care of me, and
attend to all my wants and wishes.

On the morrow, he writes :

This day we have a family gathering at Mr. Gray's, at dinner, and music in the evening, the old gentleman being a great
amateur.   To-morrow morning I take my departure in the
nine-o'clock train for Washington, where the cars take me in
less than two hours.   I shall leave Baltimore with regret, for
they have made me completely at home here, and I have
passed my time very much to my taste ; having a capital
library to retire to when I wish to be alone, or to exercise my
pen, and my old friend Phil to hover about me like a guardian
spirit—though rather a black one.

Mr. Gray is a capital specimen of the old Irish gentleman
—warmhearted, benevolent, well informed, and, like myself,
very fond of music and pretty faces, so that our humors jump
together completely.   I believe it was our sympathies in these
two last matters which linked us together so cordially last summer, and made him exact a promise from me to visit him this
winter.

From Washington, he writes to Sarah Irving, at
Sunnyside :

I am most comfortably fixed at Mr. Kennedy's, with a capital room, and everything snug about me for writing or reading or lounging. Mrs. K. received me in her own frank, kind manner. She could not treat me better *even if she were a niece.* I understand my friend Major Jack Downing is in Washington with his family; also A—— H——, who is here pleading a cause before the Supreme Court. I found my darling little friend, Mrs. S——, on a morning visit to Mrs. K., on my arrival, so that I see I shall meet with lots of agreeable company. I wish, however, to keep out of the whirl as long as I can, that I may get among the archives of the State Department, before I am carried off my feet by engagements. On Friday evening is the President's *levee,* which I shall attend, and then I shall be launched.

And launched he was, if not immersed, as we shall see by the letters which follow :

[*To Miss Catherine Irving, Sunnyside.*]

WASHINGTON, Jan. 23, 1853.

MY DEAR KATE :

I am in the midst of terrible dissipation, and in great danger of being carried away by it, in spite of all my efforts at sober life. I have three young belles in the house with me, on a visit to Mrs. K. They are very pretty, very amiable, very ladylike, and one of them very musical; and 1 could make myself very happy at home with them, if Tom, Dick, and Harry out of doors would leave me alone ; but I am assailed with invitations of all kinds, which I find it impossible entirely to fight off.

Yesterday I made a delightful excursion, with some of our household and some of the young folks of the President's family, down the Potomac, in a steamer, to Mount Vernon. We began by a very pleasant breakfast at the President's, where we met Mr. Augustine Washington, the proprietor of Mount Vernon, who accompanied us on the excursion. The day was superb. It was like one of those Indian summer days we had just before I left home. On board the steamer we were joined by Mrs. D——, and two very agreeable ladies from Boston. Everything conspired to render our visit to Mount Vernon a very interesting and delightful one; and we returned in the steamer by four o'clock in the afternoon.

In the evening I was at the President's *levee*. It was very crowded. I met with many interesting people there, and saw many beauties from all parts of the Union; but I had no chance of enjoying conversation with any of them, for in a little while the same scene began that took place here eleven years ago, on my last visit. I had to shake hands with man, woman, and child, who beset me on all sides, until I felt as if it was becoming rather absurd, and struggled out of the throng. From the *levee* I was whirled away to a ball, where I found my friend Madame Calderon, the Spanish Minister's lady, and was getting a world of chat about Madrid and our acquaintances there, when the system of hand shaking began again, and I retreated, and came home.

It is certainly very gratifying to meet with such testimonials of esteem and cordial goodwill, but, at the same time, it is extremely embarrassing.

*   *   *   *   *   *

This morning I have taken my seat as an honorary member at a meeting of the Smithsonian Institute. It is a noble institution, and is beginning to make itself known throughout the world. The edifice is a very imposing one, of brown stone, in the Norman style of architecture, built by Renwick; the interior, excepting part of the wings, yet unfinished.

*   *   *   *   *   *

I have been much pleased with what I have seen of the President and his family, and have been most kindly received by them. Indeed, I should have a heart like a pebble stone, if I was insensible to the very cordial treatment I experience wherever I go. The only fault I find is, that I am likely to be killed by kindness.

With my best love to all at my dear little home,

Your affectionate uncle,

WASHINGTON IRVING.

January 27th, he writes to his niece Sarah :

Yesterday I was rather good for nothing, having passed a somewhat sleepless night. Still I worked all the morning in the archives of state, and had to play my part at a large dinner party at home. * * * I cannot keep my spirits up to these continual claims upon them. * * * Playing the lion has killed me. I should like to repose for a few days in my den at Sunnyside.

Washington, February 4th, he writes to his nieces at Sunnyside :

MY DEAR GIRLS :

I am in debt for several letters from home, so this must do for you all. I have, in fact, been so much taken up by hard work at the State Department, when I can manage to get there, and by the incessant demands of society in all kinds of shapes, that I have neither leisure nor mood to write. I have at times been nearly done up, and would have broken away and hurried home, but for the mine I have to dig at in the archives.

I foresee I shall be detained here some time longer, having such a world of documents to examine, and being so often interrupted in my labors. You must not think I am staying here for pleasure's sake; for pleasure, just now, I would gladly dispense with, if I could. I do manage to keep clear of most of the evening parties; but the long dinners are inevitable, and the necessity of returning visits cuts up my time deplorably.

Had I nothing to do but amuse myself, I should find Washington really delightful, for I meet pleasant and interesting people at every turn; but I have no time to follow up new acquaintances, and am only tantalized by proffered friendships which I cannot cultivate.

Mrs. Kennedy had one of her *soirées* a few evenings since, when all Washington poured in upon us. * * * On this occasion, an officer of the navy delivered to me a small paper box containing a miniature anchor. It was made from the bolt to which Columbus was chained in the prison at St. Domingo. A purser of the navy * had gouged the bolt out of the wall, and sent part of it to the National Institute of this city; the other part he designed for me. The poor fellow was taken ill, and died of the yellow fever; but his sister had executed his wishes, in having a little anchor wrought out of the relic, and had forwarded it, with a letter, to me. Both the letter and the anchor have been between six and seven years in reaching me, having lain in the hands of a naval officer at Washington. I shall treasure them up in the archives of Sunnyside. * * *

* Robert S. Moore, of Newbern, N. C.

In a letter to myself, dated February 6th, 1853, he says :

I am making a longer sojourn in Washington than I had intended, but it takes time to make the necessary researches in the archives of state. * * * I cannot say that I find much that is new among the manuscripts of Washington, Sparks having published the most interesting; but it is important to get facts from the fountain head, not at second hand through his publications.

The following is in answer to a letter which contained an allusion to a party in New York, where the amusement of the evening was moving tables—a novel and mysterious experimenting, of which the whole city was just then full :

[*To Mrs. Pierre M. Irving.*]

WASHINGTON, Feb. 10, 1853.

MY DEAR HELEN :

 *   *   *   *   *   *

I had hoped Lent, which put a stop to the balls, would likewise put a stop to the dinner parties; but the latter continue, and I stand committed for several. The last one for which I am engaged is at the President's, on Saturday week. It is to be a small social party, his huge dinners being rather unwieldy, and somewhat promiscuous. I shall accept no invitations after that, hoping then to turn my face homeward, tarrying a day or two at Baltimore on the way.

 *   *   *   *   *   *

Thackeray has delivered one of his lectures here, and delivers another to-morrow evening. I attended the first, and shall attend the next.   He is well received here, both in public and private, and is going the round of dinner parties, &c.   I find him a very pleasant companion.

I see you are in the midst of hocus pocus with moving tables, &c.   I was at a party, last evening, where the grand experiment was made on a large table, round which were seated upward of a dozen young folks of both sexes.   The table was for a long time obdurate.   At length a very pretty, bright-eyed girl, who in England would have passed for a Lancashire witch, gave the word, "Tip, table!" whereupon the table gradually raised on two legs, until the surface was at an angle of forty-five degrees, and was not easily to be put down again, until she gave the word, "Down, table!"   It afterward rose and sank to a tune, performed gyrations about the room, &c.; all which appeared very mysterious and diabolic.   Unfortunately, two or three of us tried an after experiment, and found that we could tip table, and make it move about the room without any very apparent exertion of our hands; so we remain among the unconverted—quite behind the age.

From the close of the following letter, it would seem there had been some table waltzing at Sunnyside :

[*To Miss Sarah Irving.*]

Washington, Feb. 25, 1853.

My dear Sarah :

I have just received your letter, dated 24th, by which I am happy to find all is going on well at home.

I went down, yesterday, in the steamer Vixen, with a large party, to visit the caloric ship Ericsson.   In our party were the two Presidents (Fillmore and Pierce), all the Cabinet, and many other official characters. The Ericsson appeared to justify all that has been said in her praise, and promises to produce a great change in navigation.

After inspecting the machinery, and visiting all parts of the ship, which is a noble vessel, and beautifully fitted up, we partook of a plentiful collation, and returned, well pleased, to the capital.

This morning I went down to Mount Vernon, in company with Miss Mary K——. We were joined at the steamboat by Mr. B—— and Sarah, and found Mr. Augustine Washington on board. Our visit to Mount Vernon was but for two or three hours, returning in the afternoon. I went merely for the purpose of taking one more view of the place and its vicinity, though pressed by Mr. Washington to make a longer visit.

This evening I have been at the last reception of President Fillmore. It was an immense crowd, for the public seemed eager to give him a demonstration, at parting, of their hearty goodwill.

I see you are all conjuring, and setting the tables waltzing. It is really high time for me to come home. I beg you won't set the table in my study capering. If that gets bewitched, I am undone.

Three days after, he writes to Mrs. Pierre M. Irving as follows:

I have been thinking of setting off homeward for the last week, yet here am I still lingering, and I begin to question whether I shall not make good your surmise, that I would stay until after the inauguration. I really am yearning for home;

but my friends the Kennedys will not hear of my going off until they break up their camp, which will probably be at the end of the week.

I have become acquainted with the President elect. He is a quiet, gentlemanlike man in appearance and manner, and I have conceived a goodwill for him, from finding, in the course of our conversation, that he has it at heart to take care of Hawthorne, who was his early fellow student.

Hawthorne afterward received the appointment of Consul at Liverpool—a lucrative post. Mr. Irving had never met the gifted author, but was a great admirer of his powers, and considered his novels and essays among the best productions of our literature. His letter continues:

I have a letter from Sarah S——, giving an account of the grand spectacle of the Emperor and Empress going to Notre Dame, with all their wedding retinue. It must have been a magnificent pageant.

I believe I have told you that I knew the grandfather of the Empress—old Mr. Kirkpatrick, who had been American Consul at Malaga. I passed an evening at his house, in 1827, near Adra, on the coast of the Mediterranean. A week or two after, I was at the house of his son-in-law, the Count Téba, at Granada—a gallant, intelligent gentleman, much cut up in the wars, having lost an eye, and been maimed in a leg and hand. His wife, the daughter of Mr. Kirkpatrick, was absent, but he had a family of little girls, mere children, about him. The youngest of these must have been the present Empress. Several years afterward, when I had recently taken up my abode in Madrid, I was invited to a grand ball at the house of the Countess Montijo, one of the leaders of the *ton*. On making my bow to her, I was surprised at being received by her with the warmth and eagerness of an old friend. She claimed me as the friend of her late husband, the Count Téba (subsequently Marquis Montijo), who, she said, had often spoken of me with the greatest regard. She took me into another room, and showed me a miniature of the Count, such as I had known him, with a black patch over one eye. She subsequently introduced me to the little girls I had known at Granada—now fashionable belles at Madrid.

After this, I was frequently at her house, which was one of the gayest in the capital. The Countess and her daughters all spoke English. The eldest daughter was married, while I was in Madrid, to the Duke of Alva and Berwick, the lineal successor to the pretender to the British crown. The other now sits on the throne of France.

Mr. Irving remained in Washington until after the inauguration of President Pierce, when he returned to Sunnyside.

The following letter to Mrs. Kennedy, at whose house he had been domesticated for nearly two months, was addressed to her a few days after his return. The "gentle Horseshoe" was a name Mr. Irving was fond of giving the late Secretary of the Navy, from the title of one of his novels, Horseshoe Robinson.

[*To Mrs. John P. Kennedy.*]

SUNNYSIDE, March 11, 1853.

MY DEAR MRS. KENNEDY :

I was really sad at heart at parting with you and Mary Kennedy at Washington. Indeed, had not your establishment fallen to pieces around me, I hardly know when I should have gotten away. I could almost have clung to the wreck so long as there was a three-legged stool and a horn spoon to make shift with. You see what danger there is in domesticating me. I am sadly prone to take root where I find myself happy. It was some consolation to me, in parting, that I had Mrs. H——— and the gentle Horseshoe for fellow travellers. Without their company, I should have been completely downhearted. The former was bright, intelligent, and amiable as usual ; and as to "John," you know he is a sympathizing soul. He saw I needed soothing, so he cracked some of his best jokes, and I was comforted.

I was rejoiced to find your father down stairs, and seemingly almost, if not quite as well as when I left him. My reception by him and your sister made me feel that I was in another home—or rather in another part of the family circle in which for some time past I had been flourishing so happily. * * *

I arrived in New York too late for the Hudson River Railroad cars, so I had to remain in the city until morning. Yesterday I alighted at the station, within ten minutes' walk of home. The walk was along the railroad, in full sight of the house. I saw female forms in the porch, and I knew the spyglass was in hand. In a moment there was a waving of handkerchiefs, and a hurrying hither and thither. Never did old bachelor come to such a loving home, so gladdened by blessed womankind. In fact, I doubt whether many married men receive such a heartfelt welcome. My friend Horseshoe, and one or two others of my acquaintance, may; but there are not many as well off in domestic life as I. However, let me be humbly thankful, and repress all vainglory.

After all the kissing and crying and laughing and rejoicing were over, I sallied forth to inspect my domains, welcomed home by my prime minister Robert, and my master of the house Thomas, and my keeper of the poultry yard, William. Everything was in good order; all had been faithful in the discharge of their duties. My fields had been manured, my trees trimmed, the fences repaired and painted. I really believe more had been done in my absence than would have been done had I been home. My horses were in good condition. Dandy and Billy, the coach horses, were as sleek as seals. Gentleman Dick, my saddle horse, showed manifest pleasure at seeing me; put his cheek against mine, laid his head on my shoulder, and would have nibbled at my ear had I permitted it. One of my Chinese geese was sitting on eggs; the rest were sailing like frigates in the pond, with a whole fleet of white topknot ducks. The hens were vying with each other which could bring out the earliest brood of chickens. Taffy and Tony, two pet dogs of a dandy race, kept more for show than use, received me with well-bred though rather cool civility; while my little terrier slut Ginger bounded about me almost crazy with delight, having five little Gingers toddling at her heels, with which she had enriched me during my absence.

I forbear to say anything about my cows, my Durham heifer, or my pigeons, having gone as far with these rural matters as may be agreeable. Suffice it to say, everything was just as heart could wish; so, having visited every part of my empire, I settled down for the evening in my elbow chair, and entertained the family circle with all the wonders I had seen at Washington.

To-day I have dropped back into all my old habits. * * * I have resumed my seat at the table in the study, where I am scribbling this letter, while an unseasonable snow-storm is prevailing out of doors.

This letter will no doubt find you once more at your happy home in Baltimore, all fussing and bustling at an end, with time to nurse yourself, and get rid of that cold which has been hanging about you for so many days.

And now let me express how much I feel obliged to you and Kennedy for drawing me forth out of my little country nest, and setting me once more in circulation. This has grown out of our fortunate meeting and sojourn together at Saratoga last summer, and I count these occurrences as among the most pleasant events of my life. They have brought me into domestic communion with yourselves, your family connections and dearest intimacies, and have opened to me a little world of friendship and kindness, in which I have enjoyed myself with a full heart.

God bless you all, and make you as happy as you delight to make others.   Ever yours, most truly,

WASHINGTON IRVING.

CHAPTER VIII.

THE following letter is addressed to Mrs. Storrow, at Paris :

SUNNYSIDE, March 28, 1853.

MY DEAR SARAH :

A letter received from you while I was at Washington, gave an account of the marriage procession of Louis Napoleon and his bride to the Church of Notre Dame, which you saw from a window near the Hotel de Ville. One of your recent letters, I am told, speaks of your having been presented to the Empress. I shall see it when I go to town. Louis Napoleon and Eugenie Montijo, Emperor and Empress of France !—one of whom I have had a guest at my cottage on the Hudson ; the other, whom, when a child, I have had on my knee at Granada ! It seems to cap the climax of the strange dramas of which Paris has been the theatre during my lifetime.

I have repeatedly thought that each grand *coup de theatre* would be the last that would occur in my time ; but each has

been succeeded by another equally striking, and what will be
the next, who can conjecture?

The last I saw of Eugenie Montijo, she was one of the
reigning belles of Madrid; and she and her giddy circle had
swept away my charming young friend, the beautiful and ac-.
complished —— ——, into their career of fashionable dissipation. Now Eugenie is upon a throne, and —— a volun-
tary recluse in a convent of one of the most rigorous orders!
Poor ——! Perhaps, however, her fate may ultimately be
the happiest of the two. "The storm," with her, "is o'er, and
she's at rest;" but the other is launched upon a returnless
shore on a dangerous sea infamous for its tremendous ship-
wrecks.

Am I to live to see the catastrophe of her career, and the
end of this suddenly conjured-up empire, which seems to be of
"such stuff as dreams are made of?"

I confess my personal acquaintance with the individuals
who figure in this historical romance gives me uncommon interest in it; but I consider it stamped with danger and instability,
and as liable to extravagant vicissitudes as one of Dumas's
novels. You do right to witness the grand features of this
passing pageant. You are probably reading one of the most
peculiar and eventful pages of history, and may live to look
back upon it as a romantic tale.

I have passed part of the winter at Washington, delightfully situated in the house of my friend Kennedy, who was
Secretary of the Navy.

      *   *   *   *   *   *

I was present at the going out of one Administration and
the coming in of another; was acquainted with both Presidents and most of the members of both Cabinets, and wit-

nessed the inauguration of General Pierce. It was admirable to see the quiet and courtesy with which this great transition of power and rule from one party to another took place. I was at festive meetings where the members of the opposite parties mingled socially together, and have seen the two Presidents arm in arm, as if the sway of an immense empire was not passing from one to the other.   *   *   *

At the last of this week I expect some of the family up here to my birthday, the 3d of April, when I come of age— of full age—seventy years! I never could have hoped, at such an advanced period of life, to be in such full health, such activity of mind and body, and such capacity for enjoyment as I find myself at present. But I have reached the allotted limit of existence; all beyond is especial indulgence. So long as I can retain my present health and spirits, I am happy to live, for I think my life is important to the happiness of others; but as soon as my life becomes useless to others, and joyless to myself, I hope I may be relieved from the burden; and I shall lay it down with heartfelt thanks to that Almighty Power which has guided my incautious steps through so many uncertain and dangerous ways, and enabled me to close my career in serenity and peace, surrounded by my family and friends, in the little home I have formed for myself, among the scenes of my boyhood.

With affectionate remembrances to Mr. Storrow, and love to the dear little folks,

Your affectionate uncle,

WASHINGTON IRVING.

The following letter also touches upon his three-score and ten. It is addressed to the Hon. Robert C.

Winthrop, of Boston, who had just sent him a volume of his writings, and with whom he had recently become acquainted under Mr. Kennedy's roof, at Washington, where they sojourned together for a week. It has allusion also to a sketch of him by Wilkie. Of this last, Mr. Winthrop writes: "Do you remember my telling you that I had a sketch of you, by Wilkie, in one of his published volumes? I have found it, since my return, in a volume which I purchased in London, and which was just out when I was there, in 1847. The sketch is entitled, "Washington Irving consulting the Archives of Cordova," and is dated 25th April, 1828. It forms the frontispiece to a large volume dedicated to Lord Lansdowne. The original of the sketch of you is said to be in the possession of Sir William Knighton, Bart."

SUNNYSIDE, April 4, 1853.

MY DEAR MR. WINTHROP:

I have deferred replying to your very kind and acceptable letter until I could acknowledge the receipt of the volume it announced. It has now come to hand, and I shall prize it, not only for its own merit, but as a memorial of the very pleasant time we passed together under the hospitable roof of Kennedy, at Washington; and I assure you I esteem it one of the most gratifying circumstances attending my delightful sojourn there, that it brought me into domestic companionship with you.

I regret to learn that you, like Kennedy, have been a sufferer in health since we parted, though I trust you are both fully recovered. You have no doubt been shocked, like myself, at the sad bereavement which has afflicted the worthy

Fillmore family. I almost think poor Mrs. Fillmore must have received her death warrant while standing by my side on the marble terrace of the Capitol, exposed to chilly wind and snow, listening to the inaugural speech of her husband's successor. This sad event, as you perceive, has put an end to the Southern tour, which did not seem to meet your approbation, and has left Kennedy to the quiet of his home and his library, which I should think he would relish after the turmoil of Washington.

As to myself, to echo your own words, I am "safely at Sunnyside, and in the best of health." The shadows of departed years, however, are gathering over me, for yesterday I celebrated my seventieth birthday. Seventy years of age! I can scarcely realize that I have indeed arrived at the allotted verge of existence, beyond which all is special grace and indulgence. I used to think that a man, at seventy, must have survived everything worth living for; that with him the silver cord must be loosed, the wheel broken at the cistern; that all desire must fail, and the grasshopper become a burden. Yet here I find myself, unconscious of the withering influences of age, still strong and active, my sensibilities alive, and my social affections in full vigor.

> "Strange, that a harp of thousand strings
> Should keep in tune so long!"

While it does keep in tune; while I have still a little music in my soul to be called out by any touch of sympathy; while I can enjoy the society of those dear to me, and contribute, as they tell me, to their enjoyment, I am content and happy to live on. But I have it ever present to my mind that the measure of my days is full and running over; and I feel ready at any moment to lay down this remnant of existence, with a thankful heart that my erratic and precarious career has been brought to so serene a close, among the scenes of my youth, and surrounded by those I love.

The sketch of me by Wilkie, which you tell me you have in one of his published volumes, cannot be an attempt at a likeness. I recollect the composition; the scene, I think, was at Seville. I was seated in a dusky chamber at a table, looking over a folio volume which a monk who was standing by my side had just handed down to me. Wilkie thought the whole had a Rembrandt effect, which he aimed at producing; but, if I recollect right, my face could not be seen distinctly.

Farewell, my dear Mr. Winthrop, and believe me, with no common regard,   Your friend,

WASHINGTON IRVING.

[*To Mr. Edward Gray.*]

SUNNYSIDE, April 24, 1853.

MY DEAR MR. GRAY:

The hams which you have had the kindness to send me, came safe to hand. One of them was served up to-day, at dinner. All my family partook of it with uncommon relish. Never did a ham achieve such sudden popularity. In a word, it covered itself with glory! I must get your receipt for curing hams; but there must be much in the breed of the animal, as well as in the treatment and feeding. I never attempt anything but a few green hams, in which I succeed very well; but hams so rich, high flavored, and thoroughly cured as those you have sent me, are quite beyond my art. I thank you most heartily for this specimen of what Maryland can furnish in this line. If I had the ordering of things, I should have all our pigs sent to Maryland to be *cured*, as they send patients to southern climates.

I am happy to learn from Mrs. Kennedy that your health is restored to its usual state, and anticipate the pleasure of again meeting you in the ensuing summer. Since we parted, I have celebrated my seventieth birthday, and passed that boundary beyond which a man lives by special privilege. Your example shows me, however, that a man may live on beyond that term, and retain his sensibilities alive to every-thing noble and good and pleasurable and beautiful, and enjoy the society of his friends, and spread happiness around him. On such conditions, old age is lovable. I shall endeavor to follow your example.

Ever affectionately, your friend,

WASHINGTON IRVING.

[To Mrs. Kennedy.]

SUNNYSIDE, April 24, 1853.

MY DEAR MRS. KENNEDY:

I am truly concerned to hear that Kennedy still continues unwell. He has overtasked himself, and has led a life of too much excitement for some months past, and is now in a state of collapse. He must give his mind perfect repose for a time —do as they do with the horses, when they take off their shoes and turn them out to grass. His study is no place for him just now. I think the idea a good one to make an excursion—try change of scene and a course of agreeable society. I think Mrs. S—— a capital prescription for his present case ; and the sooner you pay her your proposed visit, the better.

I should indeed like to be of your party, for I am be-

witched with the South, and Virginia has always been a poetical region with me.   But I begin to doubt whether those
high-seasoned regales of society that I have had of late, at
Saratoga and Washington, do not unsettle me a little, and
make it hard for me to content myself with the sober, everyday fare of Sunnyside.   I have now to work hard to make up
for past dissipation, and to earn any future holiday.   *   *   *

I have just been writing to your father, to thank him for
the hams, which have arrived in prime order, and to give him
an account of the brilliant manner in which one of them ac-
quitted itself at dinner to-day.   I strike my flag to him completely, and confess that, for hams, we cannot pretend to cope
with old Maryland (always saving and excepting certain *green*
hams peculiar to Sunnyside).   It gives me sincere pleasure to
learn that your father continues in his usual health.   I trust
that he has his musical evenings, and his pet minstrels to play
and sing for him.   There will never be any wrinkles in his
mind as long as he can enjoy sweet music, and have youth and
beauty to administer it to him.

I am writing late at night, and it is high time to go to bed.
So give my kindest remembrances to your sister and your husband, and believe me ever, your affectionate friend,

WASHINGTON IRVING.

The following letter, among other matters, contains
a cordial and complimentary allusion to Sparks, the
more interesting that it is entirely spontaneous, and
that it expresses a mature and unbiassed judgment of
the manner in which the task of editing " Washington's Writings " had been executed by him :

[*To Hon. Robert C. Winthrop.*]

MY DEAR MR. WINTHROP :

I thank you and Mr. Prescott for your kind remembrances
of me. It is very gratifying to be so remembered by such
men. I have heretofore consulted Frothingham's History of
the Siege of Boston, about which you speak. It merits the
character you give it, as being "the best thing written about
the Bunker Hill period." I am also much obliged to you for
the clippings which you send me from newspapers, giving
familiar anecdotes of Washington. It is surprising how few
anecdotes there are of him in his familiar life; but he was
essentially a public character, and so regulated in conduct by
square and rule, as to furnish very little of the amusing and
picturesque anecdote that we find in the lives of more irregular
men.

I doubt whether the world will ever get a more full and
correct idea of Washington than is furnished by Sparks's collection of his letters, with the accompanying notes and illustrations, and the preliminary biography. I cannot join in the
severe censures that have been passed upon Sparks for the ver-
bal corrections and alterations he has permitted himself to
make in some of Washington's letters. They have been
spoken of too harshly. From the examination I have given
to the correspondence of Washington, in the archives of the
State Department, it appears to me that Sparks has executed
his task of selection, arrangement, and copious illustration,
with great judgment and discrimination, and with consummate
fidelity to the essential purposes of history. His intelligent
and indefatigable labors in this and other fields of American

history are of national and incalculable importance. Posterity will do justice to them and him.

I am glad to learn that you are supervising a lithographic portrait of our friend Kennedy, ironing out "the wrinkles and crow's feet," and fitting it to figure to advantage in the shop windows. It will rejoice the heart of his good little wife, who thinks he has never had justice done him in that line, and was half piqued at a lithographic effigy of myself, where the painter and engraver had represented me as flourishing in "immortal youth." *

Such likenesses, "corrected and amended," will do well to go with the Homes of American Authors, recently published, to give Europeans a favorable idea of literary men and literary life in this country. In commenting on that publication, a London critic observes, that "the American authors seem to court the muse to some purpose." He did not know that most of them, so well housed, had courted a rich wife into the bargain.

Ever, my dear Mr. Winthrop, yours, with great regard,

WASHINGTON IRVING.

On the 27th of May, Mr. Irving writes to Miss Mary E. Kennedy, a niece of Mr. John P. Kennedy, and one of his household at Washington:

Too much occupation has produced symptoms, of late, which oblige me to suspend literary occupation, and may exile me for a time from my study.

In sober sadness, I believe it is high time I should throw

---

* Probably the likeness prefixed to Mr. H. T. Tuckerman's article on Sunnyside and its Proprietor, in the Homes of American Authors.—ED.

by the pen altogether; but writing has become a kind of habitude with me, and, unless I have some task on hand to occupy a great part of my time, I am at a loss what to do. After being accustomed to literary research, mere desultory reading ceases to be an occupation. There is as much difference between them, in point of interest, as between taking an airing on horseback and galloping after the hounds. It is pretty hard for an old huntsman to give up the chase.

In the following June, being " ordered to throw by his pen, and abstain from head work of all kinds for a time," he left his manuscript with me to look over, and give him my impressions of the work, and set out for Kennedy's, connecting with his journey some object of advantage in inspecting the manuscripts of Mr. Washington Lewis, which had been mentioned to him as containing letters and diaries of Washington, and a visit to some places noted in Washington's history.

From Philadelphia, where his *compagnon de voyage* from New York left him, to continue on to Washington in the night train, at ten o'clock, while he retired to his room, he writes me, June 13th, as follows:

Inform my beloved family of my well-being, as well as of my extraordinary prudence and self-restraint in not continuing on in the night train with Mr. P——, to which I confess I felt sorely tempted. But I gain prudence with years, and, I trust, will in time be all that my friends could wish.

[*To Mrs. Pierre M. Irving.*]

ELLICOTT'S MILLS, June 15, 1853.

MY DEAR HELEN :

I arrived at Baltimore yesterday, between one and two o'clock, after a pretty warm and dusty ride from Philadelphia. However, as I sat by a window on the shady side of the cars, I did not suffer much from the heat.

I found Kennedy on the lookout for me. He had expected me the evening before. The family were all out of town, at old Mr. Gray's country establishment, where I am now writing. We dined at Kennedy's brother, Anthony's, in Baltimore, and had a very gay family dinner, after which we came out in the evening train, and had a beautiful drive along the lovely valley of the Patapsco, on the banks of which stream the country residence is situated. You may have an idea of the house from an engraving in Putnam's " Homes of American Authors."

We found the family all assembled round the tea table ; and a bright, happy gathering it was, there being a matter of five young ladies, guests in the house. Among the number, I was delighted to meet with one of the three young belles with whom I was domesticated at Washington—the one who plays so admirably on the piano. There was great greeting on all sides, and most especially by my warmhearted old friend, Mr. Gray.

The evening passed delightfully. We had music from Miss A——. We sat out in the moonlight on the piazza, and strolled along the banks of the Patapsco, after which I went to bed, had a sweet night's sleep, and dreamt I was in Mahomet's paradise. * * *

June 22d, he writes to Miss Sarah Irving, from Cassilis, the residence of Mr. Andrew Kennedy :

Mr. John Kennedy and myself left Ellicott's Mills yesterday (Monday) morning, in the train which passed at nine o'clock. * * * We had an extremely hot drive of about a hundred miles, but through lovely scenery. The railroad follows up the course of the Patapsco to its head springs, and a romantic stream it is throughout. The road then crosses some fine, open, fertile country on the summit of Elk Ridge, and descends along the course of Reynolds's Creek and the Monocacy to the Potomac, all beautiful. At Harper's Ferry we changed cars, and pushed on to Charleston, where we found Mr. Andrew Kennedy waiting for us with his carriage. A drive of about a mile and a half brought us to his seat, whence this letter is dated. Here I am, in the centre of the magnificent valley of the Shenandoah, the great valley of Virginia. And a glorious valley it is—equal to the promised land for fertility, far superior to it for beauty, and inhabited by an infinitely superior people—*choice*, though not chosen.

      *   *   *   *   *   *

To-morrow I expect to go, in company with the two Mr. Kennedys, on a visit to Mr. George Washington Lewis, who has a noble estate about twelve miles off, where we shall remain until the next day.

I have several places to visit in this vicinity, connected with the history of Washington, after which we shall push on to the mountains, where we shall find a cooler temperature. * * *

During this absence, I was at Sunnyside, mounting guard, as he terms it, and reading over his Life of Washington in manuscript, then nearly completed to the commencement of the Administration. I wrote to him that I was proceeding with the Life of Washington with an interest that seemed almost surprising to myself; and that I could not have believed that so much of freshness and new interest could be thrown about a subject so often gone over. The following is his reply:

CASSILIS, June 25, 1853.

MY DEAR PIERRE:

Your letter of the 19th, received two or three days since, has put me quite in spirits. From your opinion of my manuscripts, I begin to hope that my labor has not been thrown away. Do not make a toil of reading the manuscripts, but take it leisurely, so as to keep yourself fresh in the perusal, and to judge quietly and coolly of its merits and defects.

I have paid my visit to Mr. George Washington Lewis, to inspect the manuscripts in his possession. His seat (Audley). is about twelve or fourteen miles from this. Andrew and John Kennedy accompanied me. We went on Wednesday, and returned on Thursday. The visit was a most agreeable one. We were hospitably entertained by Mr. Lewis, who is a young man of engaging appearance and manners. * * * His mother, however, is the real custodian of the Washington reliques and papers, which she laid before me with great satisfaction. I did not find much among the manuscripts requiring note. In less than an hour I had made all the memoranda necessary. * * *

Yesterday I drove out with the Kennedys, to visit two

other establishments of the Washington family in this neighborhood, the proprietors of which had called to see me during
my absence at Audley.   These visits are all full of interest;
but I will tell you all about them when we meet.   *   *   *

To-day we are to visit some other places of note in the
neighborhood.   On Monday, the day after to-morrow, I set off
with Mr. John Kennedy and his bachelor brother, Pendleton
Kennedy, for the mountains.

I must again apologize for my wretched scrawl; but it
seems hard work for me to extract any ideas out of my weary
brain, which is as dry as " a remainder biscuit."

I hope you will continue to mount guard at Sunnyside
during my absence.

>With love to all, your affectionate uncle,

>>WASHINGTON IRVING.

The next day, in replying to a letter of Mrs. Irving
giving him some account of affairs at Sunnyside, where
we were sojourning, and speaking encouragingly of his
manuscript Life of Washington, he remarks:

I never shall be able, I fear, to give it the toning up which
a painter gives to his picture before finishing it.   I am afraid
my head will not bear much more work of the kind.   It gives
me hints, even when I am scrawling letters.

[To Miss Kate Irving.]

BERKELEY SPRINGS (BATH), July 1, 1853.
MY DEAR KATE:

I received, yesterday, your letter of Sunday and Monday
last, and rejoice to find you have all survived the late intense

weather. I have been for four or five days in this watering place, which is in a small valley among the mountains, and, as far as my experience goes, one of the hottest places in the known world. You will be surprised to learn, however, that my greatest amusement, during the heat of the day, is at the ten-pin alley, and that I am getting quite expert at bowling. The perspiration it produces is awful, and only to be allayed by the cool baths for which this place is famous.

To-morrow I trust to emerge from this oven, and to return with Mr. Andrew Kennedy to Cassilis, where I shall be once more within the reach of cooling breezes. * * *

Tell Robert [the gardener] I charge him not to work in the sun during the hottest hours of the day, should this intense warm weather continue. He injured himself by it last summer; and I would not have anything happen to him for all the hay in the country. * * *

Farewell. The weather is so hot that I cannot write, nor do anything else but play at bowls and fan myself.

With love to all, your affectionate uncle,

WASHINGTON IRVING.

On the 6th of July, I wrote him that I had concluded the perusal of his manuscript the day before, and that the impression I communicated in my former letter had gained strength by what I had since read. "Familiar as I am with the story," I add, "I have been equally surprised and gratified to perceive what new interest it gains in your hands. I doubt not the work will be equally entertaining to young and old." The following is his reply:

MY DEAR PIERRE:

I have just received your letter of the 6th, which I need not tell you has been most gratifying and inspiriting to me. I thank you for writing it; for I was looking most anxiously and dubiously for your verdict, after reading the narrative of the war, in which the interest, I feared, might suffer from diffusion, and from the difficulty of binding up a variety of enterprises and campaigns into one harmonious whole. I now feel my mind prodigiously relieved, and begin to think I have not labored in vain.

I left Bath shortly after I wrote to Kate. We had intended a tour among the Alleghanies, but the intense heat of the weather discouraged us, and we determined to postpone that part of our plan to another season.

Returning to Cassilis, we passed a few days more under the hospitable roof of Mr. Andrew Kennedy, where I saw something of a harvest home in the noble valley of the Shenandoah.

Leaving Cassilis on Wednesday morning, we arrived here before sunset. * * *

Tell Sarah I have received her letter of the 1st July, but cannot answer it at present. To tell the truth, though my excursion has put me in capital health and spirits, I find I cannot handle the pen, even in these miserable scrawls, without feeling a sensation in the head that admonishes me to refrain. Think, then, how gratifying it must be to me to learn from your letter that I may dispense from any severe task work in completing my historical labor.

I feel that my working days are over, and rejoice that I have arrived at a good stopping place.

At this period, he did not think of continuing the
Life through the history of the Administration, but
proposed to make the inauguration of Washington his
" stopping place."   Hence his premature felicitation
that he had reached the end of his " working days."
He was yet to give a great deal of handling even to
the part he deemed finished ; but when he returned to
Sunnyside, it was with the desire and intention of preparing the Life at once for the press—an intention
frustrated by the condition of his health.

CHAPTER IX.

FOR some time before he went to Virginia, in June, 1853, Mr. Irving had to lay aside the pen almost entirely, "having overtasked myself," he says, " and produced a weariness of the brain that renders it an irksome effort even to scrawl an ordinary letter." On his return, though in excellent general health, he found himself still unable to resume his literary occupations, and thereupon determined to set off for Saratoga, the waters of which were of such service to him the preceding year, and might be this; " though," he says, " I believe all that I require is a good spell of *literary abstinence.*"

He did not remain long at the Springs. " I feel a little fatigued with the bustle of the place," he writes, August 6th, a few days after his arrival, " and the very attentions I receive begin to be a task upon my spirits."

The following letter, written after his return home, will continue the story of his travels. His reminiscence of the Ogdensburg of his boyhood will recall a similar passage in another letter in the third chapter of the first volume.

[*To Miss Mary E. Kennedy.*]

SUNNYSIDE, Sept. 8, 1853.

MY DEAR MISS KENNEDY:

Indisposition has prevented me from replying earlier to your welcome letter of the 4th August, which I received about three weeks since, on my return from Saratoga.

*   *   *   *   *   *

The hot weather was as intolerable at Saratoga as I had found it at Berkeley Springs; so, after passing about ten days there, I set off on a tour with your uncle John, who wished to visit the F——s, at Buffalo. We went by the way of the lakes, and had a magnificent *sail* (if I may use the word) down Lake Champlain in a steamer to Plattsburg, whence we made a night journey by railroad to Ogdensburg. Here we passed part of a day—a very interesting one to me. Fifty years had elapsed since I had visited the place in company with a party of gentlemen proprietors, with some ladies of their families. It was then a wilderness, and we were quartered in the remains of an old French fort at the confluence of the Oswegatchie and the St. Lawrence. It was all a scene of romance to me, for I was then a mere stripling, and everything was strange, and full of poetry. The country was covered with forest; the Indians still inhabited some islands in the river, and prowled about in their canoes. There were two young ladies of the party to sympathize in my romantic feelings, and we passed some happy days there, exploring the forests, or gliding in canoes on the rivers.

In my present visit, I found, with difficulty, the site of the old French fort, but all traces of it were gone. I looked round on the surrounding country and river. All was changed. A populous city occupied both sides of the Oswegatchie; great steamers ploughed the St. Lawrence, and the opposite Canada shore was studded with towns and villages. I sat down on the river bank, where we used to embark in our canoes, and thought on the two lovely girls who used to navigate it with me, and the joyous party who used to cheer us from the shore. All had passed away—all were dead! I was the sole survivor of that happy party; and here I had returned, after a lapse of fifty years, to sit down and meditate on the mutability of all things, and to wonder that I was still alive!

From Ogdensburg we made a voyage up the St. Lawrence, through the archipelago of the "Thousand Islands," and across Lake Ontario to Lewistown, on the Niagara River, where we took a carriage to the Falls. There we passed an insufferably hot day, and parted in the evening—your uncle to go to Buffalo, I to Cayuga Lake to visit one of my nieces; whence I went to Syracuse to visit Mrs. B——, and then hastened homeward. All this tour was made during a spell of intensely hot weather, that deranged my whole system. The consequence was, that, the day after my return home, I was taken down with a violent fever and delirium, which confined me several days to my bed. *   *   *

He had hardly got rid of his fever, and was still in a state of great debility, when he addressed the following letter to the friend and travelling companion with whom he parted at Niagara Falls :

[*To Mr. John P. Kennedy.*]

SUNNYSIDE, Aug. 24, 1853.

MY DEAR KENNEDY :

After much weary travelling by land and water, by night and day, through dust and heat and " fell morass," I reached home on Wednesday last, and almost immediately broke down. Whatever it was of evil that had been lurking in my system for some time past, took vent in a spell of chills, fever, and delirium, which hung over me for several days, and has almost torn me to rags. I avail myself of a tolerably sane fragment of myself which is left, to scrawl these lines.

You will now perceive, my dear Horseshoe, that when I was a little techy under your bantering at Niagara, it was not the fault of your jokes—which were excellent, as usual—but because I was too miserably out of tune to be played upon, be the musician ever so skilful.

I trust this outbreak of malady, when I get through with it, will carry off with it all the evils that have been haunting my system for some time past, and that, when next we meet, I shall relish your jokes with my usual hearty zest, even though, by singular chance, they should happen to be bad ones.

I fear, however, I shall not be strong enough to go sight-seeing with you in New York; and, indeed, have seen so much of the Crystal Palace in my delirium, that I am afraid the very sight of it would bring on a paroxysm.

I look forward, however, to a visit from you all at my

"small contentment," where, however I may be, my nieces will be happy to entertain you in their own modest way, on our rural fare—"a couple of shortlegged hens, a joint of mutton, with any pretty little tiny kickshaws," or, peradventure, with a juicy ham sent to me from the banks of the Patapsco, by a much-valued and somewhat musical friend who flourishes in that quarter. To that excellent friend, and his two inestimable daughters, give my most affectionate remembrances.

"Thine evermore," my dear Horseshoe, "while this machine is to him."

GEOFFREY.

Very soon after the date of this letter, Mr. Irving received the visit to which he was looking forward from Mr. and Mrs. Kennedy, and Mr. and Miss G——, who passed the day at Sunnyside. "I do not know," he writes to Miss Kennedy, "when I enjoyed a day more thoroughly. I only wish you had been here, to make the party complete."

The following extract contains an interesting mention of the rural cemetery in which, "after life's fitful fever," he was himself to sleep. It is addressed to his niece in Paris, as he was on the point of setting off on another visit to Maryland and Virginia:

[*To Mrs. Storrow.*]

SUNNYSIDE, Sept. 29, 1853.

*   *   *   *   *   *

I have had one solemn and sacred duty to perform, of late; which was, to remove from New York the remains of such of

the family as were interred in the vault in front of the Brick
Church, in Beekman street. That street was to be widened,
and, of course, the churchyard invaded. I have always appre-
hended some such event, and am glad it has taken place while
I am here to protect the ashes of those I loved from desecration. I accordingly purchased a piece of ground in a public
cemetery established within a few years on the high ground
adjacent to the old Dutch church at Beekman's millpond, com-
monly called the Sleepy Hollow Church. The cemetery, which
is secured by an act of the Legislature, takes in a part of the
Beekman woods, and commands one of the most beautiful
views of the Hudson. The spot I have purchased is on the
southern slope, just on the edge of the old churchyard, which
is included in the cemetery. I have had it enclosed with an
iron railing, and shall have evergreens set out around it. It is
shaded by a grove of young oaks.

There I have seen the remains of the family gathered together and interred, where they cannot be again disturbed;
and a vast satisfaction it was, to have rescued them from that
restless city, where nothing is sacred.

As I was selecting this place of sepulture, I thought of
Byron's lines:

> " Then look around,
> And choose thy ground,
> And take thy rest."

I have marked out my resting place by my mother's side, and
a space is left for me there.

This may seem to you rather a melancholy theme for letter
writing. Yet I write without melancholy, or, rather, without
gloom. I feel deeply gratified at having been able to perform

this duty, and I look forward with serene satisfaction to being gathered at last to a family gathering place, where my dust may mingle with the dust of those most dear to me.

God bless you, my dear Sarah. I owe my dear little Kate a letter, but have not time at present to answer it. Give my love to her and the other young princesses, and my affectionate remembrances to Mr. Storrow.

Your affectionate uncle,

WASHINGTON IRVING.

P. S.—I set off on my expedition this afternoon, and expect to be absent nearly all October.

I give some letters written during this excursion, the first dated, as will be seen, the night of his departure, at a hotel named in his honor in New York:

[*To Miss Sarah Irving.*]

IRVING HOUSE, Friday Evening, Sept. 29, 1853.

MY DEAR SARAH:

I hasten to inform you of my well-being, as I know you will be anxious. I arrived in town safe, and proceeded to the Irving House, where I asked for a room. What party had I with me? None. Had I not my lady with me? No; I was alone. I saw my chance was a bad one, and I feared to be put in a dungeon, as I was on a former occasion. I bethought myself of your advice, and, when the book was presented, wrote my name at full length—from Sunnyside. My dear Sarah, I was ushered into an apartment on the first floor (second story), furnished with rosewood, yellow damask, pier glasses, &c.; a sumptuous bedroom, with a bed large enough for an alderman and his wife; a bathroom adjoining. In a word, I am accommodated completely *en prince*. The negro waiters all call me by name, and vie with each other in waiting on me. The chambermaid has been at uncommon pains to put my rooms in first-rate order; and, if she had been pretty, I absolutely should have kissed her; but as she was not, I shall reward her in sordid coin. Henceforth I abjure all modesty with hotel keepers, and will get as much for my name as it will fetch. Kennedy calls it travelling on one's capital.

I am at a loss where to go this evening—the Crystal Palace, Julien's, or the opera. I shall let you know, before I go to bed, my decision in the matter.

My dear Sarah, I have just returned. It is near twelve o'clock. They have made such a fire in my sitting room, that it is roasting to sit there; and I am sleepy, so I must be brief. I determined to go to the opera; but, on the way, as it was early, I strolled into the St. Nicholas Hotel, to take a look at it. It beats everything of the hotel kind I have ever seen. I wandered up stairs and down stairs and into the ladies' saloon. Such splendor; such extent; such long corridors and vast saloons; and such crowds of well-dressed people and beautiful ladies! In the course of my rambles, I came upon Mr. Baldwin, who is boarding there. He took me all about to see the wonders of the house, and, among other places, took me into the bridal chamber, about which so much has been said. It is very magnificent, but, I am told, has never been occupied excepting by a Californian prince and his bride.

On the 17th of October, a day or two after his arrival at the residence of Mr. Andrew Kennedy, near

Harper's Ferry, Mr. Irving set off with that gentleman and his brother, Mr. John P. Kennedy, for Winchester, whence they extended their excursion to Greenway Court, once the residence of old Lord Fairfax, the early patron of Washington, and an occasional resort of the latter in his youthful days. In the following letter the reader is furnished with an amusing account of the expedition to these historic points:

[*To Miss Sarah Irving.*]

CASSILIS, Oct. 21, 1853.

MY DEAR SARAH:

The expedition to Winchester and Greenway Court, in company with Messrs. John and Andrew Kennedy, was very pleasant. We went to Winchester by railroad, and then hired a carriage and an old negro coachman to take us to Greenway Court, once the residence of old Lord Fairfax, and a resort of Washington in his younger days. We set off from Winchester in the afternoon. The distance to Greenway Court was said to be about twelve miles, but the roads so bad that it would be impossible to return to Winchester the same evening. What was to be done? Greenway Court was no longer habitable. There was no good country inn near at hand. Mr. Andrew Kennedy determined to seek quarters at the house of a Mr. Nelson, who resided about three miles from the Court, and with whom he was acquainted. We hoped to reach his house before sunset, so as to seek quarters elsewhere should we fail to find them there. We had a delightful afternoon drive, through a fine country diversified by noble forests in all the glory of their autumnal hues. I saw some of the noblest specimens of oaks I have ever seen in this country. The roads, in many places, were very bad. We travelled slowly. The sun went down in great splendor, and the landscape soon began to darken. Our black John knew nothing of the situation either of Greenway Court or of Mr. Nelson. We made inquiries along the road, but received replies which rather perplexed us. It grew quite dark before we reached a gate, which, we were told, opened into Mr. Nelson's grounds. We drove across two or three broad fields—opened as many common country gates. Nothing had the appearance of the approach to a gentleman's seat. I began to feel dubious. It seemed very much of an intrusion, for three persons to drive up to a gentleman's house after dark, and ask quarters for the night. The Kennedys laughed at my scruples. It was the custom in Virginia. Mr. Nelson would be glad to receive us. "Perhaps," said I, "he may not have room." "Oh, yes; he has lately enlarged his house. You will find yourself in clover." We drove on. No signs of a house. We might have mistaken the road. At length we saw a light twinkling at a distance. It appeared to be from a small house. More consultation. This might not be Mr. Nelson's; or he might not have enlarged his house. For my part, I was so fatigued, that I declared myself resigned to quarters in a barn, provided Mr. Nelson would allow me a little clean straw. The road gradually wound up to the house. As we approached, the moon, rising above a skirt of forest trees, lit up the scene, and we saw a noble mansion crowning a rising ground, with grand portico and columns, and wings surmounted with battlements. We drove up to the door. A negro boy came forth, like a dwarf from an enchanted castle. Mr. and Mrs. Nelson were both from home! What was to be done? It was too late to go wandering about the country in quest of other quarters.

Would Mr. and Mrs. Nelson be home soon? Oh, yes; they had gone to make a visit in the neighborhood, and would be back to tea. Mr. Nelson's mother-in-law was in the house; that would do. We alighted; entered a spacious hall upward of twenty feet wide, with a beautiful circular staircase; thence into a noble dining room, where the tea table was set out, but nobody present. After a time, the mother-in-law made her appearance. Mr. John Kennedy was slightly acquainted with her, and introduced us. She was very civil, and by no means disposed to set the dogs on us. I began to have hopes of something better than the barn. After a time, Mr. and Mrs. Nelson came home. They accosted us in true Virginia style. Mr. Nelson claimed some acquaintance with me. He reminded me of his having introduced himself to me three years before, at the Revere House in Boston, when I was on there with the G——s; and said he had a prior acquaintance, having been one of a committee of the students at the University of Charlottesville, who, about twenty years since, waited on me at the hotel to invite me to accept a public dinner.

In a word, we were made at once to feel ourselves at home; invited to pass several days there. Mr. Nelson would take us all about the country, and make us acquainted with all his neighbors.

We had glorious quarters that night. The next day Mr. Nelson took us to Greenway Court. Had a large party of the neighboring gentlemen to meet us at dinner; and it was with great difficulty we got away in time to return in the evening to Winchester.

So much for my expedition to Greenway Court.

To-morrow I set off, with Mr. and Mrs. Kennedy, on our return to Ellicott's Mills, and, in the beginning of next week,

shall take my departure for New York, to be at my post at
the Astor Library on Wednesday.

The following is an extract from a letter to Mrs.
Kennedy, written after his return home:

How comes on the "house that Jack built"—or is to build?
I envy Kennedy the job of building that tower, if he has half
the relish that I have for castle building—air castles, or any
other. I should like nothing better than to have plenty of
money to squander on stone and mortar, and to build chateaux
along the beautiful Patapsco with the noble stone which
abounds there; but I would first blow up all the cotton mills
(your father's among the number), and make picturesque ruins
of them; and I would utterly destroy the railroad; and all the
cotton lords should live in baronial castles on the cliffs, and the
cotton spinners should be virtuous peasantry of both sexes, in
silk skirts and small clothes and straw hats, with long ribbands,
and should do nothing but sing songs and choruses, and dance
on the margin of the river.

Of late, I have gratified my building propensity in a small
way, by putting up a cottage for my gardener and his handsome wife, and have indulged in other unprofitable improvements incident to a gentleman cultivator. A pretty country
retreat is like a pretty wife—one is always throwing away
money in decorating it. Fortunately, I have but one of those
two drains to the purse, and so do not repine.

I see you are again throwing out lures to tempt me back to
Baltimore, and sending me messages from M—— D—— and
dear little "Lu;" and I have a letter from Mr. Andrew Kennedy, inviting me to come to Cassilis and the Shenandoah,

when I am tired of the Hudson. Ah, me! I am but mortal man, and but too easily tempted; and I begin to think you have been giving me love powders among you—I feel such a hankering toward the South. But be firm, my heart! I have four blessed nieces at home hanging about my neck, and several others visiting me, and holding me by the skirts. How can I tear myself from them? Domestic affection forbids it!

CHAPTER X.

THE following letter was addressed to Mrs. Kennedy, just as her husband was about to start on a Southern tour with Mrs. Fillmore, the late President, which was to have taken place the previous spring, but was prevented by the death of Mrs. Fillmore. Mr. Kennedy had intimated a wish that Mr. Irving should accompany them; "but I have no inclination," he writes, "to travel with political notorieties, to be smothered by the clouds of party dust whirled up by their chariot wheels, and beset by the speechmakers and little great men and bores of every community who might consider Mr. Fillmore a candidate for another presidential term." "Douce Davie," mentioned in the letter, was the name of a horse his correspondent

used to ride, and which he had often mounted at Ellicott's Mills :

SUNNYSIDE, Feb. 21, 1854.
MY DEAR MRS. KENNEDY :

*   *   *   *   *   *

I met Mr. Meredith in town on Saturday last, and he told
me that Kennedy had been unwell. If it is that affection of
the head of which he complained last year, tell him I have
found, in my own case, great relief from homœopathy, to
which I had recourse almost accidentally, for I am rather slow
at adopting new theories. I can now apply myself to literary
occupation day after day for several hours at a time, without
any recurrence of the symptoms that troubled me. In fact,
my head seems to be as hard as ever it was—though perhaps
somewhat heavier.

You tell me Kennedy is about to set off with Mr. Fillmore
on his Southern tour, and would like to have me for a companion. Heaven preserve me from any tour of the kind ! To
have to cope at every turn with the host of bores of all kinds
that beset the paths of political notorieties ! To have to listen
to the speeches that would be made, at dinners and other occasions, to Mr. Fillmore and himself; and to the speeches that
Mr. Fillmore and he would make in return ! Has he not found
out, by this time, how very borable I am ? Has he not seen
me skulk from barrooms, and other gathering places, where he
was making political capital among the million ? Has he forgotten how, last summer, a crew of blatant firemen, whose
brass trumpets gave him so much delight, absolutely drove me
into the wilderness ? No, no. I am ready at any time to
clatter off on Douce Davie into the woods, with the gentle
Horseshoe, or to scale the Alleghanies with him (barring

watering places) ; but as to a political tour, I would as lief go campaigning with Hudibras or Don Quixote.

You ask me how I have passed my time this winter. Very much at home—dropping into town occasionally to pass a few hours at the Astor Library, but returning home in the evening. I have been but once or twice at the opera, and to none of Julien's concerts. Still my time has passed pleasantly in constant occupation ; though I begin to think that I often toil to very little purpose, excepting to keep off *ennui*, and give a zest to relaxation.   *   *   *

The letter which follows, was written on his seventy-first birthday, to the wife of a nephew rather delicate in health, and a great favorite, who had been for some time housed at Sunnyside, and was now "roughing it about the world." It was in reply to a letter from Montgomery, Ala., in which she gave an account of her pilgrimages :

[*To Mrs. Sanders Irving.*]

SUNNYSIDE, April 3, 1854.

MY DEAR JULIA :

Sarah has engaged that I shall write a postscript to her letter ; but I am in a sad state of incompetency to do it. My faculties seem benumbed, probably from the long spell of dismal, wintry weather we have *enjoyed* for the last fortnight. It is quite tantalizing to read your account of your roses and rhododendrons, and the budding and blossoming of spring in the " sweet south country " through which you have been pilgrimaging. I should have liked to be with you in your voyage up the Tennessee. I begin to long for a wild, unhackneyed river, unimproved by cultivation, and unburdened by commerce.

To-day is my seventy-first birthday, and opens with a serene, sunny, beautiful morning. * * *

I have wished a thousand times, my dear Julia, since your departure, that you were with me, making your home under my roof, as you do in my heart; and I never wished it more strongly than at this moment. I feel very much this long separation, and grieve that it is likely to be so much prolonged, and that you are moving to farther and farther distances from me. I wish S—— could have some employment near at hand, so that you could take up your abode with me entirely.

In a letter to Mrs. Irving, then on a visit with me to North Carolina, dated April 6th, after giving some account of his dissipations during a week's sojourn in town, he writes:

Another of my dissipations was an evening at the dancing school, where I was very much pleased and amused. I met your friend Mrs. M—— there, whom I found very agreeable, and who made me acquainted with her bright little daughter. The scene brought my old dancing-school days back again, and I felt very much like cutting a pigeon wing, and showing the young folks how we all footed it in days of yore, about the time that David danced before the ark.

The next morning, where should I breakfast but at Judge Duer's! It was to meet Mr. Lawrence, the English portrait painter, who has come out with letters from Thackeray, and I don't know who all, and is painting all the head people (some of whom have no heads) in town. It was a very agreeable breakfast party, three or four gentlemen besides Mr. Lawrence and myself; but what made it especially agreeable, was the presence of two of the Miss —— ——. My dear H——, I was delighted with them—so bright, so easy, so ladylike, so intelligent! H—— has one of the finest, most spiritual faces I have seen for a long time. Why, in heaven's name, have I not seen more of these women? We have very few like them in New York. However, I see you are beginning to laugh, so I will say no more on the subject.

In April, he receives a note from a neighbor, informing him that the Postmaster General " acceded to the wishes of all the inhabitants of Dearman, save himself, to have the name of Dearman changed to Irvington." Dearman was the original name of the village and railroad station a few hundred yards south of Sunnyside. It was known thereafter as Irvington.

May 30th, he is " on a two-days' visit at the old bachelor nest of his friend Mr. Gouverneur Kemble, in the very heart of the Highlands, with magnificent scenery all around him ; mountains clothed with forests to their very summit, and the noble Hudson moving along quietly and majestically at their feet."

June 16th, Mr. Hueston writes him for a contribution to the Knickerbocker Gallery, a complimentary tribute to Louis Gaylord Clark, for twenty years editor of the *Knickerbocker Magazine*, and trusts he will be able to furnish it by the 1st of July. On the 21st of the same month, Mrs. C. M. Kirkland throws herself on his gallantry for a ten-line scrap—the sweeping of his portfolio—that might be read aloud at a literary and musical festival that had been devised at Milwaukie, as a means to raise three hundred dollars toward an institution for the education of young women at the West. After being read aloud, the article was to be sold to the highest bidder. Both requests were complied with, and articles sent.

June 29th, he writes to Kennedy, with "a head confused and almost stupefied with catarrh;" that this had "been rather an unfortunate season with him, having had two returns of his old complaint, chills and fever; the last just as he was on the way to attend a wedding of a grandniece, at which all the ten tribes of the family were assembled."

In the following letter we have an account, among other things, of a visit to Idlewild, the home of N. P. Willis:

[*To Mr. J. P. Kennedy.*]

SUNNYSIDE, Aug. 31, 1854.

MY DEAR KENNEDY:

Wherever this letter finds you, whether in your tower on the banks of the Patapsco, at your brother's in the Shenandoah Valley, or with that rare old cavalier, your uncle Pendleton, in his favorite resort, the cool hollow of Berkeley Springs, may it find you in the enjoyment of good health and good spirits.

*   *   *   *   *   *

I am concerned to learn that Mr. Gray's health has been feeble of late, and that he has had days of suffering and "nights of prolonged nervous distress." Your account of his firm presentiment that he was to close his earthly career on his birthday, the 16th of last July, of his business arrangements for the event, and the calm serenity with which he awaited it, is really touching and beautiful. It only proved how truly worthy he is of length of days; for none is so fitted to live as he who is well prepared to die. God send him many more years, with a body as free from pain as his mind is from evil or his heart from unkindness. He has everything that should accompany old age,

"As honor, love, obedience, troops of friends;"

and he is an instance how lovable old age may render itself.

I lately made a day's excursion up the Hudson, in company with Mr. and Mrs. M—— G—— and two or three others, to visit Willis in his poetical retreat of Idlewild. It is really a beautiful place, the site well chosen, commanding noble and romantic scenery; the house commodious and picturesque, and furnished with much taste. In a word, it is just such a retreat as a poet would desire. I never saw Willis to such advantage as on this occasion. * * * Willis talks and writes much about his ill health, and is really troubled with an ugly cough; but I do not think his lungs are seriously affected, and I think it likely he will be like a cracked pitcher, which lasts the longer for having a flaw in it, being so much the more taken care of.

      *   *   *   *   *   *

I have been passing the summer entirely at home, determined not to travel any more in hot weather. I have had no return of the chills and fever, that paid me a slight visit early in June, and am now in fair health for such a green old gentleman. I wish I had Douce Davie here to mount occasionally,

for Gentleman Dick is in such disgrace that my womankind
will not hear to my mounting him any more. The last time I
did so, he took a start from hearing a young horse in a pasture
galloping alongside of the fence, and, fancying it to be a chal-
lenge to a race, set off *ventre a terre*, and gave me a run of
nearly three miles before I could bring him to a stop. Fortunately, I had a fair road; everybody and everything turned
aside, and made way for me; and Dick showed such speed and
bottom, that I am thinking of entering him for the cup at the
next races.

God bless you, my dear Kennedy. Yours very faithfully,

WASHINGTON IRVING.

It was nine months before he again mounted the
back of Gentleman Dick; and the equestrian mis-
chance that then befell him, will be told in its place.
I introduce, now, Mr. Willis's account of a conversation with him about Moore, the poet, which took place
on his late visit to Idlewild:

We chanced to be present, the other day, when Washington Irving took up the defence of the memory of Tom Moore.
So noteworthy an outpouring, as it was, of a generous and
genial nature—properly eloquent in defence of the friend with
whom he had exchanged cordialities, and over whose grave he
would not, therefore, see an ill weed grow unplucked—we
wished, at the time, that the summer wind would play reporter,
and tell the whole world of it. The subject was started by
Irving's being rallied on having been such a Brummel, while in
London, as to have served Moore for a model in dress; as

appeared by a passage in one of his letters, giving directions to his publisher to look up Irving's tailor to make him a coat.

"Ah," said Geoffrey, with one of his genial lightings-up of the face still handsome, "that was owing to the mere chance of Moore's having been with me, one morning, when I went into Nugee's. And I have often thought of it since, by the way, as a curious instance of the bringing together of opposite classes in England. We were strolling down St. James street, and Moore just stepped in with me while I ordered a coat. Seeing that Nugee did not know him, I stepped between the two, and said, 'Really, gentlemen, two such very distinguished men ought to know each other! Mr. Nugee, this is Mr. Thomas Moore; Mr. Moore, Mr. Nugee!' Upon which, Nugee, who was worth one hundred and fifty thousand pounds at least, came forward, bowing almost to the ground in his excessive humility, and could not find words enough to express his sense of the honor of such an introduction.* He was delighted with it, too, and thanked me warmly for it afterward. 'Good creature!' he said of Moore; 'good creature!'—using the phrase very popular in London, at that time, to express great admiration. Yes," continued Irving, musingly, "there was that tailor, worth a magnificent fortune, and he would come to your lodgings with the coat he had made, to try it on! I remember his flattering way of looking

---

* Irving thus provided a customer for the tailor. In Moore's Diary occurs the following passage: "Nugee called with the first _sketch_ of my coat, to try it on. Said he would dress me better than ever I was dressed in my life. 'There's not much of you, sir,' he said, 'and therefore my object must be to make the most I can of you.' Quite a jewel of a man, this Nugee. Have gone to him in consequence of my former tailor being bankrupt."

at me, and expressing his interest when I called upon him, on
my return from the Continent, to order something. 'Not looking quite so well, my dear sir; not quite so well! Take care
of yourself, dear Mr. Irving; pray, take care of yourself!
We can't spare you yet.'

" But they do Moore the greatest injustice in denying him
a sincere affection for his wife. He really loved her, and was
proud of her. I *know* it," continued Irving, very emphatic-
ally. " When we were in Paris together, I used to go out
and breakfast with him; and most delightful those breakfasts
were. And I remember being with Moore when his friends
Lord and Lady Holland had just arrived; and Lady Holland
told Tom *they* were coming out the next day to breakfast, and
she wished particularly to see little Bessy. 'They shall have
the breakfast,' said his wife, when he told her, 'but they *won't*
see little Bessy!' She said it very archly, but with the posi-
tiveness of an habitual independence, for she *would* not be
patronized by great folks! Moore admired this, though he
used to say it was quite beyond what he was capable of himself. But she *did* yield to him occasionally, and go out with
him to parties—once, particularly, exciting her husband's greatest admiration by the way her quiet and self-possessed manner
completely baffled the condescension of Lady L——. Her
ladyship had intended to be excessively cordial; but the simple
way in which 'little Bessy' took it as a matter of course,
turned the balance of dignity altogether. Moore spoke of it
delightedly afterward. Oh, they have cruelly misrepresented
that man! He was an honorable, highminded fellow, and, in
some trying money matters particularly, he showed the greatest disinterestedness and liberality. He has been shamefully
wronged since his death."

Thus vindicatorily of his friend spoke the just and kind Geoffrey Crayon a day or two since; and we are glad to record it while the dark wing of the poet's renown is uppermost. For, says Milton,

"Fame has two wings—one black, the other white;
She waves them both in her unequal flight."

To Mrs. Kennedy he writes, from Sunnyside, August 31st:

*   *   *   *   *   *

You ask me whether the homœopathics still keep me quite well. I really begin to have great faith in them. The complaint of the head especially, which troubled me last year, and obliged me to throw by my pen, has been completely vanquished by them, so that I have fagged with it as closely as ever. * * *

My nephew, P. M. I., is about to build a cottage in my immediate vicinity, I having given him a site for the purpose—one of my fields, which lies on the south side of the lane leading down to my dwelling.

[*To John P. Kennedy.*]

SUNNYSIDE, Oct. 5, 1854.

MY DEAR KENNEDY:

Your letter has remained too long unanswered; but I find it impossible to be regular and prompt in correspondence, though with the best intentions and constant efforts to that effect. I condole with you sincerely on the loss of your mother, for, from my own experience, it is one of the losses which sink deepest in the heart. It is upward of thirty years since I lost mine, then at an advanced age; yet I dream of her to this day, and wake up with tears on my cheeks. I think the advanced age at which she died endears her memory to me, and gives more tenderness and sadness to the recollection of her. Yet, after all, a calm and painless death, closing a long and well-spent life, is not a thing in itself to be lamented; and, from your own account, your mother's life was happy to the end; for she was, you say, "well conditioned in mind and body," and one of her last employments was to perform for her grandchildren on the piano. * * * What a blessing it is to have this feeling for music, which attended your mother to the last! It is indeed a sweetener of life, and a fountain of youth for old age to bathe in and refresh itself.

[*To Mr. J. P. Kennedy.*]

SUNNYSIDE, Nov. 22, 1854.

MY DEAR KENNEDY:

Your last letter was in cheerful contrast to those which preceded it. I had heard, in a circuitous way, of Mrs. Kennedy's illness, and was about to write to you on the subject, when I received from you the intelligence that she had routed the enemy; was "gathering strength with her accustomed energy of action;" walked, rode, and ate with a determination to be as well as ever; and that you hope she would even be better than ever. I rejoice in your bulletin, and trust that she and her allies, the doctor and quinine, will be more prompt and complete in their triumph than the allied powers in the Crimea, with whom you have compared them.

I am glad to find, also, that Mr. Gray continues to falsify his predictions, and to grow fat and hearty in spite of himself. I trust nature will continue to make him a false prophet in this respect; she is very apt to surprise valetudinarians with a latent fund of longevity of which they had no conception. I think, if he were to take a jaunt to New York, and hear Grisi and Mario through their principal characters, it would be like a dip in the fountain of youth to him.

I have had some delicious treats since their arrival in New York. I think Grisi's singing and acting would be just to Mr. Gray's taste. There is a freshness and beauty about her, in voice and person, that seem to bid defiance to time. I wish Mr. Gray could see her in Semiramide, and in Rosina (Barber of Seville), which exhibit her powers in the grand and the comic. I had always seen her in the former, and considered her a magnificent being. It was only lately, on my last visit to town, that I saw her in comedy, when she played Rosina twice, and surprised me by the truthfulness with which she could assume the girl, and the unforced whim and humor with which she could illustrate all her caprices. But, to perceive her thorough excellence in this part, one must be able to discern every play of her countenance, and especially of her eye. Her acting, like all great achievements of art, is worthy of especial examination. It is a perfect study. Like all great achievements of art, it is delightful from its simplicity.

The Semiramide and the Barber of Seville, as now performed in New York, are worthy of a winter's journey from Baltimore.

Just before I left town, there was a semi-centennial anniversary of the New York Historical Society. Indeed, I stayed in town to be present at it ; but, when the time arrived, my incorrigible propensity to flinch from all public ceremonials and festivals came over me. I mingled in the crowd, and heard Bancroft's erudite address from the "auditorium," but kept clear of the banquet which took place afterward. Among

the dignitaries and invited guests on the stage, I saw our friend
Winthrop, who, I find by the papers, made an eloquent speech
at the banquet. This I regret not to have heard. I have
never heard him speak in public, but have heard much of his
talent for public speaking; and I think, from what I have seen
of him, he would be apt to acquit himself well and grace-
fully. * * *

With affectionate remembrances to Mr. G——, Miss
G——, and your (much) better half,

Yours, my dear Kennedy, very truly,

WASHINGTON IRVING.

[*To Mrs. Storrow, at Paris.*]

SUNNYSIDE, Nov. 23, 1854.

MY DEAR SARAH:

Your last letter has taken me over many scenes of former
travel, and brought up delightful recollections. Switzerland,
the Rhine, and the southern parts of Germany bordering on
the Tyrol, with the quaint old towns and cities, Baden-Baden,
Strasburg, Ulm, Augsburg, Salzburg, &c., &c. Did you, when
at Baden-Baden, visit those awful chambers, or dungeons,
under the old castle, one of the seats of the "Vehm Gericht,"
or Secret Tribunal—that mysterious and tremendous associa-
tion that once held such sway over Germany? I do not know
whether they are generally shown to strangers; but, having
read a great deal on the subject of that secret institution, I
sought them out, and visited them with thrilling interest. You
say you found my name written in the visitors' book at Augsburg, *thirty-two* years since. Had there been a visitors' book
at Zurich of sufficiently ancient date, you might have met my
name written there *forty-nine* years since, as I made a visit to

it in 1805, in the course of my first European tour; and well do I recollect how much I was charmed with it, and how willingly I would have lingered there.

You do not say whether, when at Salzburg, you visited the famous salt mine, and made a subterranean excursion. I presume you did not, as you would have found it rather "awsome," as the Scotch say, though I was very much interested by it. Salzburg and its vicinity struck me as a very region for legendary romance. I presume you recollect the Untersburg, or Wanderburg, a few miles from Salzburg; within which, according to popular tale, the Emperor Charles sits in state, with golden crown on his head and sceptre in his hand. In the interior of the same mountain are palaces and churches and convents and gardens and untold treasures, guarded by dwarfs, who sometimes wander, at midnight, into Salzburg, to say their prayers in the cathedral. No doubt Kate has come across all this in the course of her German studies, and was able to put you on the track of these wonders. Before the breaking out of any war, the Emperor Charles issues out of the mountain with all his array, and marches round it with great blast and bray of trumpet, and then returns into his subterranean palace. I wish you could have seen a procession of the kind. It would have surpassed all the state of the mongrel emperors and empresses in whom you delight.

*   *   *   *   *   *

Give my love to the princesses, who, I understand, are growing in grace as in years. You are devoting yourself to their education. Do not attempt to make remarkable women of them. Let them acquire those accomplishments which enliven and sweeten home, but do not seek to fit them to shine in fashionable society. Keep them as natural, simple, and unpretending as possible; cultivate in them noble and elevated sentiments, and, above all, the feeling of veneration, so apt to be deadened, if not lost, in the gay, sensuous world by which they are surrounded. They live in the midst of *spectacle;* everything around them is addressed to the senses. The society with which they mingle is all of a transient kind—travelling Americans, restless seekers after novelty and excitement. All this you must bear in mind, and counteract as much as possible, by nurturing home feelings and affections, habits of thought and quiet devotion, and a reverence for grand and noble and solemn and sacred things.

Give my kindest remembrances to your husband, and believe me, my dear Sarah, ever your affectionate uncle,

WASHINGTON IRVING.

CHAPTER XI.

A NEW-YEAR SALUTATION—PUBLICATION OF WOLFERT'S ROOST—EXTRACTS FROM
SOME OF THE NOTICES—ANECDOTE RESPECTING MOUNTJOY—PUBLICATION OF
VOL. I OF THE LIFE OF WASHINGTON—AN EQUESTRIAN OVERTHROW—LETTER
TO JOHN P. KENNEDY—LETTER FROM BANCROFT ON RECEIPT OF VOL. I OF
LIFE OF WASHINGTON—DETERMINES TO COMPLETE THE WORK—PASSAGE FROM
LETTER TO MRS. STORROW—IMPATIENT TO GET VOL. II READY FOR THE
PRESS—REPLY TO INVITATION FROM MOSES THOMAS—LETTER TO JAMES K.
PAULDING.

THE new year finds Mr. Irving again at Cassilis,
in the valley of the Shenandoah, where he had
gone to attend a wedding of a niece of Mr. Kennedy.
A letter to one of the inmates of his little home, dated
January 1st, opens with this characteristic salutation
from the country seat where the nuptials were to be
celebrated : " My dear Kate, a happy New Year to
you, and all the family. So there, I've caught you
all."

There was generally a strife, at Sunnyside, who
should be first to bid " Happy New Year."

Soon after his return, the volume entitled " Wolfert's Roost " was issued from the press. This work
derives its title from what was the first name given by
the author to his residence of Sunnyside—the Roost

(or Rest) of Wolfert Acker, "one of the privy council-lors of the renowned Peter Stuyvesant," who retreated to this "quiet and sheltered nook" after the subjuga-tion of New Amsterdam by the English. The opening piece of the volume, consisting of three chronicles, gives a humorous description of "the little old-fash-ioned stone mansion, all made up of gable ends, and as full of angles and corners as an old cocked hat;" and recounts the remarkable inhabitants it has had at various periods of history; and how it came to be the keep or stronghold of Jacob Van Tassel, a valiant Dutchman, during the dark and troublous times of the Revolutionary war; and how, finally, the eventful little pile was selected for the haunt or sojourning of Diedrich Knickerbocker.

The reader, familiar with the letter to the editor of the *Knickerbocker*, with which the series of articles contributed by Mr. Irving to that magazine began, will detect in these opening chronicles a striking simi-larity to parts of that communication, upon which these quaint and amusing legends have evidently been remodelled. The rest of the volume is but a collection of tales and sketches long before published in that periodical, with the exception of "The Creole Vil-lage," "The Widow's Ordeal," and "A Contented Man," which were given originally in annuals. The work appeared early in February, and proved, no doubt, to the majority of its readers, a new publica-tion; to the young particularly, who could hardly have

been familiar with the contents of any of the papers of
which it is composed. The volume was greeted in the
highest terms by the press and the public on both sides
of the Atlantic. "It would not be easy to overpraise
this American miscellany," is the commencement of
some favorable comments of the London *Athenæum*.
"There is as much elegance of diction, as graceful a
description of natural scenery, as grotesque an earnestness in diablerie, and as quiet but as telling a satiric
humor, as when Geoffrey Crayon first came before the
English world, nearly forty years ago," says the London *Spectator*. "This volume," writes a critic in the
columns of the *New York Courier and Enquirer*,
"will be almost equally welcome to those who have
and those who have not read the papers of which it is
composed. * * * It was well to collect these scattered waifs of his genius while he himself was by to
superintend the labor. * * * He has given to the
world few productions more charming than 'Wolfert's
Roost' and the 'Sketches in Paris in 1825.'"

The *Evening Post* cites the second paper on the
Birds of Spring as "a special favorite." "It is the
one which relates the history of the boblink, or bob-
o'lincoln, from his first appearance as a gay warbler in
the fields of the Northern States, through his various
changes; becoming a reed bird in the marshes bordering the rivers of the Middle States, and finally a rice
bird at the South, where he degenerates into a fat
epicure, and is shot for the table. The rest of the

sketches and narratives," it adds, " have all the characteristics of Irving's graceful genius, and are worthy to
be placed by the side of his 'Sketch Book,' composed
long years since."

A notice in the Boston *Telegraph* says: " We think
it superior to any of his previous works in one respect
—that of wide range and variety. There is some
one or more papers in the new volume, which bring to
mind each of the author's former works. It seems as
if, when he published his previous imaginative works,
he had laid aside one or more papers from each of
them, and that here they were. Thus there are Spanish and Moorish legends, which remind us of the
' Alhambra ' and the ' Conquest of Granada ;' Dutch
stories, reminding one of portions of the ' Sketch
Book,' ' Tales of a Traveller,' and of the ' History of
New York.' It is, in fact, a volume which contains
' representative ' papers of all his former works."

Of the varied effusions of this compilation, a great
favorite with many was the unfinished narrative of
" Mountjoy ; or, Some Passages out of the Life of a
Castle Builder." This first appeared in the *Knickerbocker* in 1839, but it was written in England prior to
the publication of the first number of the Sketch Book,
in 1819. He read it to Leslie when the artist was in a
tired mood, and, receiving from him little encouragement to proceed, threw it aside, and never touched it
again. It was in vain that Leslie tried afterward to
put him in heart about it. He was effectually discour-

aged. I have little doubt that Ogilvie was shadowed forth in this piece under the character of Glencoe, as he afterward sat to Leslie for the portrait of Don Quixote.

The publication of the first volume of the Life of Washington soon succeeded the appearance of " Wolfert's Roost." In regard to the size and form of this long-expected biography, it had been his intention to publish it only in the octavo form ; but it was so decidedly the judgment of his publisher that the duodecimo form would be the most in demand, from being uniform with his other works, that a sort of compromise was effected, by which it was to appear in both forms together. To enforce the propriety of his views in favor of the duodecimo edition, his publisher writes him, January 11th, at Sunnyside, where he had now returned : " You are aware we printed an edition of Columbus in octavo, to range with Prescott's Works ; but of these we have never sold but two hundred and fifty copies ; while about eleven thousand have been sold of the duodecimo."

The author, at the age of seventy-two, had just got through correcting the proofs of the first volume, when he met with his second accident from his horse Dick, to which allusion was made in a previous chapter. He had not mounted him since his former accident ; but on this day, April 18th, 1855, a favorite young lady friend calling at the house on horseback, he could not resist the temptation to try him once again, and accom-

pany her on a short ride. His " womankind," as he
styled his nieces, sought to dissuade him, but he was
not to be overruled. He had gone but about two hundred yards on the main road, when the animal became
so restless that he was induced to turn about, and,
leaving his companion at the head of the lane, retrace
his steps alone toward home, resolving within himself,
as he told me, never to get astride of Master Dick
again. This purpose was hardly formed, before the
unquiet beast suddenly became ungovernable, and,
starting off at full speed, rushed madly down the hill.
His rider tried the curb in vain. He did not heed it ;
and, continuing his frantic pace through the cottage
gate, tore his way into an evergreen that overhung the
road, and, stumbling, fell himself, and threw his rider
with violence to the ground, about a hundred feet from
his own door. Luckily, no limbs were broken, but his
head received a severe bruise, and his chest was sorely
wrenched by the violence of the overthrow, so that for
two days he could not be moved in bed without great
pain, and could not rise up or turn without assistance.
This was about the eighth or ninth escape he had had
from somewhat similar accidents on horseback or in
carriage since he built the cottage.

His physician, Dr. John C. Peters, of New York,
who was immediately sent for, on coming in, asked him
how he felt. The reply was ludicrously expressive :
" I feel as if an attempt had been made to force my
head down into my chest, as you shut up a spy-

glass." To an inquiry of one of his nieces how he felt now, after his position had been changed in bed, though he was still in great pain, "First rate," was the reply, making the motion as if touching his hat, and showing that he had in mind the answer of a poor starving soldier to Lieutenant Strain, when his party was perishing for food, and he was asked by his officer how he was. Lieutenant Strain had shortly before been at the cottage, and told the touching anecdote. The next day he was somewhat less helpless, and, though he could not rise up or turn directly, yet, "by a good deal of circumlocution," as he oddly expressed it, he was able to move himself. His humor never seemed to desert him, even in his most painful moments.

On the third day, though still feeling "somewhat battered and bruised," he got up very unexpectedly, and dressed and shaved himself; and, a day or two after, wrote the following reply to an inquiry of Kennedy about the accident:

[*To John P. Kennedy.*]

SUNNYSIDE, April 23, 1855.

MY DEAR KENNEDY:

The telegraphic report was, as usual, exaggerated. I have been thrown from my horse, but not as dangerously hurt as reported. Thanks to a hard head and strong chest, I have withstood a shock that would have *staved in* a sensitively constructed man. My head was pretty well battered, and came nigh being forced down into my chest, like the end of a telescope ; and my chest is still so wrenched and sore, that I am like one suffering with the asthma. But I have left my bed, and am on my legs again. It's all the doings of that rascal, Gentleman Dick, who, knowing my fondness for him, has played me all kinds of tricks. This is the second time he has fairly run away with me, but at least the tenth time he has attempted it. The first time I kept my seat, but this time he was determined I should not ; so he ran me among trees, and we both came down together. I have cut him off with a shilling.

The worst result of the accident (he writes to a niece who had expressed great concern about it from abroad) was, that I had to sell my favorite saddle horse, Gentleman Dick, or there would have been no peace in the household, the " womenkind " were so clamorous against the poor animal. Poor Dick ! His character was very much misunderstood by all but myself. He was one of the gentlest, finest tempered animals in the world. But a scamp of a coachman had played tricks with him, and made him so timid, that he was apt to get into a panic, when suddenly he would take the bit between his teeth, and trust to his heels for safety. I am now looking out for a quiet, sober, old-gentlemanlike horse, if such a thing is to be met with in this very young country, where everything is so prone *to go ahead.*

May 20th, 1855, Mr. Irving writes to me : " I enclose a letter, just received from Murray, which I will thank you to hand to Mr. Putnam. You will see that some negligence or omission in forwarding advance sheets to London may mar my interests in that quarter. But no matter. If my work be well received by the public, I shall be content, whatever be the pecuniary profits."

The letter from Murray informed him that he had placed the advance sheets of " Washington" in the hands of Bohn, on " a promise of £50, and a hope of something more if he could keep the field to himself ; but added that there was risk of perfect copies coming over from America before Bohn could complete his edition, in consequence of there being some pages missing from the proof sheets sent over. " It is quite absurd," he says, " to think of sending sheets of a book otherwise than in duplicate sets."

If there were demand for a large edition, he would print one himself, in conformity with the terms of his last letter ; " but," he writes, " I fear the publication in volume will be fatal to a large edition. The prospects of literature seen athwart the war are not encouraging, and I am disposed, consequently, to publish as little as possible."

This volume treats of the earlier part of Washington's career previous to the Revolution, ending with his arrival at the camp before Boston as Commander-in-Chief.

Mr. Irving, as usual, had been a good deal depressed about the work, and had avoided looking over it since its publication ; but the following cordial letter from Bancroft helped to put him more in conceit of it, and made him hope that the Life of Washington would not be the death of him, as he sometimes used to say he feared it would.

DEAR IRVING:

Your volume, of which I gained a copy last night, and this morning have received one made still more precious by your own hand, shortened my sleep last night at both ends. I was up late and early, and could not rest until I had finished the last page. Candor, good judgment that knows no bias, the felicity of selection, these are yours in common with the best historians. But, in addition, you have the peculiarity of writing from the heart, enchaining sympathy as well as commanding confidence; the happy magic that makes scenes, events, and personal anecdotes present themselves to you at your bidding, and fall into their natural places, and take color and warmth from your own nature. The style, too, is masterly, clear, easy, and graceful; picturesque without mannerism, and ornamented without losing simplicity. Among men of letters, who do well, you must above all take the name of FELIX, which so few of the great Roman generals could claim. You do everything rightly, as if by grace; and I am in no fear of offending your modesty, for I think you were elected and foreordained to excel your contemporaries.

Ever, dear Irving, most truly yours,

GEORGE BANCROFT.

The letter of the distinguished historian was soon followed by other notices and letters, which conspired to relieve the sort of nightmare solicitude he had felt about the work, and determined him to complete it.

He had before wellnigh given up the idea of carrying it any farther than the inauguration of Washington as President, the history of the Administration admitting of so little personal or picturesque detail that he feared he could give it no interest. He lost his indifference, however, about the completion of the Life, with the success of the first volume, and now determined, at whatever expense of labor, to go through with the whole.

The following close of a letter to Mrs. Storrow, dated June 27th, 1855, gives, in his own characteristic vein, a picture of a summer evening at Sunnyside:

* * * I am writing late at night, as I have to go to town on business in the morning. It is a beautiful moonlight night, and I have been kept up late by the young folk; having two of P. P. I——'s daughters with me—Hatty and sweet little Nelly; and they have been with the young G——s, cruising by moonlight on the Tappan Sea, in a beautiful yacht which G—— has recently bought. It puts me in mind of the water parties in former days, in the Dream, with the H——s, B——s, &c., when the old chorus used to be chanted:

> "We won't go home till morning,
>   Till daylight doth appear."

It is a different yacht and a different generation that have taken up the game, and are now sailing by moonlight and singing about the Tappan Sea. So rolls the world.

In September, Mr. Irving was all impatience to get his second volume of " Washington " ready for the

press. " I live only in the Revolution," said he to me.
" I have no other existence now—can think of nothing
else. My desire is to give everything vividly, but to
avoid all melodramatic effect. I wish the incidents to
be brought out strongly, and speak for themselves ;
but no hubbub of language, no trickery of phrase,
nothing wrought up."

He had made great additions to the " Life " since I
had read it before. I spoke with admiration of his
narrative of the battle of Princeton. " It is very difficult," said he, " to give a clear account of a battle.
Bancroft told me he was bothered about his battles,
but Prescott likes them. I study it thoroughly, to
seize the strong point, then dip my brush in the paint,
and color up for that."

September 27*th.*—I accompanied him to the complimentary festival to authors and booksellers at the
Crystal Palace. A carriage was sent for him to No.
33 Lafayette Place, where he was staying. We got in,
and were to call for Bishop ——, at No. —— ——
street. When we got near, I asked Mr. Irving if
he knew the Bishop. " No. Don't you ? " " No."
" Well, then, let's get out. It will be very awkward
to be in the carriage with him." P——'s lad, who
accompanied the carriage on the driver's seat, expostu-
lated. " Mr. P—— had sent him expressly with the
carriage. Would not like it." " But I *must* get out."
" But Mr. P——" " Never mind Mr. P——. I want
to have my way, not his." So down we got, and

walked from Twentieth street to the Crystal Palace, entering on Fortieth street. Mr. Irving could not endure the thing, as he drew near, but, after he got in, spent a pleasant evening. Was especially delighted at meeting Moses Thomas, his old bookseller, now a prosperous auctioneer in Philadelphia.

October 5th.—I was reading with Mr. Irving, in his study, the proof of some of the early pages of his second volume of " Washington," which had gone to the press about a week before. He was, at the same time, engaged in retouching and adding to the battle of White Plains; was desirous, he said, to exhibit the Revolution in its motley character, and give the play of human nature throughout.

Some days after, I drove over to Chatterton Hill with him, to visit the battle ground, he taking his manuscript account of it with him. While engaged in the survey, an old man, on a mealy-mouthed horse with white eyebrows, came up, and, informing us that he was the owner of the property, asked if we did not wish to buy it; he was too old to take care of it. Mr. Irving told him he was too old to buy it. On our way down, met a bright-eyed lad about six or seven years of age. " Stop—stop a moment," said he; " let me see what money I have," pulling out his purse. " I must buy those eyes. My little fellow, what will you take for those eyes ? " The little fellow stood aghast with amazement. " Well," said he, " here's sixpence for you, at any rate."

The anecdote is of a piece with that related by Mr. Davis, of the lad at Saratoga, and, though trivial, serves to illustrate his peculiar fancy for drolling with and mystifying children.

November 13th.—I went up to the cottage, to return the next day. Found Mr. Irving correcting proof of second volume of "Washington." Very glad of my visit. Had recast and improved the chapter about Lee's tardy movements to join Washington. Spoke of the raciness of Lee's character historically. "A game flavor about it," he said. Made a less flowing narrative, by giving the extracts from letters, and dates, but gave strength and accuracy to the detail. The character of Washington grew upon him constantly. Gave me the first chapters of the third volume to read. Was determined to push on with that the moment he finished the second.

November 21st.—Mr. Irving had been some days in the city, preparing the last chapters of the second volume of "Washington" for the press. Was busy on the last chapter but one when I called, soon after breakfast. Had been reading, in a morning paper, a report of the address of the Rev. Dr. De Witt, the night previous, before the Historical Society, in which there was a touching allusion to his Life of Washington, followed by loud cheers, and to himself, as "one whose modesty was only increased by the weight of public commendation." "I do not know," said he, adverting to it, "when anything has gratified me so much as this mention of me by old Dr. De Witt. I must write to him, and express to him what I feel."

I called again in the evening, and asked him if he had added to the close of the second volume, as he had thought of doing in the morning. " No ; I was too weary. Oh ! I shall be so glad to throw off the harness, and take a roll on the grass."

At the moment of completing his second volume, he received from Mr. Charles L. Brace some manuscript Hessian journals, which had been copied for the Historical Society, and which led him to recal and revise some of his proofs, and make some additions and alterations.

The following letter to his early Philadelphia publisher, Moses Thomas, was in reply to an invitation to attend a literary dinner in that city, and a request that he would make his home at his house on the occasion :

[*To Moses Thomas.*]

SUNNYSIDE, Dec. 15, 1855.

MY DEAR THOMAS :

I thank you heartily for your kind and hospitable invitation to your house, which I should be glad to accept did I propose attending the Godey Complimentary Dinner; but the annoy·ance I suffer at dinners of the kind, in having to attempt speeches, or bear compliments in silence, has made me abjure them altogether. The Publishers' Festival, at which I had the great pleasure of meeting you, was an exception to my rule, but only made on condition that I would not be molested by extra civilities.

I regret that on that occasion we were separated from each other, and could not sit together and talk over old times. However, I trust we shall have a future opportunity of so doing. I wish, when you visit New York, you would take a run up to Sunnyside. The cars set you down within ten minutes' walk of my house, where my " womenkind " will receive you (figuratively speaking) with open arms ; and my dogs will not dare to bark at you.

Yours ever, very truly,

WASHINGTON IRVING.

To the same Moses Thomas he wrote, from Liverpool, March 3d, 1818, prior to the appearance of the Sketch Book, when he was just getting himself into habits of study and literary life, from which he had been so long divorced :

I notice what you say on the subject of getting up an original work ; but I am very squeamish on that point. Whatever my literary reputation may be worth, it is very dear to me, and I cannot bring myself to risk it by making up books for mere profit.

The following is addressed to his old friend and literary compeer, at his residence on the east bank of the Hudson, about eight miles above Poughkeepsie, where he had been living since his retirement from public life, as Secretary of the Navy, in 1841. In this picturesque seclusion, which he had left to visit the city but once since it became his abode, he resumed his literary activity; and here the veteran author, the senior of Mr. Irving by more than four and a half years, gave to the press two novels, " The Old Continental," in 1846, and " The Puritan's Daughter," in 1850, at the ripe age of seventy-two. At the date of his application to Mr. Irving for his autograph, to be presented to a peerless beauty, he had passed his seventy-seventh year—a circumstance to be borne in mind in reading the reply :

[*To James K. Paulding.*]

SUNNYSIDE, Dec. 24, 1855.

MY DEAR PAULDING :

I enclose an autograph for the " paragon of a young lady," whose beauty you extol beyond the stars. It is a good sign that your heart is yet so inflammable.

I am glad to receive such good accounts as you give of yourself and your brother, "jogging on together in good humor with each other and with the world." Happy is he who can grow smooth as an old shilling as he wears out ; he has endured the rubs of life to some purpose.

You hope I am " sliding smoothly down the hill." I thank you for the hope. I am better off than most old bachelors are, or deserve to be. I have a happy home ; the happier for being always well stocked with womenkind, without whom an old bachelor is a forlorn, dreary animal. My brother, the " General," is wearing out the serene evening of life with me ; almost entirely deaf, but in good health and good spirits, more and more immersed in the study of newspapers (with which I keep him copiously supplied), and, through them, better acquainted with what is going on in the world than I am, who mingle with it occasionally, and have ears as well as eyes open. * * *

I have had many vivid enjoyments in the course of my life, yet no portion of it has been more equably and serenely happy than that which I have passed in my little nest in the country. I am just near enough to town to dip into it occasionally for a day or two, give my mind an airing, keep my notions a little up to the fashion of the times, and then return to my quiet little home with redoubled relish.

I have now my house full for the Christmas holidays, which I trust you also keep up in the good old style. Wishing a merry Christmas and a happy New Year to you and yours, I remain, my dear Paulding, yours ever, very truly,

WASHINGTON IRVING.

CHAPTER XII.

PUBLICATION OF VOL. II OF LIFE OF WASHINGTON—LETTER FROM PRESCOTT—
LETTER TO HENRY T. TUCKERMAN—LETTER OF CHARLES L. BRACE ON VOL. II
—LETTER TO BANCROFT—LETTER TO JOHN P. KENNEDY—LETTER TO GOUVER-
NEUR KEMBLE—PUBLICATION OF VOL. III.

THE second volume of the Life of Washington, which brings the history down from the period of his taking command of the army—a year before the Declaration of Independence—to the close of the successful campaign in New Jersey, in January, 1777, was issued in December, 1855.

The following letter from Prescott, who had just received a copy, will be read with interest. In the opening paragraph, the distinguished historian alludes to a complimentary letter from Mr. Irving on his Philip the Second. Henry Brevoort, so touchingly referred to at the close, had been dead some years.

[*From W. H. Prescott.*]

BOSTON, Jan. 3, 1856.

MY DEAR FRIEND:

Since the publication of Philip the Second, I may truly say nothing has given me greater pleasure than your kind note, and the cordial manner in which you speak of my labors. Ever since I have been old enough to distinguish good from evil in literary composition, your writings have been my familiar study. And if I have done anything that deserves half the commendation you bestow on me, it is in a great measure from the study I have made of you, and two or three others of the great masters of our language. Every one who knows me, knows that this is true. You may understand, then, how well I am pleased to obtain your unsolicited approval.

I have been gladdened by the sight of the second volume of your great work, which came to us a few days since. You are a good deal quicker on the trigger than I can be. You must have had a quantity of the material already potted down for posterity. It is very tantalizing to the reader, this fashion of publishing by instalments of a volume or two at a time, and people complain if they are not turned out as rapidly as romances. Macaulay used to tell the story of a young lady of his acquaintance, whom he met the week after his first two volumes appeared, who said to him: "I have just finished your volumes, Mr. Macaulay, and now we are all ready for another two!"

You have done with Washington just as I thought you would, and, instead of a cold, marble statue of a demigod, you have made him a being of flesh and blood, like ourselves—one with whom we can have sympathy. The general sentiment of the country has been too decidedly expressed for you to doubt for a moment that this is the portrait of him which is to hold a permanent place in the national gallery.

What naturally was of especial interest to me in your first volume, was that *pons asinorum*, over which so many have stumbled—the battle of Bunker Hill.* You have gone over it in a way which must satisfy the most captious critic. The silly question as to the command, has been a much vexed question in New England, as you are aware. I don't know whether you ever heard of the amusing fact of three folio volumes of affidavits of *survivors* having been taken by the late William Sullivan, bearing particularly on that matter. At his death, they were presented by his brother, Richard Sullivan, to the Massachusetts Historical Society. A committee was appointed by that body to examine their contents, and to report respecting them. The report was, that the testimony was so contradictory in its nature, that it would rather perplex than enlighten the historian; and the volumes were returned to Mr. Sullivan. A good commentary, this, on the value of even contemporary evidence.

But your kind note should not bring down such an avalanche on your head. Its date from Sunnyside reminds me of the pleasant day I passed in company with your early friend Brevoort, and mine of later years. It is long since I made a visit to New York; and when I have had occasion to pass a day there, the forms of those who used to greet me kindly, and who have gone forever, are sure to come up before my eye.

May you be among the number of those who are spared, and long spared, dear Mr. Irving, to delight the world by your writings, and enjoy the love and gratitude of your countrymen.

Believe me, always, very truly and affectionately, yours,

WM. H. PRESCOTT.

---

* It had been a moot point, in New England, whether General Putnam or Colonel William Prescott, the grandfather of the historian, had the chief command at the battle of Bunker Hill.

The battle of Bunker Hill, of which Prescott relates his amusing anecdote, is given near the close of
the first volume. The second volume carries the narrative down to the victories of Trenton and Princeton.

To a very kind letter from Mr. Tuckerman, soon
after the publication of his second volume, he sends the
following reply, giving some insight into his own views
and plan in the treatment of his theme:

[*To Mr. H. T. Tuckerman.*]

SUNNYSIDE, Jan. 8, 1856.

MY DEAR MR. TUCKERMAN:

I thank you most heartily for your letter, which, I frankly
assure you, was very seasonable and acceptable, being the first
intimation I had received of the fortune of the volume I had
launched upon the world. It was very considerate and
obliging in you to seek to relieve me from the suspense of
"waiting for a verdict;" which, with me, is apt to be a time
of painful doubt and self-distrust. You have discovered what
I aimed at, "the careful avoidance of rhetoric, the calm, patient, and faithful narrative of facts." My great labor has
been to arrange these facts in the most lucid order, and place
them in the most favorable light, without exaggeration or embellishment, trusting to their own characteristic value for effect.
Rhetoric does very well under the saddle, but is not to be
trusted in harness, being apt to pull facts out of place and
upset them. My horse, Gentleman Dick, was very rhetorical,
and showed off finely; but he was apt to run away with me,
and came near breaking my neck.

I have availed myself of the license of biography, to step
down occasionally from the elevated walk of history, and

relate familiar things in a familiar way; seeking to show the prevalent passions and feelings and humors of the day, and even to depict the heroes of Seventy-six as they really were— men in cocked hats, regimental coats, and breeches; and not classic warriors, in shining armor and flowing mantles, with brows bound with laurel, and truncheons in their hands. But enough of all this. I have committed myself to the stream, and, right or wrong, must swim on or sink. The latter I will not do, if I find the public sustain me.

The work, as I am writing it, will inevitably overrun three volumes. I had supposed, originally, that it would not, though I did not intend that number should be specified in the title page. It was specified by my publisher, who will put an author's incidental surmises into print, and make positive promises of them.

Should I have occasion to avail myself of the papers you so kindly put at my disposition, concerning Gouverneur Morris, Early American Society, &c., I shall have no hesitation in applying to you for them. In the mean time, let me repeat how very sensibly I feel the generous interest you have manifested in my literary success on the present occasion.

Yours, very truly,

WASHINGTON IRVING.

C. L. Brace, author of various interesting works, writes, January 22d, of the second volume:

MY DEAR MR. IRVING:

I do not see why one should not acknowledge a pleasure, when one has so enjoyed it; and I want to say how intensely interesting your second volume of "Washington" is. I have

read it as I would read a romance. To me it is history alive.
I enter into the feelings and struggle and uncertainties of the
actors, so that I feel, as it were, doubtful of the issue. * * *
Washington looms out grandly in this volume ; much more so
than in the first, naturally. It is the most living picture we
have ever had of him, and shows, best of all, the incessant
difficulties of his work. It is strange, too, how you have made
those battles *real*. I have read them often, and never had any
clear idea at all of them ; now they are indissolubly associated
with the places. You have again made the Hudson classic
ground. I predict without a doubt that this will be the Washington of the people—especially of the young people. As a
boy, I should read it like Robinson Crusoe or Captain Cook's
Voyages.

To a letter from Bancroft, congratulating him on
the success of his second volume, he replies :

My dear Bancroft :

I thank you sincerely for your cordial and well-timed note.
It is always an anxious time with an author when he has just
launched a volume, and is waiting for a verdict ; and especially
with one like myself, apt to be troubled with self-distrust. I
never was more troubled with it than in the prosecution of my
present task, when I am occasionally venturing, in a somewhat
familiar way, upon themes which you will treat in such an
ampler, nobler, and more truly historical style. Indeed, I am
putting to sea at a hazardous time, when you and Macaulay
and Prescott (with his grand Spanish Armada) are afloat.
However, I am ready to drop my peak whenever any of you
come into the same waters.

Give my best thanks to Mrs. Bancroft for her favorable opinion of my volume. As Sir Fretful Plagiary says, the women are the best judges, after all.

Ever, my dear Bancroft, yours most heartily,

WASHINGTON IRVING.

February 23*d*, 1856.—I returned to the city from a visit of ten days at the cottage. Mr. Irving was busy at the third volume of "Washington," which was going through the press. About one hundred pages were printed when I came down. He had been reconstructing the narrative of Burgoyne's expedition, and the affair of Schuyler and Gates. His head troubled him occasionally, and he seemed to feel the pressure of such a task at his time of life. Rewrote three or four pages after he had got the proof; viz., Signs of an Approaching Enemy at Ticonderoga. Seemed to feel, at times, an uneasy consciousness that he might not get through with his labor. "I am constantly afraid," he said to me the morning I came down, "that something will happen to me," alluding to his head. Never saw him so impatient at the encroaching demands of letters upon his valuable time. "Oh! these letters— these letters! They tear my mind from me in slips and ribbons."

He had received, the day before (Washington's birthday), from his publisher, the present of a new table for his study. It had a good many drawers, and sundry novel conveniences, the use of which he did not readily comprehend. "You will be bothered with your very conveniences," said I. "Yes. I must get everything in a mess, and then I'll go on comfortably."

The letter which follows, is in reply to one from Mr. Kennedy, announcing the death of his wife's father, Mr. Edward Gray:

[*To Mr. J. P. Kennedy.*]

SUNNYSIDE, March 22, 1856.

MY DEAR KENNEDY:

The sight of your letter, just received, with its black seal and edgings, gave me a severe shock, though I thought I was prepared for the event it communicated. The death of my most dear and valued friend, Mr. Gray, is a relief to himself, and to the affectionate hearts around him who witnessed his prolonged sufferings; but I, who have been out of the hearing of his groans, can only remember him as he was in his genial moments, the generous and kind-hearted centre of a loving circle, dispensing happiness around him.

My intimacy with him, in recent years, had fully opened to me the varied excellence of his character, and most heartily attached me to him. My dear Kennedy, my intercourse with your family connection has been a great sweetener of the last few years of my existence, and the only attraction that has been able to draw me repeatedly from home. And in all this I recognize the influence of the kind, cordial, sympathetic character of Mr. Gray. To be under his roof, in Baltimore or at Ellicott's Mills, was to be in a constant state of quiet enjoyment to me. Everything that I saw in him, and in those about him; in his tastes, habits, mode of life; in his domestic relations and chosen intimacies, continually struck upon some happy chord in my own bosom, and put me in tune with the world and with human nature. I cannot expect, in my brief remnant of existence, to replace such a friend, and such a domestic circle rallying round him; but the remembrance will ever be most dear to me.

Give my most affectionate remembrance to your wife and her noble-hearted sister, and believe me, my dear Kennedy,

Ever yours, most truly,

WASHINGTON IRVING.

A few weeks before the date of the following letter, Mr. Irving had written to Gouverneur Kemble that his gardener had been constructing a hothouse, and preparing a piece of ground, sheltered by a fence, where he expected to effect great things; and that, if he had any cuttings or plants of grapes and figs to spare, and could send them to him by railroad, he would make his gardener very happy:

[*To Gouverneur Kemble.*]

SUNNYSIDE, April 23, 1856.

MY DEAR KEMBLE:

The roots and cuttings sent by your gardener arrived safe, and are all properly disposed of. I should like to have a few more cuttings for out of doors, and a black Hamburg or two, if you have any. I shall raise some of the grapes under glass, having a small hothouse which will accommodate a few. I hope your visit to Washington was pleasant and profitable, and that you will be favored with a seat in the Cabinet, or a foreign mission in this or the next Presidency.

I am happy to learn that your lawn is green. I hope it

will long continue so, and yourself likewise. I shall come up, one of these days, and have a roll on it with you.

Yours ever, my dear Kemble,

WASHINGTON IRVING.

April 24th, 1856, he writes to his niece, at Paris, "at a late hour of the night, after a hard day's work":

I have about two thirds of my third volume of "Washington" in type, and shall be heartily glad when the whole volume is completed; when I will give myself repose before I commence another. It is a toilsome task, though a very interesting, and, I may say, delightful one. It expands and grows more voluminous as I write, but the way it is received by the public cheers me on; for I put it to the press with more doubt and diffidence than any work I ever published. The way the public keep on with me is a continual wonderment to me, knowing my own shortcomings in many things; and I must say I am sometimes surprised at my own capacity for labor at my advanced time of life—when I used to think a man must be good for nothing.

The third volume, embracing the period from the commencement of the year 1777 to the retirement of Washington into winter quarters in 1779, appeared in July, 1856.

CHAPTER XIII.

BEFORE I proceed to introduce the letters which are to follow, I must invite the reader to travel back with me to the little episode in Mr. Irving's life, his intercourse with the Fosters, at Dresden. From motives of delicacy, I had imposed on myself a reserve as to some particulars of that intimate companionship; and, as no mention had been made of it among the letters and extracts which Mrs. Fuller had been kind enough to furnish me, I had hesitated to betray my consciousness that the imperfect memorial of his early life, found in his secret drawer after his death, was addressed to Mrs. Foster. Of this I had undoubted evidence, as well from other circumstances as from the names of Emily and Flora appearing in the manuscript. From an entry in Mr. Irving's diary, while at Prague, in June, 1823, mentioning the writing and sending to Mrs. Foster, from that city, a letter " giving anecdotes of self," I had surmised that the faded manuscript, so long preserved, was a transcript from that letter. I now learn, from the journal of Mrs. Flora Dawson, which has strangely enough made its appearance in the English edition of the third volume of my biography, that I erred in this conjecture, and that the written sheets were brought to the family by Mr. Irving himself, at Dresden, and left for their perusal, under a sacred promise that the manuscript should be returned to him ; that no copy should be taken, and that no eyes but theirs should ever rest upon it—a promise, adds the same authority, faithfully kept.

From this, I perceive that the sheets in my possession, instead of being a transcript from a letter, as I had supposed, are part of the original manuscript, here mentioned as having been left and reclaimed.

In the first volume of my work, I had already introduced some affecting passages from this memorial, bearing upon the history of his early attachment, and had supposed that I had given all that would be of interest to the general reader ; but as the London publisher of the biography, to whom the advanced sheets were sent, has taken the surprising liberty of introducing two whole chapters, making seventy-nine additional pages, at the end of the third volume, without my knowledge or consent, giving some further particulars of the author's life at Dresden, I feel it necessary again to recur to the subject. This new matter, to which the bookseller has resorted as a device to obtain

a copyright, consists mainly of the journals of Mrs.
Fuller and Mrs. Dawson, the Emily and Flora of those
days. While there is much that is of interest in their
record of those "pleasant days," as Mr. Irving calls
them in a letter which is to follow—the last he ever
wrote to the family—there are some things in the journal of Mrs. Dawson a little calculated, though no
doubt unintentionally, to mislead, or rather to be misunderstood.

A notice of the English edition of my work, which
met my eye in the London *Quarterly* before I had
been able to see the English copy, or had any intimation of the nature of the additions intruded upon it,
mentioned, to my surprise, that Mr. Irving had aspired
to the hand of Miss Emily Foster, at Dresden, and met
with a "friendly but decided rejection of his addresses." On receiving the English copy, I find that
Mrs. Dawson makes no positive assertion of the kind ;
but, while she claims for her sister, from Mr. Irving, a
degree of devotion amounting to "a hopeless and consuming attachment," she goes on to say : "It was fortunate, perhaps, that this affection was returned by *the
warmest friendship only*—(the italics are her own)—
since it was destined that the accomplishment of his
wishes was impossible, for many obstacles which lay in
his way."

While I am not disposed to question, for a moment,
the warmth or sincerity of his admiration for the lady,
that he ever thought of matrimony at this time is

utterly disproved by a passage of the very manuscript to which the sister refers, as addressed to her mother, and of which she errs in supposing that I had in possession only the first and last sheets. A more careful reference to the first volume of the biography, will show her that *only the first and last sheets were missing,* and that there remained sixteen consecutive pages. In that manuscript, after recounting the progress and catastrophe of his early love, forever hallowed to his memory, and glancing at other particulars of his life, with which the reader has already been made familiar, all given with the frankness and unreserve of perfect confidence, he closes, by saying :

You wonder why I am not married. I have shown you why I was not long since. When I had sufficiently recovered from that loss, I became involved in ruin. It was not for a man broken down in the world, to drag down any woman to his paltry circumstances. I was too proud to tolerate the idea of ever mending my circumstances by matrimony. My time has now gone by ; and I have growing claims upon my thoughts and upon my means, slender and precarious as they are. I feel as if I had already a family to think and provide for.

The reader will perceive from this passage, addressed to Mrs. Foster, at Dresden, after months of intimate friendship, what color there is for the assertion that Mr. Irving ever made advances for the *hand* of Miss Emily Foster, however great or undisguised may have been his admiration for her. That the "warmest friendship" existed between them, is fully shown from the tone of the letters which follow, written thirty-three years after their sojourn at Dresden. Their last meeting, alluded to in the letter, which I now lay before the reader, was in London, in 1832, shortly before his return to America, after his prolonged absence of seventeen years.

[*From Mrs. Emily Fuller to Washington Irving.*]

May 25, 1856.

MY DEAR MR. IRVING:

I think I ought to begin by telling you who is writing to you—Emily Foster, now Emily Fuller; and I address you, after so long a time, because I hope that my eldest boy Henry may have the happiness and advantage of meeting you, and making your acquaintance personally, as he has long ago by hearsay. I have been renewing former days. I have lately been reading over my old Dresden journal, where you are a part of our daily life, and feel it all over again so completely, I cannot believe all the time since has really passed. Then, too, in the course of last winter, we were all living with you in the Alhambra. We were reading it out loud in the evenings, and the sunshine and moonlight and fountains and Lindaraxa's garden became almost more real than the real fire and winter evenings. We also read the Sketch Book and Bracebridge Hall, and I really thought they came upon me more fresh and more delightful than even the first time I read them—the touching expressions, and the arch, pretty humor—I could see you, your *own self*, as we read, and your very smile. How I should like to hear from you, dear Mr. Irving! I married soon after we met in London. Do you remember you used to come, and often spend the evening with us in Seymour street? And now I have four boys and one little girl. They are all so good and promising as to add much to our happiness. Two of them are still at school. * * * My eldest has a great desire to settle in the States, with a friend who goes out with him—a very nice, gentlemanly young man. * * * I wish you would give us your advice as to situation, &c. Climate would be one of the first considerations; and they wish to go as far West as would be convenient. * * *

I must not exceed my space. It will be such a real happiness to hear from you. Do tell me about yourself, dear Mr. Irving. You do not know how much and often I think of you.   Yours ever, most truly,

EMILY FULLER.

To this letter Mr. Irving sent the following reply, which came to me from Mrs. Fuller with the extracts given in a former volume, and accompanied by her own beautiful testimonial to his character, in a letter to myself, already before the reader:

[*To Mrs. Emily Fuller.*]

SUNNYSIDE, July 2, 1856.

MY DEAR MRS. FULLER:

You can scarcely imagine my surprise and delight, on opening your letter and finding that it came from Emily Foster. A thousand recollections broke at once upon my mind, of Emily Foster as I had known her at Dresden, young, and fair, and bright, and beautiful; and I could hardly realize that so many years had elapsed since then, or form an idea of her as Mrs. Emily Fuller, with four boys and one little girl. * * * I wish you had given me a few more particulars about yourself, and those immediately connected with you, whom I have known. After so long an interval, one fears to ask questions, lest they should awaken painful recollections.

By the tenor of your letter, I should judge that, on the whole, the world has gone smoothly with you. Your children, you tell me, are all "so good and promising, as to add much to your happiness." How much of what is most precious in life is conveyed in those few words! You ask me to tell you something about myself. Since my return, in 1846, from my diplomatic mission to Spain, I have been leading a quiet life in a little rural retreat I had previously established on the banks of the Hudson, which, in fact, has been my home for twenty years past. I am in a beautiful part of the country, in an agreeable neighborhood, am on the best of terms with my neighbors, and have a house full of nieces, who almost make me as happy as if I were a married man. Your letter was put into my hands just as I was getting into the carriage to drive out with some of them. I read it to them in the course of the drive, letting them know that it was from Emily Foster, the young lady of whom they had often heard me speak ; who had painted the head of Herodias, which hangs over the piano in the drawing room, and who, I had always told them, was more beautiful than the head which she had painted; which they could hardly believe, though it was true. You recollect, I trust, the miniature copy of the head of Herodias which you made in the Dresden Gallery. I treasure it as a precious memorial of those pleasant days.

My health is excellent, though, at times, I have tried it

hard by literary occupations and excitement. There are some propensities that grow upon men with age, and I am a little more addicted to the pen than I was in my younger days, and much more, I am told, than is prudent for a man of my years. It is a labor, however, in which I delight; and I am never so happy of an evening, as when I have passed the whole morning in my study, hard at work, and have earned the evening's recreation.

Farewell, my dear Mrs. Fuller. If any of those of your family whom I ever knew and valued are at hand, assure them that I ever retain them in cordial remembrance; and believe me, ever, my dear Emily Foster, your affectionate friend,

Washington Irving.

I shall give, in an Appendix to this volume, the whole of the new matter so unwarrantably obtruded at the end of the third volume of the English edition of my work, published by Mr. Richard Bentley.

My next letter is one from Dickens to Mr. Irving, introducing a relative, glancing at a capital story of Mr. Irving of a dinner at Holland House, in which a clergyman's leg was a feature, and giving a comic yet touching anecdote of poor Rogers in his eclipse:

[From Charles Dickens.]

Tavistock House, London, July 5, 1856.

My dear Irving:

If you knew how often I write to you, individually and personally, in my books, you would be no more surprised in seeing this note, than you were in seeing me do my duty by that flowery julep (in what I dreamily apprehend to have been a former state of existence) at Baltimore.

Will you let me present to you a cousin of mine, Mr. B——, who is associated with a merchant's house in New York? Of course, he wants to see you, and know you. How can *I* wonder at that? How can anybody?

I had a long talk with Leslie at the last Academy dinner (having previously been with him in Paris), and he told me that you were flourishing. I suppose you know that he wears a moustache—so do I, for the matter of that, and a beard too— and that he looks like a portrait of Don Quixote.

Holland House has four-and-twenty youthful pages in it now—twelve for my lord, and twelve for my lady; and no clergyman coils his leg up under his chair all dinner time, and begins to uncurve it when the hostess goes. No wheeled chair runs smoothly in, with that beaming face in it; and ——'s little cotton pocket handkerchief helped to make (I believe) this very sheet of paper. A half-sad, half-ludicrous story of Rogers is all I will sully it with. You know, I dare say, that, for a year or so before his death, he wandered, and lost himself, like one of the Children in the Wood, grown up there and grown down again. He had Mrs. Procter and Mrs. Carlyle to break-fast with him, one morning—only those two. Both exces-sively talkative, very quick and clever, and bent on entertain-ing him. When Mrs. Carlyle had flashed and shone before him for about three quarters of an hour on one subject, he turned his poor old eyes on Mrs. Procter, and, pointing to the brilliant discourser with his poor old finger, said (indignantly), "Who is *she?*" Upon this, Mrs. Procter, cutting in, deliv-ered—(it is her own story)—a neat oration on the life and writings of Carlyle, and enlightened him in her happiest and airiest manner; all of which he heard, staring in the dreariest silence, and then said (indignantly as before), " And who are *you ?* " * * *

Ever, my dear Irving, most affectionately and truly, yours,
                                        CHARLES DICKENS.

While engrossed, as far as incessant interruptions would permit, by the task of preparing his fourth volume of the Life of Washington for the press, he writes a letter to his niece, at Paris, of which I extract some interesting passages. The " Pierre " mentioned in the first extract is not the editor, but the eldest son of his brother Ebenezer, Pierre Paris Irving, an Episcopal clergyman, who had recently returned to his parochial duties from a brief excursion in Europe, which had extended to the Orkneys.

[*To Mrs. Storrow.*]

SUNNYSIDE, Oct. 27, 1856.

* * * After Pierre's return from France to England, he made an expedition to the end of the world—in other words, to the Orkneys! It was in those islands that the branch of the Irving family from which we are descended vegetated for centuries; once having great landed possessions, ultimately losing them.

Pierre found a highly intelligent circle of society existing at Kirkwall, the capital of the Orkneys, principally composed of persons from Edinburgh, holding official stations. He was hospitably entertained by them, in a style of elegance which he had not expected in that remote region.

At Shapinsha, the island whence my father came, Pierre was shown the house in which he was born, and whence he emigrated about a century since. It is a house of modest pretensions, and still bears its old name of Quholme (pronounced Home). In the flourishing days of our family, it must have owned the greater part of Shapinsha. Mr. Balfour, the present proprietor, received Pierre very hospitably in his noble residence of Balfour Castle, and submitted to his inspection a chest full of deeds and documents of several generations, showing how, by piecemeal, the landed property passed out of the hands of the Irvings, and centred in those of the family which at present hold it. Pierre brought home one of those documents, given to him by Mr. Balfour, three or four centuries old, bearing the name of one of our ancestors, with the old family arms of the Three Holly Leaves. He also brought home a genealogy of the family, which some official gentleman, curious in antiquarian research, had digested from deeds and other documents existing at the Orkneys, and in the public archives at Edinburgh. This genealogical table, which is officially certified, establishes the fact of our being descended from the Irving of Bonshaw, who gave shelter to Robert the Bruce in the day of his adversity.

* * * You are going to pass the winter at a city I never visited—Florence. At the time I was in Italy, a cordon of troops was drawn round Tuscany, on account of a malignant fever prevalent there, and I was obliged to omit the whole of it in my Italian tour. I also failed to see Venice, which I have ever regretted.

Your letter of last June mentions your being just returned from an excursion of four days to Touraine. It recalled a tour I once made there with your uncle Peter, in which, besides visiting the places you speak of, we passed a day or two in the beautiful old chateau of Ussy, belonging to the Duke of Duras, the Duchess having given me a letter to the concierge, which put the chateau and its domains at my disposition. Our sojourn was very interesting. The chateau had a half-deserted character. The Duke had not fortune enough to keep it up in style, and only visited it occasionally in the hunting season. There were the traces of former gayety and splendor—a private theatre, all in decay and disorder; an old chapel turned into a granary; state apartments, with stately family portraits in quaint, antiquated costumes, but some of them mouldering in their frames. I found, afterward, that the Duchess had hoped I might be excited to write something about the old chateau in the style of Bracebridge Hall; and it would indeed have been a fine subject.   *   *   *

CHAPTER XIV.

THE letter which follows is addressed to a young author, to whom Mr. Irving had before written encouragingly in acknowledgment of the presentation of his first work :

[*To Mr. Charles Lanman.*]

SUNNYSIDE, March 2, 1857.

MY DEAR MR. LANMAN :

I am suffering a long time to elapse without acknowledging the receipt of the copy of your work* which you have had the kindness to send me, and expressing to you the great delight I take in the perusal of it. But when I remind you that I am approaching my seventy-fourth birthday ; that I am laboring to launch the fourth volume of my Life of Washington ; and that my table is loaded with a continually increasing multitude of unanswered letters, which I vainly endeavor to cope with, I

---

* Adventures in the Wilds of America.

am sure that you will excuse the tardiness of my correspondence.

I hope the success of your work has been equal to its
merits.   To me, your "Adventures in the Wilds" are a continual refreshment of the spirits.   I take a volume of your
work to bed with me, after fagging with my pen, and then I
ramble with you among the mountains and by the ·streams in
the boundless interior of our fresh, unhackneyed country, and
only regret that I can but do so in idea, and that I am not
young enough to be your companion in reality.

I have taken great interest, of late, in your Expedition
among the Alleghany Mountains, having been campaigning, in
my work, in the upper parts of the Carolinas, and especially in
the "Catawba country," about which you give such graphic
sketchings.   Really, I look upon your work as a *vade · mecum*
to the American lover of the picturesque and romantic, unfold-
ing to him the wilderness of beauties and the variety of adventurous life to be found in our great chains of mountains and
system of lakes and rivers.   You are, in fact, the picturesque
explorer of our country.

With great regard, my dear Mr. Lanman, yours ever, very
truly,

WASHINGTON IRVING.

By the following brief notes to myself, it will
appear that the fourth volume of the Life of Washington was going through the press, and that he was
prone to make modifications and corrections during the
process :

SUNNYSIDE, March 20, 1857.

MY DEAR PIERRE:

Page 161 must be carefully collated with the manuscript. There are two places where I cannot supply the deficit.

I have struck out some lines in page 172, so that the chapter may end on page 173, and save the great blank in page 174. The printers appear to be fond of ending a chapter at the top of a page.

I have no doubt of getting the Inauguration into this volume; but the printers must not make blank pages unnecessarily.

SUNNYSIDE, Monday Evening.

There is a passage in, I think, De Rochambeau's Memoirs, about the sending in a flag, at Yorktown, to Cornwallis, to obtain permission for Secretary Nelson to leave the town; and about his being brought out on a litter, being old, and ill with the gout. I wish you would copy it, and send it to me with the next proofs, as I wish to make immediate use of it. You will find De Rochambeau's Memoirs in the American department of the Astor Library.

If it is not in De Rochambeau's Memoirs, it is in Chastellux; but I think it is in the former.

It was in Chastellux.

SUNNYSIDE, March 22, 1857.

I send you the page which was missing. Fortunately, I had *impaled* it, as I now do all the cancelled pages. * * *

SUNNYSIDE, Tuesday Evening.

* * * I shall send no copy for a day or two, for I am

fagged and a little out of order, and need rest; and I wish to be careful about the ensuing chapters, which I have been patching, and must revise to avoid muddling. * * * I shall be heartily glad to receive the last proof sheet.

Not long after this note was written, Mr. Irving received a visit from Mr. Charles Lanman, who had recently sent him his " Adventures in the Wilds of America," for which he makes his acknowledgment in a letter just given.   On his return to his residence, at Georgetown, Mr. Lanman gave a detail of his visit in a letter to Peter Force, Esq., entitled, " A Day with Washington Irving," which was published in the *National Intelligencer*, and enclosed in an epistle from the writer to Mr. Irving.   This is his tardy but characteristic acknowledgment :

[*To Charles Lanman, Georgetown, D. C.*]

SUNNYSIDE, May 9, 1857.

MY DEAR MR. LANMAN :

I have been too thoroughly occupied in getting a volume of my work through the press, to acknowledge, at an earlier date, your letter of March 24th, respecting your letter* which has found its way into the *Intelligencer*.   I can only say, that I wish you had had a worthier subject for your biographic pen, or that I had known our conversation was likely to be recorded; I should then have tasked myself to say some wise or witty things, to be given as specimens of my *off-hand table talk*.   One should always know when they are sitting for

* A letter to Peter Force, Esq.

a portrait, that they may endeavor to look handsomer than themselves, and attitudinize.

I am scrawling this in great haste, merely that your letter may not remain longer unacknowledged; and am, very truly, your friend,

WASHINGTON IRVING.

The letter which follows is addressed to Mr. Henry T. Tuckerman, in acknowledgment of his volume of "Biographical Essays," which Mr. Irving had pronounced, in a previous letter, written on a partial perusal, the best work he had given to the public, and one that must greatly advance his reputation :

[*To Mr. H. T. Tuckerman.*]

SUNNYSIDE, Jan. 26, 1857.

MY DEAR MR. TUCKERMAN :

I wrote to you, some days since, on the subject of your new work, when I had read but a part of it. I have just finished the perusal of it, and cannot rest until I have told you how thoroughly I have been delighted with it. I do not know when I have read any work more uniformly rich, full, and well sustained. The liberal, generous, catholic spirit in which it is written, is beyond all praise. The work is a model of its kind.

I have no doubt that it will take a high stand in England, and will reflect great credit on our literature, of which it will remain a lasting ornament.

Congratulating you, with all my heart, on this crowning achievement of your literary career I remain, yours, very cordially and truly,

WASHINGTON IRVING.

The fourth volume of the Life of Washington was published in May. The first letter he received on the subject was from Bancroft, who pronounced the picture he had drawn of Washington " the most vivid and the truest " that had " ever been written." To a warm, congratulatory letter from Mr. Frederick S. Cozzens, author of the humorous " Sparrowgrass Papers," a resident of Yonkers, about eight miles south of Sunnyside, he sends the following characteristic reply :

SUNNYSIDE, May 22, 1857.

MY DEAR MR. COZZENS :

Your letter has been most acceptable and animating ; for letters of the kind are not, as you presume, " common to me as blackberries." Excepting a very cordial and laudatory one from Bancroft, yours is the only one, relative to my last volume, that I have yet received. Backed by these two letters, I feel strong enough to withstand that self-criticism which is apt to beset me and cuff me down at the end of a work, when the excitement of composition is over.

You speak of some misgivings which you felt in the course of my literary enterprise, whether I would be able to go through with it, and " end as happily as I had begun." I confess I had many misgivings of the kind myself, as I became aware of the magnitude of the theme upon which I had adventured, and saw " wilds immeasurably spread " lengthening on every side as I proceeded. I felt that I had presumed on the indulgence of nature in undertaking such a task at my time of life, and feared I might break down in the midst of it. Whimsical as it may seem, I was haunted occasionally by one of my own early pleasantries. My mock admonition to Diedrich Knickerbocker not to idle in his historic wayfaring, rose in judgment against me : "Is not Time, relentless Time, shaking, with palsied hand, his almost exhausted hourglass before thee ? Hasten, then, to pursue thy weary task, lest the last sands be run ere thou hast finished thy history of the Manhattoes."

Fortunately, I had more powers of endurance in me than I gave myself credit for. I have attained to a kind of landing place in my work, and, as I now rest myself on the bank, feel that, though a little weary, I am none the worse for having so long tugged at the oar.

And now, as the winter is past, the rains are over and gone, and the flowers are appearing upon the earth, I mean to recreate myself a little, and may, one day or other, extend my travels down even to Yonkers, but will always be happy to welcome you to Sunnyside.

With kindest remembrances to Mrs. Cozzens, believe me, very truly, your obliged friend,

WASHINGTON IRVING.

I bring this chapter to a close with the two following letters ; the first written by Prescott after completing the perusal of the fourth volume of the Life of Washington, and the last by Motley, about to leave the country, and whom Mr. Irving never met. Motley had recently achieved a brilliant fame by his " Rise of the Dutch Republic ;" and, after some modest demur to which his letter alludes, had sent his volumes to Mr. Irving, who responded with a sincere and warm eulogy :

[*From Mr. W. H. Prescott.*]

LYNN, MASS., Aug. 7, 1857.

MY DEAR MR. IRVING :

I have just closed the fourth volume of your Life of
Washington. I have not hurried myself, as you see; and,
in truth, a man who travels through books with the ear, instead
of the eye, cannot hurry. I don't know whether you care
about remarks on your books from friends, though they be
brothers of the craft; but it always seems to me that, when
one has derived great pleasure from reading an author, to make
no acknowledgment is as uncourteous as for a gourmand, after
he has crammed himself with a good dinner, to go away without a civil word to his host.

My wife, who has been my reader, and myself, have indeed read with the greatest interest this your last work—an
interest which went on *crescendo* from the beginning, and
which did not reach its climax till the last pages. I have
never before fully comprehended the character of Washington; nor did I know what capabilities it would afford to his
biographer. Hitherto we have only seen him as a sort of
marble Colossus, full of moral greatness, but without the touch
of humanity that would give him interest. You have known
how to give the marble flesh color, that brings it to the resem-
blance of life. This you have done throughout; but it is
more especially observable in the first volume and in the last.
No one—at least, I am sure, no American—could read the last
without finding pretty often a blur upon the page. Yet, I see,
like your predecessors, you are not willing to mar the beautiful
picture, by giving Washington the infirmity of temper which

common report assigns to him.   Perhaps you are not satisfied
with the foundations of such a report.

I had feared, from your manner of talking, that you would
never set about the great work in earnest.   Happy for the
country that it has been at last accomplished by your pen!

It is long since I had the pleasure of seeing you, though I
often get particulars about you.   How gratified should I be, for
one of many, if you would pay a visit to our northern latitudes!   I so rarely go to New York, that, when I go, the
memory of friends like Brevoort, Wainwright, and a few
others, rises to my mind, and fills it with a melancholy feeling.

Adieu, my dear Mr. Irving.   Long may it be before *you*
are called away, and before you cease to give pleasure and
instruction to the world by your writings.

Always, very sincerely, your friend,

WM. H. PRESCOTT.

[J. Lothrop Motley to Washington Irving.]

BOSTON, Aug. 7, 1857.

MY DEAR SIR:

You must permit me to address you a single line of thanks
for the kind note you did me the honor of sending me several
days since.

To receive such warm and generous commendation from so
venerated a hand, is sufficient reward for literary labor, although it were far more severe and more successful than mine
has been.

Having been, from youth upward, among the warmest
and most enthusiastic admirers of your genius, I appreciate
entirely the generosity with which you extend to me the hand
of fellowship and sympathy.

It is your great good fortune to command not only the respect and admiration of your innumerable readers, but their affection also. A feeling of personal obligation—almost of personal friendship—mingles itself, in their minds, with the colder sentiments which are often entertained toward even a successful author.

I will not proceed in this vein, lest I should say more than you would think becoming, as addressed directly to yourself. I will only say, that when the book of which you have been pleased to speak so indulgently first appeared, I wished very much to depart, in a single instance, from the rule which I had laid down—not to send, namely, a copy to any one who was not an old personal acquaintance. I did wish very much to send you one, as a testimony of gratitude and respect from one who had been long most familiar with you, although utterly unknown to you. I refrained, however, until recently, and I am rejoiced to find that you did not consider my sending the book an intrusion.

I need not tell you how bitterly disappointed I was at missing the promised pleasure of meeting you at dinner at President King's. It is just possible that you may not know the nature of the *contretemps.* Mr. King was so kind, upon my expressing a strong desire to see you, as to invite me to New York upon a certain day, when he hoped also to have the pleasure of your company. Subsequently, by letter, he countermanded this arrangement, thinking you absent from home. Nevertheless, on the day before the appointed one, I was ready, with my trunk packed, to take the afternoon boat for New York, and went to the post office, hoping for a summons. There was nothing there, so I remained. *Five days* after the dinner, I received from Mr. King a telegraphic dispatch *via*

Nahant (where I had not been for several days), notifying me that you were to dine with him "to-morrow"—that to-morrow having already crept, with its stealthy pace, into the regions of eternal yesterday. Alas! I *must* say, in the bitterness of my spirit,

> " The best laid schemes of mice and men
>   Gang aft a-gley,
> And leave us nought but grief and pain
>   For promised joy ; "

for the pleasure which I anticipated has been turned into a perpetual "grief and pain." I indulge the hope of meeting you, however, after my return.

I leave this country on the 12th of this month. If I can be of any service to you in England or France, during my residence there, I need not say how much it will gratify me to be of use to you. My address is, "Care of Baring Brothers & Co."

Meantime, with sentiments of the most sincere respect and regard, I remain, your obliged friend and servant,

J. Lothrop Motley.

The following brief correspondence between Mr. Irving and S. Austin Allibone, of Philadelphia, author of the "Dictionary of Authors," is not without interest :

[*To Washington Irving.*]

Philadelphia, Oct. 28, 1857.

Dear Sir:

Last night, or rather this morning—for it was after midnight—I was deeply engrossed with your graphic picture of your own residence in the Alhambra in the spring of 1829.

It occurs to me to send you the descriptive title of Owen Jones's illustrations of the Alhambra. May I venture to ask, whether the thrilling sketch of your midnight "night-walking" through the halls of the Alhambra is an account of a real ramble, or whether it is partly a fancy picture, founded on fact? It is certainly one of your best *passages*, and that is saying a great deal.

I am, dear sir, very truly yours,

S. AUSTIN ALLIBONE.

[*To S. Austin Allibone.*]

SUNNYSIDE, Nov. 2, 1857.

MY DEAR SIR :

We have in the Astor Library a copy of Owen Jones's work illustrative of the Alhambra. I have lately seen a number of photographs of various parts of the Alhambra, which I believe are intended for publication. They will give a perfectly truthful idea of the old pile.

The account of my midnight rambles about the old palace is literally true, yet gives but a feeble idea of my feelings and impressions, and of the singular haunts I was exploring.

Everything in the work relating to myself, and to the actual inhabitants of the Alhambra, is unexaggerated fact.

It was only in the legends that I indulged in *romancing ;* and these were founded on materials picked up about the place.

With great regard, my dear sir, yours very truly,

WASHINGTON IRVING.

CHAPTER XV.

A LITERARY HARVEST—ENGAGED ON HIS FIFTH VOLUME—LETTER TO MRS. STOR-
ROW—THE CRISIS OF 1857—CONVERSATIONS—KEMBLE—COOKE—COOPER—
DARLEY AND DIEDRICH KNICKERBOCKER—WASHINGTON ALLSTON—LETTER TO
BANCROFT—LETTER TO PROFESSOR LIEBER—LETTER TO MISS J. I. GRINNELL
—THE ATLANTIC CABLE—INDISPOSITION—LETTER TO A JUVENILE CORRE-
SPONDENT.

THE year 1857 had been a calamitous year for persons engaged in trade ; and Mr. Irving, who had
been in suspense in regard to his publisher's affairs,
found it necessary to make a settlement with Mr. Putnam, and continue his connection with him on a different footing.   Their connection, thus far, had been most
advantageous to both ; but other enterprises swept
from the upright and liberal publisher the profits realized from the sale of Irving's works.   On preparing
for Mr. Irving, in December, 1857, a summary of his
sales and receipts from July, 1848—when he made his
first agreement with Mr. Putnam for the publication
of a new edition of his already published works—to
June 30th, 1857, a period of nine years, I found there
had been sold about three hundred and fifty thousand
volumes, and that he had realized about eighty thou-

sand dollars; that is, his receipts had averaged about
nine thousand dollars a year—a prolific literary harvest. At the opening of the year 1858, I wrote to
him : " The contract with Mr. Putnam, to begin April
1st, has been executed." By this contract, Mr. Putnam, who had made a full settlement of their present
business, was to act as his agent, Mr. Irving purchasing from him the stereotype plates of all his works. I
had written to him on the 31st of December : " In
taking a business retrospect of the year that is just
closing, it may be a satisfaction to you to know that
you have received from Mr. Putnam, in the course of
it, what is equivalent to twenty-five thousand dollars.
Though the close of the year has been attended with
some annoyances, I think, therefore, you may bid it
farewell with a blessing."

At the date of the following letter to his niece, at
Paris, Mr. Irving was trying, with apparent benefit, a
prescription for an obstinate catarrh, which had been
very troublesome of late. Three days after its date
(February 18th), I was led, by some anxiety in regard
to his health, to the cottage, to spend a few days. A
temporary deafness, which had been shifting from one
ear to the other, had now reached both ears, so that I
found it necessary to speak above my natural tone to
be heard by him. He was troubled, also, with difficulty of breathing, especially in making ascents, and
told me that he had been sensible, for some time, of
shortness of breath, in going up hill, to an unusual

degree.   It was evident to him that the "harp of thousand strings" was no longer "in tune."   "But I cannot complain now," said he to me, "if some of the
chords should be breaking."   That morning, for the
first time in about a month, he had taken pen in hand
and written a page on his historical task.   December
14th, he had written me that he was "in the vein,
and anxious to complete the rough draft of his final
volume."

[*To Mrs. Storrow.*]

SUNNYSIDE, Feb. 15, 1858.

MY DEAR SARAH :

Your letter of January 9th came to me like a reproach,
making me feel my delinquency in not having answered your
previous letter; but I am unavoidably a delinquent on this
score, my weary brain being overtasked by my literary under-
takings, and unable to cope with the additional claims of an
overwhelming correspondence.   I am endeavoring to accomplish a fifth volume, wherewith to close the Life of Washington, but I work more slowly than heretofore.   For two or
three years past I have been troubled by an obstinate catarrh,
but this winter it has been quite harassing, at times quite stupe-
fying me.   Recently I have put myself under medical treatment, and begin to feel the benefit of it.

Mr. Storrow must have brought you lamentable accounts
of the state of affairs in this country during the late revulsion.
He was here in the height of the storm, when we seemed to
be threatened with an almost universal shipwreck.   Happily,
the crisis is past; things are returning to order, but it will take
some time for business to regain its usual activity.   *   *   *

Fortunately, I have experienced but a very moderate loss in my investments, and my relations with my publisher have been placed on a different footing, which, I trust, will prove advantageous to us both.

I have never been more struck with the energy and elasticity of the national character, than in observing how spiritedly it has struggled with this overwhelming calamity, and is exerting itself, amid the ruins of past prosperity, to build up the edifice anew. The crisis has been felt sorely in my immediate neighborhood, among those who were largely in business, some of whom have been completely ruined; yet they have borne their reverses manfully, and are looking forward hopefully to better times.

I have a very pleasant social neighborhood; and it has been more social than usual this winter, people seeming to draw closer together and seek refuge in cordial intercourse from external evils. Indeed, I am so happy in my neighborhood, and the home feeling has grown so strong with me, that I go very little to town, and have scarcely slept a dozen nights there within the last twelve months. Perhaps it is the effect of gathering years, to settle more and more into the quiet of one's elbow chair.

*   *   *   *   *   *

You have no doubt learned, before this, that the G——s intend to set out, in June next, on a European tour. I can easily imagine what a delightful meeting it will be when you all come together. I wish they could bring you all back with them, and put an end to your protracted absence from your natural home, which I cannot help considering a protracted error.

With kind remembrances to Mr. Storrow, and love to the young folks, your affectionate uncle,

WASHINGTON IRVING.

February 19*th*, 1858, *at Sunnyside.*—Mr. Irving had been kept awake until after three by coughing, yet seemed in tolerable spirits at breakfast, and resumed his writing after it. The next day he got speaking of George Frederick Cooke, the eminent performer. " He was a great actor," he said ; " a great actor. The finest group I ever saw, was at Covent Garden, when Cooke, after long disgrace for his intemperance, reappeared on the boards to play Iago to John Kemble's Othello. Mrs. Siddons played Desdemona and Charles Kemble Cassio, beautifully. Kemble [John] had sent for Cooke to rehearse with him at his room, but Cooke would not go. 'Let *Black Jack*'— so he called Kemble—' come to me.' So they went on the boards without previous rehearsal. In the scene in which Iago instils his suspicion, Cooke grasped Kemble's left hand with his own, and then fixed his right, like a claw, on his shoulder. In this position, drawing himself up to him with his short arm, he breathed his poisonous whispers. Kemble coiled and twisted his hand, writhing to get away—his right hand clasping his brow, and darting his eye back on Iago. It was wonderful. Speaking to Cooke of the effect on me of this scene, after his arrival in New York [in 1810], 'Didn't I play up to Black Jack!' he exclaimed. 'I saw his dark eye sweeping back upon me.'

"I was at John Howard Payne's, near Corlier's Hook, the night of Cooke's arrival in New York. I was there by invitation, to meet him. Cooke came in a little flustered with drink. Was very much exasperated at the detention at the Custom House of some silver cups, possibly presents, he had brought with him, and would break forth, every now and then, with, 'Why did they keep my cups? *They knew they would melt!*' with significant emphasis. He was harsh and abusive when drunk, but full of courtesy when sober." Mr. Irving dwelt upon "the easy jollity" with which he played Falstaff. "Hodgkinson" [whom, probably, some living may yet remember on the boards of the old Park Theatre] "was a little fustian in tragedy, but capital in comedy and farce. He was finer than Cooper in Petruchio. Cooper was harsh. With Hodgkinson, you could 'see the fun at the bottom' of his treatment to Catherine."

I asked which he preferred — John Kemble, or Cooke?

"Kemble had, perhaps, more the sympathy of his audience, because he played nobler characters—Cooke, the villains; but, in his range, which was limited, he was the greatest actor."

Speaking afterward of artists, he remarked : " Jarvis tried, but failed to embody my conception of Diedrich Knickerbocker. Leslie also. Darley hit it in the illustrated History of New York. My idea was that he should carry the air of one profoundly impressed with the truth of his own History.

"Allston was always the gentleman. Would talk by the hour. Liked to talk. A capital teller of ghost stories. Would act them with voice, eyes, gesture. Had touches of gentle humor. Rather indolent. Would lie late in bed. Smoked segars. A man of real genius. A noble painter. It was a pity he came back [in 1818]; he would have risen to the head of his art—been the greatest painter of his day."

The foregoing, and the anecdotes which follow, I give from rough notes made at the time.

March 23d, 1858 (*still at Sunnyside*).—Mr. Irving mentioned, after breakfast, a dream of the night before, that he had killed one of the little birds that had commenced singing about the cottage, and his waking in great distress in consequence, and lighting his lamp to read off the effect. Had shot many a robin when a youngster; and, when they were skipping about the cottage, often thought with compunction how many of their *ancestors* he had killed. "Oh, uncle!" exclaimed a niece, "how could you ever shoot those innocent little things!" "Well, my dear, it wasn't the same robins that covered the babes in the wood."

March 27th, 1858.—He came down to the city for the day, in good health. Entered my office half past one, chuckling at the idea of his having just left the

Astor Library with a volume in his pocket he was using in his Life of Washington, and for once circumvented his friend Cogswell, the librarian.

April 3d, 1858, was his seventy-fifth birthday, and a family party was assembled, as usual, to celebrate it. It was a bright, beautiful, genial day. He was in fine spirits, serenely cheerful. Spoke of his happiness at feeling so well on his seventy-fifth birthday, when a little before he had been troubled with asthma and difficulty of breathing, and had begun to feel that "he had got his ticket" for the other world.

Soon after breakfast came baskets of flowers, and various other birthday offerings from the neighborhood. Later in the day, different friends dropped in with their congratulations. Altogether, the day passed off delightfully—nothing to mar it.

April 17th, 1858.—A Mr. T——, from the centre of Ohio, called at the cottage, as he stated, "simply to see Washington Irving before his return." He brought a letter from Horace Greeley, saying that he was no author, and only curious to have a look at him. Made a short visit, and proved to be a very good fellow. Began by telling Mr. Irving his first fondness for reading dated from Knickerbocker's New York. Showed no great inclination that way until his schoolmaster set him down to that. "And that," said Mr. Irving, "begot a taste for *history*." The visitor being connected with railroads, Mr. Irving spoke of the wonderful rapidity of locomotion nowadays. "Travellers now walked Broadway with the dust of the prairies on their boots." "Yes, literally," said his auditor.

I follow, with a letter to Mr. Bancroft, on receipt of a fresh volume of his History:

SUNNYSIDE, May 17, 1858.

MY DEAR BANCROFT:

I have delayed acknowledging the receipt of your volume until I should have read it through. I now thank you heartily for your kindness in sending it to me. The interest with which I have devoured it, notwithstanding the staleness of the subject with me, is a proof that you have told the story well. I was charmed with the opening of your volume: the political state of England and France; the decadence of the French nobility; the characters of the French monarchs; the beautiful sketch of Marie Antoinette; then the transition to sober, earnest New England—the "meeting of the nine committees" (p. 35), "the lowly men accustomed to feed their own cattle, to fold their own sheep, to guide their own plough—*all trained to public life in the little democracies of their towns*," &c., &c. How graphic! how suggestive! how true!

I see you place Samuel Adams in the van of the Revolution, and he deserves the place. He was the apostle of popular liberty, without a thought of self-interest or self-glorification.

There is capital management throughout all the chapters treating of the New England States, wherein you go on building up the revolutionary fire stick by stick, until, at last, you set it in a blaze.

You have a mode of *individualizing*, if I may so use the word, which gives great spirit and a dramatic effect to your narration. You make brief citations from speeches, letters, or conversations, which stamp the characters, reveal the motives, or express the actions of the persons concerned. So also with regard to States, cities, villages, communities—they are made to take a part in the drama by "word of mouth," as it were, thus saving a world of detail and circumlocution.

In this way, by turns, you vocalize the whole Union, and make the growing chorus of the Revolution rise from every part of it. I hope you will make out what I mean to say ; for I consider what I attempt to designate, a capital quality in your work of narrating.

I am delighted with the tribute you pay to the noble policy of Chatham, and the cold charity which you dispense to Lord North. "Lord North was false only as he was weak and uncertain. He really wished to concede and conciliate, *but he had not force enough to come to a clear understanding with himself.*" You have given me a hearty laugh at the expense of poor Lord North.

In a word, my dear Bancroft, I congratulate you upon the manner in which you have executed this volume. I have found it animated and spicy throughout, and take it as an earnest of the style in which you are to accomplish the history of a revolution " destined on every side to lead to the solution of the highest questions of state."

With best regards to Mrs. Bancroft, yours, very faithfully,

WASHINGTON IRVING.

The following letter, with the explanation which precedes it, was received from Professor Francis Lieber, of Columbia College, New York. As the subject

is curious, and may interest the reader, I give it in
full :

The letter of Irving, of which a copy is sent here, was
written in reply to an inquiry made by Dr. Lieber. Oscar
Peschel states, in his History of the Age of Discoveries, Stuttgart, 1848, that " Columbus brooded over the prophesying song
of the chorus in the Medea of Seneca." The words of the
chorus are :

> " Venient annis sæcula seris
>   Quibus Oceanus vincula rerum
>   Laxet, et ingens pateat tellus,
>   Tethysque novos delegat orbes,
>   Nec sit terris Ultima Thule."

> [Distant the age, but surely it will come,
>   When he—Oceanus—fettering all things,
>   Yields, and the vast earth lieth before man,
>   Tethys unveils that world, yet unknown,
>   And no more an Ultima Thule.]

Peschel, generally accurate and cautious, gives no authority
for the assumption that Columbus knew this remarkable passage ; and Dr. Lieber had asked Irving whether he knew of
any. The first portion of Irving's letter refers to this inquiry.
The latter portion of the letter has reference to the fact that
Dr. Lieber, considering, as he does, William of Nassau and
Washington akin in character, has hanging against the wall of
his entry a frame surrounding the portraits of the two great
men, placed in close connection. Over them is the sign used
by astronomers for a double star ; under them is written, *Stella
Duplex.* Around the portrait of William is his own motto :

Sœvis tranquillus in undis. Around that of Washington, the owner had the words inscribed, *Justus et tenax,* Washington never having selected a motto for himself. It was æsthetically necessary to place a sentence corresponding in place to the beautiful one of William.

SUNNYSIDE, June 3, 1858.

MY DEAR SIR:

* * * I am not aware of any authority for the fact stated, as you say, by Peschel (whose work I have not seen), that Columbus "brooded over the prophesying song of the chorus in the Medea of Seneca." I don't recollect that it is adverted to by Fernando Columbus, when furnishing the grounds of his father's belief of the existence of land in the West. Nor is there any mention of it by Columbus himself. The assertion of Peschel may have been made on what he considered a strong probability.

I am sorry Putnam could not have furnished an engraved likeness of Washington that would have matched more completely with the one you possess of William the Silent. Your idea of placing the likenesses of these illustrious men, so similar in character and virtue, side by side, is excellent; and the motto you have written round that of Washington, stamps his great merits at a blow.

Ever, my dear sir, with high respect and regard, yours, very truly,

WASHINGTON IRVING.

FRANCIS LIEBER, LL.D., &c., &c., &c.

May 26th, 1858.—Mr. Irving came to town to take leave of the G——s, about to embark for Europe in the Persia. Spent the evening at his nephew's, I. V.

W. I—— was trying to recall to his recollection a person at Birmingham whom he had met long years before. " Don't you recollect Mrs. ———, that lady who used to go to sleep in the evening?" "Ah! I am afraid I always got the start of her."

Mr. Irving's propensity to unseasonable drowsiness was quite notorious, but has been much exaggerated. A short nap after dinner was almost indispensable to prevent a struggle with sleep in the evening, unless something occurred to excite him, when he would rouse himself at once, and be ready for anything. He in reality slept less than persons ordinarily do. Even in his best health, his sleep was always fitful and interrupted; and it was remarked by those in the next room to him, that they never awoke in the night without hearing the turning of leaves in his room. He was always in the habit of reading, and even writing at times, in bed. This habit, as his physician remarked who attended him in his last illness, no doubt increased the difficulty of relieving that sleepless nervousness under which, as we shall see, he suffered so distressingly during the last year of his life.

Toward the middle of June, Mr. Irving came to town, and called at my office. He was rather out of sorts. Had not been able to touch pen to paper for three weeks. Was worried that his publisher had stated, in some circular, that the fifth volume of the Life of Washington would be ready in the autumn. Seemed half dubious whether he would ever publish a fifth volume. I reminded him of Dr. Johnson's remark, that a man could write at any time, if he only set himself doggedly to it; but he said it was not so with him, and particularly for *the effects* he was now seeking. Must bide his time.

Five or six weeks after this, I was at the cottage. Mr. Irving, in speaking of his Life of Washington, said he considered the labor of the closing volume in a measure done. The thing now was to give effects, graces. Could not create exciting detail for the volume. Could not make Washington come on the stage, and fire off a gun, as Charles Kemble did in his alteration of Richelieu. "My object now is to throw in an occasional touch here and there, as painters, after they have hung up their pieces for exhibition, sometimes give their greatest effects by a few dabs of the brush." He added: "I must deal cautiously with the party questions. I wish to stand in my history where Washington stood, who was of no party."

Walked out with him to the pond. Ducks swimming in it, with fourteen *young*. Spoke of the difficulty of raising the brood. "What with the rats, the snapping turtles, and their cursed cruelties toward one another's young, it was very hard." Just then one of the old ducks turned round, and made an assault upon the young of another, pecking it, and thrusting its head under water. "Look at that, now—look at that! I should like to have that fellow here, and wring his neck for him."

Vol. IV.—11*

The following extract is from a letter to a young niece travelling in Europe, who had written him a very pleasant account of her tour, and whose residence in the country adjoined his own :

[*To Miss Julia I. Grinnell.*]

SUNNYSIDE, Sept. 2, 1858.

MY DEAR JULIA :

    *   *   *   *   *   *

By all your accounts, you have had uncommonly propitious weather throughout your tour in England, Scotland, and Ireland, and have been able to bring off in your minds delightful pictures of scenery and places. Sightseeing is at times rather fatiguing and exhausting ; but the fatigue is amply repaid by the stock of recollections hung up in one's mental picture gallery.

While the world is turning rapidly with you, who are continually on the move, with us who remain at home it seems to be almost standing still. * * * It is quite mournful to look at your deserted mansion, with the flowering vines clambering about the columns, and no one at home to enjoy their beauty and fragrance.

We miss the evening gun of the yacht, as it returns from town. The Fourth of July would have been a *triste* day, had there not been fireworks in the evening at Mr. ———'s. Archery is at an end ; there is no more gathering on the lawn ; the bows are unstrung, the arrows sleep in their quivers, and the green bodices of the fair archers are motheaten.

I do not know what would have become of us all, and whether we should not have sunk into the spell-bound oblivion of Sleepy Hollow, if we had not been suddenly roused from our apathy by the laying of the Atlantic Cable. This has thrown the whole country into one of those paroxysms of excitement to which it is prone. Yesterday was the day set apart for everybody throughout the Union to go crazy on the subject. New York, you may be sure, was the craziest of cities on the occasion. I went down to town early in the morning, and found it already in a ferment, and boiling over, for all the country had poured into it. But I refer you to the newspapers, which you will undoubtedly see, for ample accounts of the civic rejoicings, which threw all former New York rejoicings in the shade.

I find my sheet is full, so I will conclude this scrawl, which can hardly be called anything more than an apology for a letter. Tell I—— I will answer his most acceptable letter on another occasion. Give my love to father, mother, and Fannie, and believe me, my dear, dear Julia, your affectionate uncle,

WASHINGTON IRVING.

September 12*th.*—I visited the cottage, on my return from a month's excursion, during which time I had not seen Mr. Irving. I asked him if he had been writing much at his fifth volume during my absence. " No ; I have been spell bound—have taken things to pieces, and could not put them together again." He had been suffering very much for the last few days by a return of his catarrh.

On the 18th, though still very much troubled with catarrh, cough at night, and difficult respiration, he told me he had been able to write a little. " I have to watch for a flaw—a little breeze, then spread my sails, and get on." He gave me the first six chapters, some of which he had been taking to pieces and put together again. I read them, and recommended some rejections, to which he acceded.

Told me he had got through the labor of constructing his fifth volume, but wanted to handle certain parts. Sometimes the way in which a thing should be done flashed upon him as he was going to bed, and he could not recall it the next morning. When in the mood, everything came easy ; when *not*, the devil himself could not make him write.

September 30th.—Mr. Irving came in town to remain a few days. In the evening went to Laura Keene's Theatre, to see young Jefferson as Goldfinch in Holcroft's comedy of the Road to Ruin. Thought Jefferson, the father, one of the best actors he had ever seen ; and the son reminded him, in look, gesture, size, and *make*, of the father. Had never seen the father in Goldfinch, but was delighted with the son.

The next morning I called on him just after breakfast. His catarrh not troublesome, but a disposition to cough in the *throat*. To an inquiry about his health, " Had a streak of old age. Pity, when we have grown old, we could not turn round and grow young again, and die of cutting our teeth."

He spoke of his anxiety about his fifth volume. Would like to dress up some things. Could see how they ought to be done, but lacked the power to do it. Could not " mount his horse." I said *he* saw what effects might be given, but others would not. Yes, he replied; it was a consolation to think the reader did not see what he saw.

Some days after, he gave me twenty-one chapters of the fifth volume of his Life of Washington to read. In the twentieth was the account of Genet's reception at New York. I asked him if some of the particulars were not from his own recollection as a boy. "Yes; remembered following Genet down Wall street, and envying a little boy who had a feather stuck in the side of his hat." Told me the remaining chapters would need very little handling.

Monday, October 11*th.*—Mr. Irving returned home, Mrs. I. and myself accompanying him on a visit to the cottage. He had given me, the day before, the concluding chapters of his fifth volume to read. He was still very much troubled with catarrh and shortness of breath, though his disposition to cough had yielded somewhat to a medical prescription. The next day he had no appetite at breakfast, but was heavy and languid. In the evening was still out of sorts, and apparently feverish, complaining of heat in his head. The following morning I went to the city for his physician, Dr. John C. Peters, who left for Sunnyside in the ten-o'clock train. As I was called to attend the funeral of a relative at Hyde Park on that day, I did not get back until ten at night, when I found Mr. Irving had a high fever, and was in bed. The doctor returned at midnight, and remained until the next

morning.   He pronounced it a case of intermittent
fever.   He came up again in the evening, and, when
he left in the morning, declared his patient much better every way, though still very languid.   The newspapers of the 16th reported him " dangerously ill."
Allusion being made to the paragraph as an exaggeration, he replied that he did not know ; that, at his time
of life, such attacks must always be dangerous ; that
he was fully aware of it ; that, at farthest, his time
would not be long, but his only anxiety was to retain
his mental powers while he did last ; that, at the commencement of this illness, and for the week before, his
head had felt so badly, he was apprehensive he might
have injured himself seriously in his endeavors to
finish this fifth volume ; that the pitcher might have
gone once too often to the well.   This, he said, was a
source of real anxiety to him, far more than any pain
or illness could cause.   " I do not fear death," said he ;
" but I would like to go down with all sail set."

In less than fourteen months, his pathetic aspiration
was to be fulfilled.

October 20*th*.—Mr. Irving drove out for the first
time since his illness, leaving me occupied in going
over the last volume of his Life of Washington.   I
discovered that he had omitted a notice of Washington's consent to be a candidate a second time.   On
calling his attention to it, he said he had written an
account of it, which must have got mislaid.   I told
him it would come in at the end of Chapter XV, and

he took a note of it. The next day he showed me a missing chapter, which contained what I had feared was omitted. He had been rummaging for it, and it was the last thing he had come upon. In the bewilderment of his brain previous to his illness, he had paged the work consecutively with this chapter left out.

Mr. Irving had now quite recovered from his attack, though he was still troubled with a distressing cough, which came on as soon as he laid down, and kept him awake for the greater part of the night. At breakfast, one morning, H—— was speaking of some person's illness. " Does he cough at night ? " inquired he. " No." " Oh ! then he'll get along," laughing. Determined not, as he expressed it, " to be bullied by a cold," he went to town that day, to attend the monthly meeting of the trustees of the Astor Library.

Notwithstanding his cough continued to trouble him, and destroy the comfort of his nights, he still found time and spirits for the following letter, addressed to a great-nephew not out of his teens, who was then making the tour of Europe with his parents, and had written him an account of a visit to Drum, the old homestead conveyed by Bruce to his progenitor, and still held by the family. I should scruple to give the letter entire, on account of its delicate encomium upon the youthful party to whom it is addressed, were it not that, as a whole, it presents so true an image of the writer's own heart, his tender symapthy with the young, and the ennobling influence which he sought to inspire in his communion with them.

[*To Irving Grinnell.*]

SUNNYSIDE, Oct. 28, 1858.

MY DEAR IRVING:

I will not apologize to you for leaving your letter of July 11th so long unanswered. You know my situation—how much my poor brain and pen are fagged and overtasked by regular literary labor, and by the irregular and inevitable demands of the post office, and will make indulgent allowances for the tardiness of my reply.

Your letter was most acceptable and interesting, giving such fresh, animated accounts of your travels, and expressing so naturally the feelings inspired by the objects around you. Speaking of Bothwell Castle, you say: "When I am beholding any such magnificent or interesting spot, I do not seem to be able to appreciate it enough. I take it in, but do not realize it; and this is really a painful sensation, so different from what you would expect. I stand looking, with all my eyes and senses open, and feel as though I were deficient in some one faculty which prevented me from really appreciating and enjoying all that I see."

My dear Irving, this is all *honestly* expressed, and describes a feeling which all hunters of the picturesque and historical are apt to experience in presence of the objects of their quest. They, in fact, do *realize* the scene before them, and the naked truth balks the imagination. Those raptures and ecstasies which writers of travels are so full of at the sight of wonders in art and nature, are generally the after-coinage of the brain, when they sit down in their studies to detail what they have

seen, and to invent what they think they ought to have felt.
I recollect how much I was vexed with myself, in my young
days, when in Italy, in reading the work of a French tourist,
and finding how calmly I had contemplated scenes and objects
which had inspired him with the most exalted transports. It
was a real consolation to learn, afterward, that he had *never
been in Italy*, and that his whole book, with all its raptures,
was a fabrication. I think true delight in these matters is apt
to be quiet and contemplative.

I was very much interested by your account of your visit
to Drum, the old "Stamm haus," as the Germans express it,
of the Irving family. I should have liked to have been of
your party on that occasion, having a strong curiosity about
that old family nest, ever since the Scotch antiquaries have
traced my origin to an egg hatched out of it in days of yore.

In going to town, yesterday, I had —— —— beside
me in the railroad cars, and he gave me an account of letters
just received from some of your party, by which I found you
were all safe in Paris, and in daily communion with the ——s,
——s, &c. What a joyous meeting it must have been!
What a relish of *home* it must have given you all! ——, I
have no doubt, keeps you well informed of everything going
on in the little world in which you and he mingled together.
He is a worthy, manly fellow, and I am glad you have an intimate friend of his stamp. I value him the more highly from
the manner in which he conducted himself during his absence
in Europe, and the frank, simple, unspoiled manners he has
brought home with him. And such, I trust, will be the case
with you, my dear Irving. I have always valued in you what
I considered to be an honorable nature; a conscientiousness in
regard to duties; an open truthfulness; an absence of all low

propensities and sensual indulgences; a reverence for sacred things; a respect for others.; a freedom from selfishness, and a prompt disposition to oblige; and, with all these, a gayety of spirit, flowing, I believe, from an uncorrupted heart, that gladdens everything around you.

I am not saying all this, my dear Irving, to flatter you, but to let you know what precious qualities Heaven has bestowed upon you, which you are called upon to maintain in their original purity. You are mingling with the world at large at an extremely youthful age. Fortunately, you go surrounded by the sanctity of home, in the company of your parents and sisters—a moral halo, to protect you from the corruptions of the world. I am confident, however, that your own native good sense and good taste will protect you against the follies and vices and affectations in which "Young America" is too apt to indulge in Europe; and that, while you give free scope to your natural buoyancy of spirit, you will maintain that frank, manly, modest simplicity of conduct that should characterize the American gentleman.

I wish I could write you a more interesting letter; but this, such as it is, is scrawled with some difficulty, for I am just recovered from a fit of illness, and am little fitted for the exercise of the pen.

God bless you, my dear Irving, and bring you home to us with a mind stored with profitable and delightful recollections, manners improved and refined by travel, and a heart unspotted by the world.   Your affectionate uncle,

WASHINGTON IRVING.

CHAPTER XVI.

OCTOBER 31st, 1858.—At Sunnyside. Mr. Irving
still troubled with his harassing cough. To an
inquiry of one of his nieces how he had rested the
night before, he replied: "So, so; I am apt to be rather
fatigued, my dear, by my night's *rest*." After breakfast, he was turning over, in the library, the leaves of
Dunglison's Medical Dictionary, which had been sent
him by the publisher the day before. "A very good
book to have; but what an array of maladies for this
poor machine of ours to be subject to! One almost
wonders, as he thinks of them, that any should ever
grow old."

He afterward got speaking of Sir Walter Scott.
"Oh! he was a master spirit—as glorious in his conversation as in his writings. Jeffrey was delightful,
and had *eloquent runs* in conversation; but there was
a consciousness of talent with it. Scott had nothing

of that.   He spoke from the fulness of his mind, pour-
ing out an incessant flow of anecdote, story, &c., with
dashes of humor, and then never monopolizing, but
always ready to listen to and appreciate what came
from others.   I never felt such a consciousness of happiness as when under his roof.   I awoke in the morning, and said to myself, ' Now I know I'm to be happy
I know I have an unfailing treat before me.'   We
would go out in the morning.   Scott, with his brown
pantaloons, greenish frock coat, white hat, and cane,
would go stumping along.   Would hear him ahead, in
his gruff tones, mumbling something to himself, like
the grumbling of an organ, and find it would be a
snatch of minstrelsy.   The ' Antiquary ' was the favorite of his daughter Sophia.   It is full of his quiet
humor.   What a beautifully compounded character is
Monkbarns !   It is one of the very finest in our litera·
ture.   That single character is enough to immortalize
any man.   Ochiltree also capital.   How many precious
treats have I had out of that Antiquary !   How you
see Scott's delightful humor, whether grave or gay,
playing through all his works, and revealing the
man ! "

November 11*th*.—Handed me some chapters of
Volume V, in which he had introduced some new
matter.   Hard work, he said, to fit it in.   Conversation turned to bull fights.   " I did not know what a
bloodthirsty man I was, till I saw them at Madrid, on
my first visit.   The first was very spirited, the second

dull, the third spirited again, and afterward I hardly ever missed." " But the poor horses ! " some one interposed. " Oh ! well, they were very old, and worn out, and it was only a question whether they should die a triumphal death, or be battered a few years longer. On my return to Madrid, I did not go much. The cruelty of my nature had been worn out." His conversation was, as usual, a mixture of jest and earnest.

November 18*th*.—I left Sunnyside, and came to the city, and took rooms at the Clarendon Hotel for the winter. Mr. Irving came down, on the 20th, to see Dr. Peters about a spasm which seemed to take him after he had gone to bed, and was just falling asleep. The Doctor gave him some prescription, with which he returned ; but on Monday morning (22d) he was down again, having passed a sleepless night. He went at once to the Doctor, and then came to my room at the Clarendon. Nearly out of breath when he got there. He returned again to the country, but, finding himself still nervous and sleepless, came to town a few days after, to pass some time with his friend, Mr. Barrett Ames, at 33 Lafayette Place. The distressing symptoms continued, however, accompanied, at times, with such increased difficulty of breathing, as gave us all much anxiety. He stood it very well during the day, but began to have great dread of the night. On parting with him, one night, he repeated most feelingly the passage from Othello :

> " Not poppy, nor mandragora,
> Nor all the drowsy syrups of the world,
> Shall ever medicine thee to that sweet sleep
> Which thou ow'dst yesterday."

The next day found him quite in spirits, and full of conversation as usual. Speaking of ———, a celebrated public orator, I asked him if he had ever heard him. " Only once. Liked some parts, but too apt to change his voice suddenly from low to loud, giving evidence only of the breadth and brassiness of his throat. His voice did not swell out properly from his theme. Let slip his thunder capriciously."

On the 10th of December, after an entirely sleepless night, he rose early, and went at once to the Doctor, having been so strangely affected that he was apprehensive of some impending attack, for which the Doctor assured him there was no foundation. He retired the next night with great misgivings, but slept five hours, and in the morning was very bright. His nights continued to alternate between bad and good, and, finding no improvement from the change, he began to long for his home, and, on the 18th of December, returned to the cottage, accompanied by myself and wife, it being his earnest wish that we should go up with him. From this period to his death, we were, by his desire, inmates of Sunnyside.

I give below some notes with regard to the condition of his health, which I took at the time :

Sunday, December 19th. — A sleepless night.

Knocked at the Doctor's room (who had come up in the seven o'clock train, to stay over Sunday) at one o'clock, who got up, and read and conversed with him till half past four, when he called me, at Mr. Irving's request, to relieve him. I continued with him till he got up to shave. Excessively nervous when he came down in the morning, yet told a variety of anecdotes at the breakfast table. Tried to arrange papers after breakfast, and then was driven to the church at Tarrytown "just for the drive," the Doctor accompanying him. The fact is, he was so restless, as he expressed it, he " did not know what to do with himself." After dinner, horror-haunted with the thought that he would not sleep. Went to bed at twelve, and slept four hours, I watching with him at first till a quarter past one, and, finding he did not awake, lying down on the sofa in his room. Was bright and cheerful when he awoke, and continued so during the day.

December 20*th.*—Oliver Wendell Holmes and F. S. Cozzens, of Yonkers, made a call. Mr. Irving enjoyed their visit—glad to see Holmes, whom he had never met before, but whose Autocrat of the Breakfast Table he had been reading with great zest. They stayed about half an hour. I was absent in the city. On retiring that night, soon fell asleep, but in a short time awoke, in a very nervous and restless state. I read and talked to him for an hour, when I lay down on the sofa in his room. At half past two he awoke me again. Had great difficulty of breathing, and a sort of spasmodic affection of the stomach, which roused him whenever he was falling asleep.

December 22d.—Amused himself, this morning, in looking over old papers, and answering letters, of which he wrote four before twelve. Like himself to-day.

24th.—Full of fun, humor, and anecdote. Spoke of children too wise to believe in Santa Claus. " Too wise to be happy. When I was a child, I believed in Santa Claus as long as I could, until they put snow-balls in my stockings."

December 25th.—Christmas. Horribly nervous this morning. Returning from a walk, I withdrew to my room, but he soon came up and knocked at my door, and begged to be let in to be with me. Was perfectly ashamed of himself, he said, but had a horror of being alone. I went down with him, got him to take some prescription, and then read aloud to him, till he fell asleep on the sofa. Said it was inexpressibly soothing. The fluctuation of feeling from one day to another seems incredible.

December 27th.—Horror-ridden. H—— reads him asleep after breakfast. Starts up; goes out to walk; then to drive to Dr. Creighton's, his friend and pastor, with H—— and S——, to be in motion and escape from himself.

December 31st.—A good day. Retires at eleven. Rather restless. Somewhat troubled with cough. I read to him from two to three. Slept considerable after this.   Had been altering, yesterday, a chapter about Lawrence Lewis.

A few days before, he had received from Prescott —then in health, but destined to precede him by a few months to the grave—the following letter :

BOSTON, Dec. 28.

MY DEAR MR. IRVING :

I was sorry to hear, a few days since, that you had not been quite so well as usual of late.   I hope that this note will find you in better health.   I remember, when my first two volumes of the History of Philip II came out, you wrote me a very kind note about them.   I have just published a third volume ; and, as you seem to have taken an interest in the subject, I have done myself the pleasure to send a copy of it to Putnam for you.   I shall think myself fortunate if it should serve to amuse a leisure hour.   Yet, pressed as you have been of late years, leisure would seem to be the last thing likely to be at your disposal.   At all events, I pray you not to take the trouble to make any acknowledgment of the little *cadeau*, but to accept it as a proof of the sincere admiration and regard which I have always felt and must ever feel for you.

Believe me, dear Mr. Irving, very truly, your friend,

WM. H. PRESCOTT.

The early part of January, Mr. Irving seemed much improved.   Less difficulty of breathing and nervousness.   Was greatly interested in reading the third volume of Prescott's Philip II, just sent him by the author.   Thought his account of the trampling out of the poor Moriscoes admirably done, but there was too much of it.   Better to have generalized, as there were no grand features.   Miserable skirmishes of handfuls of men.   No romance like the wars when the Moors and Spaniards were pitted against each other.

January 12th.—His nervousness returned.   Again haunted with the idea that he could not sleep.   Strange disease, which seemed to want reality, and yet the most distressing.   He was unwilling to go to his room at bedtime, but lay down on a sofa in the parlor, Dr. Peters occupying another until four o'clock, when I relieved him.   He slept about three hours out of his " den," as he styled his bedroom.   For three or four nights after this he continued to occupy the sofa in the parlor at night, having a horror of his own room.

January 15th.—Called me into the library to show me how he had been muddling again, as he expressed it, with the Life of Washington.   It was a slight and improved change in the collocation of some sentences, taking them from Chapter X, and introducing them in Chapter XI.   At two, he came into the library, where I was, frightfully nervous.   To relieve his inquietude, he forced himself to do some copying.   Afterward I read to him, and he fell asleep temporarily.   Reading aloud to him was the only thing that seemed to quiet these nervous attacks.   The Doctor came up from the city at five P. M., intending to return at eight, but yielded to Mr. Irving's entreaty to stay the night.   He prevailed on him to lie down in his bedroom at six, and he slept until one; and afterward got a little sprinkling of sleep, as he expressed it. The faithful Doctor still encourages us and himself with the hope that this is only a morbid condition of the nervous system, which may pass off; but I have at times an ominous feeling as if we were watching his decline. He also has, no doubt, his misgivings.

It was very remarkable, that at this very time, when filled with dread of the night, and anxious that all should sit up very late, to shorten it as much as possible, he was never more delightful in conversation than during those long evenings. The excitement of his mind seemed to increase his powers, just as persons in a fever are often more brilliant than at any other time. All the interesting scenes of his life seemed to pass before him—a thousand anecdotes of persons and things of which you had never heard, related in the most graphic manner, and filled, at times, with all his old fun and humor. Scenes and quotations from favorite authors were constantly presenting themselves, and were given with a depth of feeling that added wonderfully to their effect.

Those evenings were a perfect treat, though always sad from our certainty that they boded a wakeful night.

January 18*th*.—He came into the library at half past twelve, and told me he had had " such a soothing, balmy morning, to repair his poor, tattered nerves." How different in manner and appearance from the excited state in which, a few days before, he had rushed in to give vent to his restlessness! The contrast was very touching.

I started for the post office at two, and, when I returned, I found him in the library, and apparently, except in his thin, worn visage, as well as ever. He wrote, to-day, the character of Knox, at the close of Chapter I, and told an amusing anecdote in his usual vein of facetiousness. I am to put Volume V to press to-morrow. The Doctor came at five. His patient soon after fell asleep. Awoke after three hours, and told story of Wilkie playing picture, at Madrid, at some fancy ball—in costume—putting one hand on pommel of his sword, and extending the other, as he had seen it in some old painting; occasionally would "step out of his frame" to talk to some one, and then go back.

The next day continued calm, and free from nervousness throughout the day. I gave to Mr. Putnam, the publisher, the first three chapters of Volume V of the Life of Washington. Came up in the seven o'clock train with the Doctor. Mr. Irving had slept after dinner, but was wakeful toward bedtime. A wretched night. The Doctor up almost the whole night reading to him, and administering soothing medicines, until, as Mr. Irving told him, it seemed to him he had taken medicines enough in his stomach to put a whole congregation to sleep.

The next day had no appetite at dinner, but told a

story of the Irishman who shot an owl, and thought he had killed a cherubim. Then, with a sudden change of mood, dropped his hands despairingly. Had "such a feeling of dismay come over him at the thought of the dismal, sleepless night before him." His thoughts centred in the want of sleep. Went to bed at eleven, with a foreboding that he would "sleep no more" that night, but was mistaken. Drowsed through the night, and was calm and tranquil at morning.

Read "The Professor at the Breakfast Table," in the February number of the *Atlantic Monthly*, just come in, and was very much pleased with it. "Holmes has a full, rich vein—so witty, and so much drollery. Am delighted to have made his acquaintance." I brought up, that day, the first proof of Volume V— sixteen pages—of the Life of Washington.

January 24th, Evening.—Turning to me, at half past ten: "You'll be near me to-night?" "Certainly." "I begin to feel, as bedtime approaches, that old dread of my own room and the night." "But," said one of his nieces, "you ought not to feel it to-night; you've been sleeping so quietly on the sofa, you'll have a good night, and will soon sleep again." "I know it, my dear; but there is no arguing with these things. They are incontrollable. They come and go like the wind. When you are all about me here, I can sleep quietly; but when I get to my own room, and you are all gone, and I think all are asleep but myself, then comes over me this strange dread again. You recollect" (turning

to me) " the scene among the tombs, in The Mourning
Bride :

> ' Give me thy hand, and let me hear thy voice;
> Nay, quickly speak to me, and let me hear
> Thy voice. My own affrights me with its echoes.' "

Nothing could exceed the expressive manner in which
he repeated this exclamation of Almeria to Leonora, in
that passage of Congreve's tragedy to which Dr. Johnson gave such high praise.

January 26th.—Rather faint and nervous at bedtime, but some preparation which the Doctor had left
seemed to have a good effect. I took the " porch
room," as it is called, next his, to be at hand, and he
went to his room with a feeling that he would have a
good night. I kept awake until midnight, listening for
a possible call, and then fell asleep. At a quarter past
three he came into my room in great nervous agitation.
Had not been able to sleep. I returned with him to
his room, where I remained until half past six, administering to him some medicine, after which he became
composed and quiet.

January 30th.—I showed him the *Evening Post*,
containing news of Prescott's death. Had recently
written to Prescott, after reading his third volume of
Philip II; and Prescott, but a few days before, had
expressed to Cogswell (in Boston) his gratification at
the letter.

The next day he walked out, and was seized, on his

return, with a violent spasm of shortness of breath, the most distressing and alarming he had yet had, though it did not continue so long as some others.

February 1*st*.—I went to the city, and came up in the five o'clock train, bringing proof from page 58 to page 68. Found he had been engaged anew upon the character of Washington, which he had already completed, and had become nervous under the operation. In the evening he gave me the whole draft, and told me to arrange the pages; that he was determined to bother himself no more with it. I commended the resolution, and told him it answered as it was before. When I examined and arranged it, the next morning, I found he had improved the commencement. I put the papers together, and kept them away from him.

His shortness of breath seemed now to recur at more frequent intervals. The Doctor prescribed, as an experiment—what had also been suggested by Holmes, on his late visit — " Jonas Whitcomb's Remedy for Asthma," a teaspoonful in a wineglass of water, to be taken every four hours. A good night was the result.

February 3*d*.—Went to bed at half past ten, apparently calm. At eleven had a severe attack of coughing, which lasted an hour, and left him excessively nervous. Hearing his indistinct moans, I asked if anything distressed him. " Yes ; this harassed feeling—these long, long, long hours till morning." Tried to read in Miss Pardoe's Court of Louis XIV. Would explode upon the baseness, the despicable meanness of the French monarch.   More and more nervous as morning approached.

The next day looked very haggard.   Fell into a doze about midnight, which continued half an hour. Slept again until half past two, when he awoke with a strange feeling of faintness at the stomach, as if he were dying.   Said to me he was just dying, when he awoke, stretched forth his hand, and took a sip of some liquid, which revived him.   " I would have been gone in another minute."

For two or three days this excessive nervousness continued.   He told me I must bear with him—we must all bear with him; his state was a deplorable one, and sometimes he knew he must appear like a child.   Read aloud to us—as if to escape from himself—some scenes in "As You Like It."   Told anecdote of Kemble, in his personation of Jaques, embodying in the part the passage descriptive of his moralizing about the deer.   Nothing could be more affecting than his struggles against this overmastering nervousness; it was so new to him, so opposed to his healthy and heroic nature—to the whole character of his past life—that it seemed impossible for him to yield to its dominion.

February 7th.—A better day.   Was speaking with admiration of the Yacht Voyage—" Letters from High Latitudes," by Lord Dufferin, which he had finished a few days before.   Wished he had another book to read by the same author—such a fine spirit in it.   Felt still more interest in it now that he knew the author to be the son of Mrs. Norton. Then spoke of her captivating beauty, when he first saw her at the house of some lady of quality, on his return from Spain to London, in 1829.

Mr. and Mrs. H—— and Mrs. S—— call between one and two. Very pleasant, and like himself.

February 14*th.* — The Doctor, on coming up, thought him better than he had been since he was first taken with this nervous excitability. Assured me he had no fears of softening of the brain, and hoped to date his continued amendment from that day.

The next day continued better. Remarked, in the morning, he was so well he was almost frightened; afraid it was a weather breeder. Slept in an upright position on the sofa, after tea, a couple of hours, but no rest after he retired. In the morning was sad, and out of spirits at the "wearing, wearing, wearing" night he had spent. Quite discouraged, though his asthmatic symptoms had very much abated of late, and his catarrh disappeared.

About two hundred pages of his fifth volume of the Life of Washington were now printed. He wrote a few lines relative to the composition of the Farewell Address—the only time he had touched it since it went to press, with the exception of some passages in the character of Washington.

February 27*th.*—Notwithstanding his improvement in other respects, his restless nights continued, his "poor, fluttering nerves," as he expressed it, scarcely allowing him any quiet. Could hardly summon resolution to go, at night, to his "haunted chamber," as he termed his sleeping apartment, from the brooding phantoms that, like Poe's Raven, seemed perched above the door. When I entered it, at eleven, to take my station on a sofa for the night, I found he was shunning his bed, and pacing up and down the room with great restlessness. He begged me not to leave the room, but to "stick by" him; it was a great comfort to know I was there.

The next day I took to the city two of the last four chapters of his Life of Washington. On my return to the cottage, at five P. M., accompanied by the Doctor, I found that he had been engaged for two or three hours in the morning on his last chapters. Wished to retain them, to re-dress the concluding portion. Had a very comfortable day.

March 9th.—Seemed to have been losing ground for the last few days. Still held on to the last chapter of " Washington," though the printers were nearly up to it. On the 15th, he put the finishing touch to it. The next day was sadly out of spirits. Had had difficult respiration much more frequently of late; within the last day or two, almost constantly.

March 17th.—Asked me if the last chapter of the Life of Washington was printed last night. "Yes." " Well, I never got out a work in this style before, without looking at the proof sheets. In better health,

I could have given more effect to parts; but I was afraid to look at the proofs, lest I should get muddling." That afternoon drove up to Mr. Bartlett's, to leave with Mrs. B., in compliance with her previous request, the pen with which he wrote the last words of his Life of Washington.

March 18*th*.—I returned from the city at five, accompanied by the Doctor. Learned that Mr. Irving had had more than usual of coughing and labored breathing. Told the Doctor, on his leaving, at seven o'clock, that he was quite discouraged; that he did not see that he was getting any better, and did not know where all this was to end. It was the first time he had spoken with such discouragement to the Doctor. His presence had generally a cheering influence, and we always remarked that he appeared better when he was with him, than at any other time, and often made too light of his symptoms. The Doctor seemed a little taken aback by his desponding tone. Had three hours of sound sleep on the sofa before going to bed, and about three hours afterward, with transient intermissions of wakefulness.

March 20*th*.—Slept from half past three to four p. m., on the sofa, when a neighbor called. Great difficulty of breathing when he left, which continued, with spells of coughing, until bedtime. On taking up his candle to retire for the night, " Well, as the ghost in Hamlet says, ' The time has come when I to sulphurous and tormenting flames must render up myself.' "

March 23d.—Received a newspaper from Lewisburg, Pa., containing notice of the death of a Mrs. Chamberlain, aged ninety, formerly of New York, and a friend and correspondent of his sister Anne, who had died in 1808. The sister was alluded to in flattering terms. Mr. Irving broke forth into warm eulogy of her wit, sensibility, and humor—" delightful in every mood." " I was very meagre, when a child, and she used to call me a little rack of bones. How fond I was of having her sing to me, when an infant, that pathetic ballad of Lowe :

> " The moon had climbed the highest hill
> That rises o'er the source of Dee."

How it used to make me weep, and yet I was constantly begging her to sing it." His love of music was a passion with him through life.

March 25th.—Wrote the following note—a copy of which has been sent me since his death—to a lady who had requested permission to dedicate to him a work, entitled " Domestic Annals of the Revolution," but the title of which was afterward changed to " Recollections of the Revolution " :

[*To Miss Lydia Minturn Post.*]

SUNNYSIDE, March 25, 1859.

DEAR MADAM :

Your note of March 9th, being directed to Tarrytown instead of Irvington, has been slow in reaching me. You have my full consent to the dedication of your forthcoming " Domestic Annals of the Revolution" to me, if you think it would be of advantage to the work, or a gratification to yourself. I only request that the dedication be extremely simple, and void of compliment.

With great respect, yours, very truly,

WASHINGTON IRVING.

April 2d.—Received, in the morning, a letter from a young senior at Chapel Hill, N. C., telling him he had been so delighted with his four volumes of the Life of Washington, that he had read them over repeatedly, and now wrote to beg him, not only for his own sake, but for the sake of the country, to write an account of the Presidential career and closing days of Washington at Mount Vernon. " Here is a request," said he, " that I think I will gratify at once." The whole of the fifth volume was already printed, and waiting only the Preface, which was completed that very morning, before the receipt of the letter. He spoke sadly of his condition, as if he were failing. Great restlessness at night, with brief snatches of sleep.

April 3d.—His birthday—seventy-six this day. A dull, cheerless morning; overcast at dawn, and raining before seven. After breakfast, he showed me his Spanish Chronicles in manuscript—Don Pelayo, Fernando el Santo, &c. In the midst of our conversation, a bunch of flowers was brought in from Robert, the most faithful of gardeners, a present for his birthday.

Later, a beautiful bouquet from Mrs. ——— followed.
" Beautiful flowers," he exclaimed, " to a withered old
man ! " The dinner table was decked with the bouquet, and the dessert enriched with various delicacies,
presents from loving neighbors. All tried to be cheerful at dinner ; but at the close, after a spasm of coughing had driven him from the room, and we felt the uncertainty of another birthday with him " on this bank
and shoal of time," all rose from the table in tears.

He had a paroxysm of coughing and distressed respiration at eleven, when he went to bed ; but it passed
off with the smoking of a medicated cigarette. He
then fell asleep for a few minutes, and awoke inclined
to be terribly depressed and nervous, as the night before ; " but," said he to me, " I will try to combat it."
He fell asleep again, and when he awoke, at two, he
was composed, and read and dozed through the rest of
the night without cough or labored breathing.

CHAPTER XVII.

MR. IRVING'S health continued to fluctuate.
Throughout the month of April there seemed
to be a decided improvement, though he still had, at
intervals, a return of his distressing nights. One
symptom appeared, which gave us a good deal of
anxiety, being quite new. It was a bewilderment on
waking, which sometimes continued for half an hour
or more; an uncertainty as to exactly where he was,
and an idea that strange persons had been in the room
—his dreams probably mingling with his waking. On
the whole, however, he seemed much better; and, on
the 20th, told me, on retiring to his room for the night,
that he thought he could now get along by himself;
but, on my assenting, immediately recalled the opinion, and said perhaps I had better remain a night or
two longer. Fell asleep for about fifteen minutes, then
awoke, and had a deplorably nervous night. He con-

tinued to improve, however, and, on the 27th, determined to be present at the monthly meeting of the trustees of the Astor Library, but was prevented by rain. It was now more than four months since he had been in the city.

May 1st.—Read Henry T. Tuckerman's account of the Portraits of Washington, in the Appendix to the fifth volume. Pronounced it quite an acquisition.

On the 4th, went to town, and returned at half past seven, the better for the journey. Occupied his room alone that night.

May 9th.—Received the following letter from Bancroft, in acknowledgment of Volume V of Life of Washington :

Sunday, May 7.

DEAR IRVING :

Your publisher sent me, late yesterday, your fifth volume, to which I must entreat you to add your autograph, in evidence of the intention, which Putnam vouched for. I did not go to bed till I had finished all the last half of the volume; and my first moment this morning is to tell you with what delight, and, I add in all soberness, emotion, I read it. The narrative is beautifully told, in your own happy diction and style, felicitous always; never redundant; graceful, and elegant. The throbbings of your heart are as marked and perceptible along the pages as in anything you ever wrote. But the charm is, the loveliness that your portraiture sheds round the venerable patriot in his retirement. Much as I have read and studied about Washington, I was taken by the novelty that your ever fresh and warm manner has thrown about your sketch. Your hero dies like the sun in his beauty in a cloud-less sky.

After reading to the end, I began at the beginning. You have charmingly shown Washington's dislike of state; and you have hit off John Adams's character in perfection at a single touch. Having had many letters sent me about Randolph, I looked up your account of that sad matter; and I think your statement is a model of candor, indicating just the extent of Randolph's indiscretion, and no more; and I think the letter of contrition, which you insert, tends to exonerate Randolph from the deeper imputation, for it shows, at bottom, an honest heart, though his judgment may have grievously erred.

The sketch which Washington gives of Hamilton, on preferring him for the post next himself in the army, is the finest tribute ever paid to Hamilton's rare combination of talents. * * * But I shall weary you; only I could not delay telling you how admirably you have, in my judgment, combined, in this volume, grace of style, freshness, candor, and all the good qualities that make you the delight of your friends and the pride of the country.

I am ever, dear Irving, very heartily yours,

GEORGE BANCROFT.

May 10*th*.—Received a letter from John P. Kennedy, proposing his going on a trip to St. Louis with the Baltimore and Ohio Railroad Company, which he declines, as follows:

[*To John P. Kennedy.*]

SUNNYSIDE, May 11, 1859.

MY DEAR KENNEDY:

I have had to decline the very tempting invitation of Mr. Prescott Smith in behalf of the Baltimore and Ohio Railroad Company. In fact, I am not in a condition to undertake the expedition proposed. I have been under the weather all winter, suffering from an attack of asthma, and a nervous indisposition brought on by overworking myself in endeavoring to bring my literary task to a conclusion. Thank Heaven, my fifth volume is launched, and henceforth I give up all further tasking of the pen. I am slowly regaining health and strength, and am having my natural rest at night, for I suffered wretchedly from sleeplessness. Within the last two or three weeks I feel quite encouraged; but I still have to take great care of myself, for asthma is constantly dogging at my heels, and watching every opportunity to get the mastery over me.

In my present precarious state of health, I can make no engagement that would take me far from home; and can therefore make you no promise of accompanying you to the mountains, or even of visiting you at Ellicott's Mills. In fact, I have been but once to New York since last Christmas, and that was only a few days since; and have not been able to jollify even at little parties in my immediate neighborhood.

Give my affectionate remembrances to Mrs. Kennedy and Miss Gray, and believe me, my dear Kennedy, ever very truly, yours,

WASHINGTON IRVING.

May 13*th*.—Received a very kind and delightful letter from Professor C. C. Felton, of Cambridge,

Mass., who had just been reading his fifth volume of
the Life of Washington, and expressed great pleasure
in the perusal. Read the letter aloud, and said it was
particularly gratifying to get such testimonials from
such men, as he had found it impossible to repress
great misgivings with regard to the last volume, which
he had never been able to look at since it was finished.
His illness came on the very next day. Indeed, he
was then unfit to write ; and he had constantly had in
his mind the recollection of the Archbishop of Granada, in Gil Blas, whose Homilies were thought to smell
of the apoplexy. His old love of fun revived with the
recollection, and he went to his library for the book,
and read the story aloud with great zest.

About this time, the papers had announced the
death of Baron Alexander Humboldt, at the age of
ninety-one, with the following published card from
him, dated Berlin, March 15th, 1859, curiously illus-
trating some of the penalties of celebrity :

Laboring under extreme depression of spirits, the result of
a correspondence which daily increases, and which makes a
yearly average of from sixteen hundred to two thousand letters
and pamphlets on things entirely foreign to me—manuscripts
on which my advice is demanded, schemes of emigration and
colonization, invoices of models, machinery, and objects of natural history, inquiries on balloons, demands for autographs,
offers to nurse or amuse me—I once more publicly invite all
those who desire my welfare, to try and persuade the people
of the two continents not to be so busy about me, and not to

take my house for the office of a directory, in order that, with
the decay of my physical and intellectual strength, I may enjoy
some leisure, and have time to work.   Let not this appeal, to
which I only resorted with reluctance, be interpreted with ma-
levolence.

ALEXANDER VON HUMBOLDT.

"I met Humboldt often in society in Paris.   A
very amiable man.   A great deal of *bonhommie*."

May 17th.—Mr. Irving had a very severe attack of
shortness of breath, and was so sadly nervous in the
evening, that I resumed, for the nonce, my station in
his room at bedtime.   The difficulty of breathing continued by turns through the night.   He got up and sat
in his chair at daybreak, when it subsided.   He then
read me an interesting and touching letter just received from William C. Preston, ex-Senator of the
United States, his old travelling companion in Scotland, now paralytic, but with all his brilliant powers
yet unimpaired.

Those nights, when I look back upon them, seem a
strange mingling; for, between the paroxysms of distress, he would seize on anything to divert his own
thoughts, or to relieve what he feared must be the
weariness of those who were watching with him.   He
would read or relate anything that interested him at
the moment, and so endeavor to cheat the hours till
day.   I give the letter:

[*William C. Preston to Washington Irving.*]

CHARLOTTESVILLE, VA., May 11, 1859.

MY DEAR SIR :

Seeing, in yesterday's *National Intelligencer* (the only paper that I now read), that you had been ill, but were recovered, I was prompted to write to you at once what an unabated interest I cherish for you.   My last communication with you was an act of kindness to me, in sending some letters of introduction for my friend Hampton, to Europe.   Hampton did wiser than to go to Europe; he got married, and keeps your letters as precious autographs.   Those that I have had from you have long since been begged or stolen from me by piecemeal, and I have often had an enhanced consideration, when it was known that I had been an acquaintance of Washington Irving; for I don't believe that any man, in any country, has ever had a more affectionate admiration for him than that given to you in America.   I believe that we have had but one man who is so much in the popular heart.

On reading this notice in the *Intelligencer*, I found in my memory (what, for aught I know, may be common to old men) a sort of *mirage*, which made distant objects rise above those more near.   My mind at once recalled Jones of the Brinn and Loch Katrine, and it was only upon reflection that I recalled your visit to me in the War of Nullification, and subsequently, during our war in the Senate against General Jackson.   In those tumultuary scenes I was an excited actor, and fretted my hour amid them.   The curtain fell; new scenes were brought forward, and I have sat exhausted in the dark recesses of the theatre, the pageant gone, and sad realities about me—sickness and sorrow.

I had not thought you so old as the paper announces you to be. I knew you were somewhat my senior forty years ago, but, for some years, I have felt older than anybody seemed to me to be. A paralytic stroke may well be counted for twenty years, which makes me eighty-five.

What a noble capital your Life of Washington makes to your literary column! The paper says you are busily at work. I am sorry to think that you are vexing yourself with further labors; you have fairly won the privilege of rest. Your honorable labors have been crowned with most honorable rewards. Whatever your country's love and admiration can give, has been bestowed. I indulge the wish, therefore, that the Life of Washington, which inseparably connects your name with his, may have no interposing object, and that your labors may be mere amendments in minute touches, giving a more perfect polish, where, although the public eye may perceive no want of it, your own delicate perception may suspect it.

I am, my dear sir, ever, your affectionate friend,

WM. C. PRESTON.

I anticipate to give Mr. Irving's reply in this place, though it was delayed nearly three months:

[*To William C. Preston.*]

SUNNYSIDE, Aug. 9, 1859.

MY DEAR PRESTON:

I have suffered a long time to elapse without a reply to your most kind and welcome letter, but the state of my health must plead my apology. For many months I have been harassed by an attack of asthma, accompanied by sleepless nights, which deranged my whole nervous system. I have had to give up all literary occupation, and to abstain as much as possible from the exercise of my pen even in letter writing. I am slowly recovering, but will have to be very careful of myself. Fortunately, I have finished the Life of Washington, about which you speak so kindly, and now I shall no more tax myself with authorship.

Your allusions to Jones of the Brinn and Loch Katrine, brought up a host of recollections of pleasant scenes and of pleasant adventures which we enjoyed together in our peregrinations in England and Scotland, in our younger days. I often recur in thought to those ramblings, which furnish some of the most agreeable day dreams of past times, and, if I dared to indulge my pen, could call up many an amusing incident in which you figured conspicuously. But this scribbling I must postpone to some future day, when I am less under the thraldom of nerves and the asthma. At present, I merely scrawl these few lines to assure you of my constant and affectionate remembrance.

I believe our present Minister in Spain is a cousin of yours. I am glad to hear he is likely to prove popular there. A lady correspondent in Madrid, well acquainted with the Court circle, speaks in very favorable terms both of the Minister and his lady.

Farewell, my dear Preston. Believe me, though at present a very lame correspondent, yet, as ever,

Yours, very faithfully,
WASHINGTON IRVING.

May 23*d.*—Mr. Irving went to the city, by special invitation, to see Church's picture of The Heart of the

Andes. It was the last day of the exhibition, and the
room was crowded. Delighted with it. Pronounced
it glorious—magnificent!—such grandeur of general
effect with such minuteness of detail—minute without
hardness; a painting to stamp the reputation of an
artist at once.

The next night woke at two, in great distress from
difficulty of breathing, which continued for an hour
and a half. Went to the city to see Dr. Peters, who
called in Dr. Hosack to hold a consultation. Dr. P.
sought to encourage him with an account of Mr.
———, who had been a sufferer with asthma for forty
years, and whom they thought near his end, of late,
and, when he and his family were prepared for it, he
suddenly rallied, and was getting as well as he had
been before. His only comment was: " Ah, Doctor,
why didn't you let him go? Why call him back to
such suffering?"

Mr. Cogswell related to me the following anecdote:
Mr. Irving called at his room in the Astor Library, not
many months since, and, finding him sick abed, and
alarmingly ill, hurried off for his physician, Dr. Bar-
ker. One of his jokes, after Cogswell got well, was,
that, in going for the Doctor, he thought he would just
stop at the undertaker's on his way, and order a coffin;
and now he had the coffin on his hands.

On his return from the city, he retired, at bedtime,
to his room alone, as he had done for some nights past.
The doors were open, and perceiving, in the night, that

he was restless, I went in. The next morning, at breakfast, he remarked that he felt my coming in quite as a reprieve. After dinner, said to me: "I shall have to get you to mount guard again to-night. I am ashamed to ask it, but you cannot conceive what an abject coward this nervousness makes of me." I assured him of my readiness to resume my post.

June 2d.—Looked better, and had a comfortable day. Drove out with Mrs. J——. On his return, at twelve o'clock, found here his old friend, Gouverneur Kemble, who had come to see him and urge him to make him a visit. Kemble greeted him very cordially. "Why, you are looking——" "Very badly," interposed Mr. Irving. "But better than I expected to see you." Kemble stayed to dinner. Mr. Irving, at parting with him, accompanied him to the door, and bade him "good-by" with a "God bless you!"

When he returned to the parlor, his eyes were filled with tears, and he burst forth with a gush of feeling. "That is my friend of early life—always unchanged, always like a brother; one of the noblest beings that ever was created. His heart is pure gold." He was deeply affected. He had been, as he generally was in the society of those he liked, except when in immediate suffering, very cheerful during the dinner, and, excited and gratified by the visit, Mr. Kemble could form no idea of his situation. This proved to be their last meeting.

The next day he was very nervous, and sadly dis-

couraged. Said he had nearly given up all hope of
recovery or improvement, and only trusted that he
would not be left a burden long. After dinner, drove
out with H——. This depression continued through
the whole drive. " I've always dreaded," he remarked,
" beyond anything, becoming a confirmed invalid, and
a burden to those about me." " But you will never be
that," was the reply. " What do you call this ? I see
no relief to it. This cough prevents my sleeping, and,
with such nights, how can I be better ? And poor
——, too—what a tax on him ! " " He does not consider it so." " Well," he rejoined, " I trust he may
not have the burden long."

About this time, Mr. Irving received a letter from
Henry T. Tuckerman, who had been looking forward
with special interest to the concluding volume of his
Life of Washington, showing how agreeably it struck
him, by the following notice, which he enclosed :

The appearance of the concluding volume of Irving's Life
of Washington has been looked for with unusual interest.
Varying, as its subject matter does, from what went before—
shifting from military to political interest—it was thought, by
those cognizant of biographical art, that it would prove difficult
for the author to narrate Washington's administration with the
same simple directness which lent such emphasis to the story
of the war. But Mr. Irving has equally succeeded here.
Without swerving from his original plan, he has faithfully told
the facts, avoided, with consummate skill, the discussion of
mooted questions, kept strictly to his sphere of biography—

giving exactly enough about the French Revolution, alliance, and difficulties, Jay's treaty and its consequences, Jefferson's intrigues, Genet's impertinence, the state of parties and the course of opinion, as was absolutely necessary to explain Washington's position, difficulties, and conduct—and nothing more.   And he keeps the hero himself constantly in view—treats of events as they affect him, and not general history ; in a word, as throughout the work, he makes us partake of the consciousness of Washington more than the sentiment of party or the theories of politicians.   It is as the squabbles of his Cabinet, the sarcasms of the press, the events in Europe influence his peace, purposes, and feelings, that we know them ; and, by thus rendering domestic and foreign affairs subordinate to the delineation of his great subject, the harmony, unity, and clear significance of the biography are admirably preserved.   *   *   *

By the Preface, we learn that, more than thirty years ago, the Life of Washington was suggested to Mr. Irving by a famous Edinburgh publisher.   Its execution was postponed ; but the period which sees the work complete could not be more favorable for its useful influence and its successful achievement.   It is a graceful and noble consummation of a literary career of half a century—a high service both to our national literature and our civic wants—the greatest of which is to keep fresh to eye, mind, and heart, the matchless example herein unfolded in a spirit and with a candor parallel with its own purity and truth.

To the letter with the above enclosure, Mr. Irving made the following reply :

[*To Mr. H. T. Tuckerman.*]

SUNNYSIDE, June 8, 1859.

MY DEAR MR. TUCKERMAN:

I have suffered a long time to elapse without acknowledging the receipt of your letter enclosing a printed notice of my fifth volume, which you had furnished to the press. My only excuse is, that, since I have got out of regular harness, I find it exceedingly difficult to bring myself to the slightest exercise of the pen.

I cannot sufficiently express to you, my dear Mr. Tuckerman, how deeply I have felt obliged by the kind interest you have manifested on various occasions, and in a variety of ways, in me and my literary concerns. It is truly gratifying to be able to inspire such interest in the mind of a person of your stamp and intellectual character.

Your remarks on my last volume were especially inspiriting. Unnerved, as I was, by a tedious indisposition, I had come to regard this volume with a dubious and almost desponding eye. Having nothing of the *drum and trumpet* which gave bustle and animation to the earlier volumes, I feared it might be considered a falling off. Your letter has contributed to put me in heart, and I accept with gratitude your congratulations on what you pronounce a "happy termination" of my undertaking.

Ever, my dear Mr. Tuckerman, with great regard, your truly obliged friend,

WASHINGTON IRVING.

CHAPTER XVIII.

I RECUR to my notes taken at the time for a
brief record of the last months of the author's
existence.

June 13th.—A lowering day, but Mr. Irving again
improving. His days, of late, have presented quite a
contrast to that wretched 3d of June, and he has apparently been gaining ever since.

Received a note from General V. P. Van Antwerp,
of Iowa, and Colonel John T. Heard, of Massachusetts, two of the Board of Visitors, consisting of sixteen, now in session at the United States Military
Academy at West Point, enclosing a highly complimentary resolution to himself, and proposing, if agreeable, to call on him in a body the next day, when they
should adjourn, to tender to him, in their collective capacity, " the homage due to one whose long life had

been distinguished by sterling virtues, and who wore with becoming gracefulness the laurels which labors successfully devoted to literature had placed upon his brow."

Such a mark of consideration, from a body consisting of members from the different States of the Union, could not but be deeply gratifying, yet he was all in a flutter about it. " I must stop this at once ! " he exclaimed, and immediately went to the library and wrote a letter to General Van Antwerp, expressive of his very high sense of the intended compliment, but pleading his inability to cope with the visit, from long ill health and nervousness.

General Van Antwerp had intimated, in his note, that some of the Board had expressed fear that this " simple demonstration, not intended for publicity," might be an annoyance, and that if, for any reason, it should be either distasteful or inconvenient, a private note to him would suffice to explain the reason.

Mr. Irving was quite relieved when he had written his note, and got our approval. All dreaded the threatened visit, as likely to bring back or rather aggravate his nervousness.

June 19*th.*—Gentle and playful—something almost childlike in his manner. Asked whose the passage that was running in his head, " Fair laughs the morn," &c. I showed it to him in Gray's Bard. Inquired, then, if I could recollect the author of two lines that had lingered — disconnectedly — in his memory for years :

> " She asked of each wave, as it reached the shore,
> If it ever had touched the ship's tall side."

They are very suggestive. I had never met them. Very cheerful at dinner. Walked round the brook lot in the afternoon. In the evening took his seat in the parlor, and opened a book to read. Had been some time at a loss for a pleasant book. " I'm reduced to my favorite author." " What is it ? " is asked. " The fifth volume of the Life of Washington. I think I'll read it now. I have not looked at it since it was put to press."

June 22d.—Mr. Irving wretchedly nervous. I went to town, to bring up Dr. Peters in the afternoon train. The Doctor found him looking much better than he expected. As usual, he appeared better while the Doctor was there, but more nervous again after he left. He had a wretched night. I remained with him till three o'clock, when I retired for an hour. On my return, I found him struggling with one of those strange hallucinations he could not easily dispel. Had started up from sleep with an impression of some poor family he had to take care of. The impression, or the effect of it, seemed to cling to him, though he knew it was a fallacy. He had his mind and consciousness perfectly, as he said, and yet he could not shake it off. The effect of it continued for an hour. Very singular.

June 23d.—A necessary engagement taking four of the inmates to town, H—— remarked to him, before breakfast, that S—— would remain and read to him, and lull him to a good long sleep. " Ah ! my dear, I wish, indeed, it might be a *long* sleep ! "

June 24th.—I went to town, and returned with a letter for Mr. Irving, marked " Private," and post-marked Charleston, S. C. He did not break the seal that evening, but the next morning, after a restless, sleepless night, he opened it, without adverting to the postmark, and found it to contain only a newspaper slip from the Charleston *Mercury* of June 21st, with a finger mark pointing significantly to the following extract :

When a man sets himself down to write history, no one, of course, can deny him the privilege of drawing from the facts such inferences as he pleases; but the facts themselves he is bound to relate exactly as they occurred. Now, to apply the above rule, Mr. W. Irving has just published his last volume of " Washington's Life," and, in a paragraph devoted to the consideration of Washington's will, he discourses thus :

" On opening the will, it was found to have been carefully drawn up by himself; and, by an act in conformity with his whole career, one of its first provisions directed the emancipation of his slaves on the decease of his wife. It had long been his earnest wish that the slaves held by him in his own right should receive their freedom during his life ; but he had found that it would be attended with insuperable difficulties on account of their intermixture by marriage with the dower negroes, whom it was not in his power to manumit under the tenure by which they were held.   *   *   *   Though born and educated a slaveholder, this was all in consonance with feelings and principles which he had long entertained."

Now, what says the will itself? (see Appendix 4, at the end of the volume :)

" On the decease of my wife, it is my will and desire that all the slaves I hold in my own right shall receive their free-dom. To emancipate them during her life would, though ear-nestly wished by me, be attended with insuperable difficulties, on account of their intermixture by marriage with the dower negroes, and excite the most painful sensations, if not disagree-able consequences to the latter, while both descriptions (of negroes) are in the occupancy [!] of the same proprietor [!]— it not being in my power, under the tenure by which the dower negroes are held, to manumit them."

So far about the will. In order, however, to show that Washington had, long previously to his death, and in direct conflict with his education, become perfectly Northernized, Irving quotes—and fairly, too—several letters to different friends; omitting, nevertheless, or possibly overlooking one, which, for the comfort of all Northerners, and of Mr. I. him-self especially, shall be given—an extract—below :

" *May 10th*, 1786.—The benevolence of your heart, my dear Marquis Lafayette, is so conspicuous on all occasions, that I never wonder at any new proofs of it; but your late pur-chase of an estate in Cayenne, with a view of liberating the slaves on it, is a generous and noble proof," &c.

" Would to God a like spirit might diffuse itself generally into the minds of the people of this country; but I despair of seeing it. Some petitions were lately presented to the Virginia Legislature, for the abolition of slavery, but they could scarcely obtain a READING."

Query : Will not a perusal of the above extracts very effectually convince any one, capable of the " combination of two ideas," that Washington was in principle essentially a Northerner—that is, he was ready, in order to advance the " glorious liberty and equality of man "—ready to confiscate the property of—other people—his wife's negroes, for instance —after his death, though.

After I had finished reading the extract aloud, " Did you ever read," said he, " such an unmeaning thing ? " He supposed, at first, it was from a North- ern paper, and that some extreme opponent of slavery had meant to impute suppression or concealment of Washington's full opinions, when he thought his ex- tracts covered the whole ground. But on a more care- ful perusal than I gave it at first, I perceived it was from a Southern source, and that the object was to show, not that Washington was entitled to *more* credit than the biography had awarded him for his opinions on slavery, but was open to a grave stigma for his con- duct, in directing, by will, the emancipation of his slaves. " As if," said Mr. Irving, when I showed him its Southern source, " the greatest reproach you could make against a man was that he was opposed to sla- very. Did you ever know such fools ? "

Eminently national in his feelings, a lover of his whole country, keenly alive to everything that con- cerned the honor and good name of the Republic, he was not without foreboding at the signs of the times, and the disposition evinced in this instance to immolate Washington on the altar of slavery, seemed to him portentous.

June 28th.—In the afternoon, a call from Miss A—— H——, Miss G——, of Boston, Mr. W——, of Boston, and Rossiter, the artist. Miss H—— thought he looked very feeble, and was much changed. Afterward, F. S. Cozzens, author of The Sparrowgrass Papers, &c., called, his wife, and a little daughter of four years of age, and remained until half past nine. Something was said by Cozzens about his sitting for a likeness to Mr. Thomas Hicks, the artist, to accompany a representation of the literary class in some contemplated grand painting, in which the various classes—commercial, scientific, &c.—were to be represented. Mr. Irving replied, that he was dwindling away so fast, that he would soon make an excellent subject for a *miniature* for Mr. Hicks, if he took miniatures.

Retired about eleven, and had one of his "perverse, wretched nights," as he styled them. From time to time would beg me to go to my room. Said that there was a forlorn comfort in having some one to groan to, but that I could not help him; that I could only lie down in the gutter with him (alluding to the story of the sot who said to a brother sot in the gutter, that he could not help him up, but would lie down beside him). A little playfulness and fun would thus blend, at times, with his extremest distress.

Toward morning he expressed a hope that this suffering might soon end. "Had never wished to live beyond a cheerful existence. His life, if prolonged, might be of value to others, and hence it was desirable; but, for himself, he was willing to go. So singular and unaccountable that he should be distressed in this way; had nothing to worry him; nothing on his mind; no concern about his worldly means or literary reputation; had had honor enough in that respect," &c.

June 29th.—I was reading Mrs. Stowe's "Minister's Wooing," then coming out in numbers in the *Atlantic Monthly*, and asked him his impression of Burr, whom she had introduced in her story. "Burr was full of petty mystery; he made a mystery of everything. When I called on him, at Baltimore, in the morning, on my way to his trial, I must come again in the evening. Five or six were in the room. He would take me in one corner, and say a word or two; another in another, and so on. I met him again at Fredericksburg, and rode with him in the stage to Richmond. I could not well make out why I was sent for. From some sounding of his, I suspected he wanted me to write for the press in his behalf, but I put a veto on that."

June 30th.—The Doctor came up, and stayed over night. Left him a new prescription—a tonic—which had a favorable effect.

July 7th.—Just before sitting down to breakfast, a

stranger called at the door, wishing to see Mr. Irving.
The servant informed him he was ill—but he had come
from a great distance, and begged to see him, if but for
a few moments. Mr. Irving, excessively troubled at
the time with shortness of breath, requested me to see
him. I went to the door, and found a very ordinary-
looking personage with a carpet bag. He asked if I
was Mr. Irving. Not Mr. Washington Irving, I told
him. He is ill, and unable to see any one. "It would
be a great gratification to see him, if but for a few
moments. Had come a great distance. Had called
four years before, but he was not at home. Trusted
he might not be disappointed." I returned to Mr.
Irving, and reported what he said. He went to the
door, and invited him into the library. The stranger
took a chair, and was going in for a long talk, when
Mr. Irving had to excuse himself, from his difficulty of
breathing. The stranger then asked for his autograph.
Mr. Irving informed him he was too distressed to write
it then, but would send it to his address, which the
stranger gave, and asked Mr. Irving his charge, saying, "It is a principle with me always to pay for such
things." "It is a principle with me," replied Mr.
Irving, sharply, "never to take pay."

He came back quite disgusted. As he detailed
this incident at breakfast, one of his auditors was reminded of an anecdote related by Longfellow, last
summer, at Nahant. A person wrote the poet, wishing him to send an acrostic, the first letters of which

should spell, " My Sweet Girl." " Write as if it were some beautiful girl with whom you were in love—just as if it were for yourself;" and at the foot of the letter were these words, " Send bill."

Had a good night, without attendance of any kind. His nervousness seems to be leaving him, and his general health to be improving. Looks better. It may be the result of a tonic which the Doctor prescribed about ten days ago.

July 10*th*.—Drove to church. A fair appetite at dinner, and very playful. " What a pity, Kate, we had not known Louis Napoleon was such a warrior when he took breakfast with us ! We might have turned the conversation on military matters." The war in Italy was then going on, in which he was much interested.

A good deal troubled with shortness of breath in the afternoon, and before retiring. On the whole, can hardly say he is gaining ground in his recovery. Though free from nervousness for the last ten or eleven nights, yet does not seem to be getting rid of this oppressed respiration, which has less of paroxysm than heretofore, but is more frequent.

July 12*th*.—Called me, in the morning, from the library to the piazza, to see " what a picture there was on the river." No wind—no tide—clusters of vessels motionless in front, making beautiful groups—clouds moving so lazily, that

" Even in their very motion there was rest ;"

the sounds of the hammer from workmen on a house at the opposite side of the river borne *distinctly* across the water. " That's the way," pointing to one of the lazy vessels in the broad sunlight, with its boom creaking to and fro, " that's the way we used to travel to Albany in former days, baking in the sun, and trying to keep within the shade of the sail. We thought it the order of things, then, to roast in summer and freeze in winter."

Remarked, at noon, that he felt he was getting on —getting well. He had expressed occasional confidence before, during an intermission of his symptoms, but never so strongly. Seemed more encouraged than he had ever been. Spent the evening on the piazza. Sturgeons leaping every few minutes. Was surprised to find them so far down the Hudson.

July 13*th.*—Has had a rather nervous and wakeful night—the first *nervous* night in a fortnight. Fears he had bragged too soon yesterday. A thunder storm began to gather just after dinner. He and I sat on the bench up the bank for a while to watch its gathering. He rather disposed to drowsiness. On returning to the house, fell into a sound sleep on the sofa, from which he awoke just before tea. At tea, seemed to be bewildered. Asked how the storm came up ; if there had been any children there that afternoon ; had been dreaming there were, and that his old friend, Leslie, recently dead, was there. A strange hallucination, such as he had occasionally during his *nervous* nights.

July 18*th*.—I brought up from the city Poe's Poems. He read over The Raven. " What a capital hit that was—such a strange, weird interest in it ! " H—— proposed that I should read it aloud. " No ; too dismal to go to bed upon." " I got one or two letters from Poe, but saw little of him. One asked permission to use certain materials of mine for a story. I gave it."

The next day a Mr. Hugh Erwin, of Nashville, called—a stranger. Conversation about Clay. Mr. Irving expressed warm admiration of Clay. Spoke of his having seen him at Washington in early life, and been strongly attracted toward him. Of his going out to take leave of him ; and Clay, mounted on his horse, accosting him with, " If I can do anything for you, let me know." " Does he suppose," thought I, " that I have been courting him all this time for a selfish object ? "

July 24*th*.—Speaking of the details of the battle of Solferino, which had just appeared in the papers : " I used to read all the details of a painful nature in wars, but now I skip them. My stomach has lost its tone ; I cannot digest horrors any longer."

August 5*th*.—Very much untuned and out of sorts. A bad night ; little sleep. Great oppression and shortness of breath during the day. I brought up from the city a fresh supply of medicine from Dr. Peters, to whom I had reported Mr. Irving's condition. He advised a continuance of the tonic remedies, particularly laying stress upon them as necessary to build him up and fortify him for the trials of the winter. Seemed to have a craving for news when I came up—anything, probably, to take off his thoughts from himself and his distress.

Had a bad night, and was excessively nervous during the whole of the next day. To one who was trying to talk to him, and get his mind off of himself: " It is a shame to depress you by my sad feelings ; but I can no more restrain these nerves than I could wild horses. Everything has such a gloomy aspect—nothing to look forward to. In this situation, I am a burden to myself and to everybody else, and would rather lie down and die. Ah! I have got to the dregs, and must take them."

August 21st.—Went to church. A good deal distressed with laboring breath after dinner. Gave H—— a letter to read, which he had received the day before from a stranger proposing to call on him. The letter was long, and occupied some time in the reading. " Oh! if he could only give me his long wind, he should be most welcome." Slept an hour or two after tea, and awoke very much distressed with shortness of breath. Great misgiving on retiring for the night. " Ah me! what a blight to fall on a man's life!"

The next morning felt better. Alluded to the common practice of swearing in the early days of New York. " Could not utter a sentence without sending a *damn* with it to give it force."

August 31*st.*—Mr. Irving paid a last visit to his friend Mr. Ames, at his country residence at Craigville, Orange County, his niece Sarah, Mrs. Irving, and myself accompanying him. He hoped to find benefit from change of air, and seemed improved at first.

Drove to Chester the next day. Very cheerful in the evening. Had seen, in some old periodical, an account of Cooper, Bryant, Tuckerman, and others, having visited the Foxes at the rooms of Rufus W. Griswold, in the year 1850, and adverted to the enigma of the manifestations. " Ah ! " said he, playfully, " the only way to get at the truth, is to bring the mediums to the stake ; that was the good old way."

September 4*th.*—Drove to a camp meeting near Oxford. Mr. Irving told, with great zest, a story of his going to a camp meeting, when a youngster, not far from Tarrytown, with a young lady. An old negro, seated on a stump, rocking to and fro, with his hands clasping his knees, looked up at them with a curious glance, supposing they had come to mock and laugh. Gave them a passing shot : " Jesus will carry de day." " If God Almighty were not too strong for de debbil, der'd be no libing in *dis* world." Two black nymphs behind, fanning themselves : " Let old Scip(io) alone. I'll warrant he'll gib dem der own."

Was very cheerful during the evening, telling various anecdotes in his old way ; but at bedtime the difficulty of breathing returned, and, with it, excessive nervousness. He had a wretched night, and the next

morning decided to return home at once. We left at
ten o'clock—he sadly discouraged. He had looked forward to this visit with great hope from change of air,
and the disappointment added to his depression. We
arrived at Sunnyside before two. He slept heavily in
the afternoon and early evening, but at ten his shortness of breath returned, and with it his distressing
nervousness.

On the 9th, he went to the city for the day on some
little business, and for the change. On his return,
found Gouverneur Kemble had called. Very sorry to
have missed him. Did not care to see new faces, or
have new faces see him; but of old faces he could not
see too much.

A day or two after, had a call from Mr. George
Sumner, who was visiting in the neighborhood. Remained to tea. Mr. Irving was scarcely able to hold
any conversation with him. Sumner reminded him of
a remark of his at Madrid, that the best things of an
author were spontaneous—the first pressure of the
grape; the after squeezings not so rich.

September 12th.—Had been awake till three; then
slept till four, after which he got no sleep. Very nervous in the morning. I took up a volume of Perci-
val's Poems, which I had just brought, and read aloud,
" She had no heart," &c. " That's very beautiful! "
said he. " Flows so naturally and easily. No hammer in that."

Speaking of an English writer whose death had

been announced in the papers, he remarked : " I never met him, and never liked him. He belonged to a Cockney clique for whom I had no relish. They used to hold junkettings at the house of my landlady, Mrs. H——, with whom I lodged soon after I went up to London to prepare the Sketch Book, and they sometimes forgot to pay for them. She told me once, when a good deal straitened, that she called at the house of one of them with her bill for wine, &c. He was absent, but she saw his wife, who told her she had not the money, and that her husband was a *man of genius*, and could not attend to such matters. " Send a bailiff after the man of genius," said I. " I know of no genius that lifts a man above his honest engagements."

September 15*th*.—Found the annexed extract, after tea, in the *Home Journal*, from the pen of N. P. Willis, which was cut out by Sarah, that he might not see it, from its allusion to his closing life :

Mr. Irving, by far the most honored man in our country, is, curiously enough, even less honored than loved. He is a marvel, if only by that difference from other men of genius— whose destiny it seems to have their last days sad. The setting of his sun is mellow, the clouds around and behind him rosier as he goes. There is another summer-day beauty, too, in his decline—the full moon of renown, after death, seen clearly even before the setting of his sun.

We have said thus much expressive of our own feeling, by way of declining more graciously the numbers of articles which have poured in upon us with the recent news of Mr. Irving's illness. From authentic sources, we learn that the report of his recent indisposition was very much exaggerated, and that he is at present in his usual condition at Sunnyside.

My record of the evening is: Played whist from eight to ten, after which Mr. Irving dozed awhile in his chair, and then retired about eleven, quite free, apparently, from the nervous apprehensions of the night before.

To keep him awake until ready to retire for the night, and to drive off disagreeable thoughts, we were in the habit of playing either whist or backgammon. Chess, of which he was fond, was too exciting. He was always a very poor player at whist, and cared nothing for the game, but was glad to seize on anything to keep him awake in the evening, lest any indulgence then should lessen his chance of sleep for the night.

September 17*th.*—Mr. Irving finishes " Quits," a novel by the authoress of the " Initials." Very much pleased with it. Has now " Cecil; or, The Adventures of a Coxcomb," which I have borrowed for him. Wants works of a continuous interest in his present condition.

September 18*th.*—Has had a good night, which makes the fourth. Apparently much better. After dinner, walks to Robert, the gardener's, to see and amuse himself with the children—his delight.

September 19*th.*—Attended a vestry meeting at

Christ Church, Tarrytown, of which he was warden
as well as vestryman. Returned before dark. Complained, at teatime, of great heat in the head. Had
something of a chill as he retired for the night. Was
evidently feverish.

The next day I called on Dr. Peters, in New York,
who came up with me in the afternoon train. Found
that Mr. Irving had fever. Had coughed a good deal
during the day. Gave him something quieting, which
allayed his cough for the rest of the evening.

Dr. Peters came up again the next afternoon. Mr.
Irving was better; and, at the dinner table, the Doctor told an anecdote of a drunkard's applying to him
for *sixpence*, though with an evident consciousness of
his own drunkenness. *Apropos* to which, Mr. Irving
related an anecdote of his walking the streets of London, smiling at the recollection of one of his own
jokes, when he was accosted by an Irishwoman: "Ah,
God bless your merry face! surely you're not the man
will refuse a poor woman a *sixpence*." He put his
hand in his pocket, and gave her—the smallest he had
—a guinea. "So much had I to pay," said he, "for
laughing at my own joke; and it served me right."

September 28*th*.—The Doctor has been up for several successive days, sometimes remaining over night.
Mr. Irving feels his kindness very deeply. Was with
him at one last night, and again from three to four
during the night, as he was very nervous. Was tor-
mented with an idea that he had a big book to write

before he could sleep. Visitors abounded to-day—eighteen or nineteen. Mr. Irving could see no one.

September 29th.—Went to bed at eleven, and had a deplorably nervous night. I had tried in vain to find a book for him to read. In his present state, it is hard for him to find entertainment in anything. Though his asthma was relieved, the lamentable nervous distress of which he was so long the victim months back, seemed to be reëstablishing itself, while he had less strength to contend with it.

One of his favorite books, during his long illness, was Slidell's Year in Spain. He read it again and again. Its graphic pictures seemed to carry him back to pleasant scenes, and out of himself. When reading to him, as we did constantly, to produce sleep, we always avoided it, as we found it excited his imagination, and roused rather than soothed him.

September 30th.—A deplorably bad night. Sadly nervous and wakeful. The Doctor came up at half past seven P. M., and remained all night. Administered opium in slight doses, to make him more amenable to the other medicines, but not to drug him.

October 2d.—Had a tolerable night, though not his quantum of sleep. Showed him a letter of his brother William, to his mother, written in October, 1787, when he was just twenty-one, giving a picture of his life on the Mohawk. Quite amused with it; then launched into a eulogium of his brother. "There was a natural richness of mind about him, that made him the most delightful of companions. How I used to delight to set him going with his world of anecdote! I knew just what key to touch." Then came an allusion to his father's pastor, "old Dr. Rodgers, with his buzz wig, silver-mounted cane, well-polished shoes, and silver shoebuckles."

October 4th.—A good night, and a good, comfortable day. No asthma now for three weeks.

October 7th.—Has had a good night, with a little more cough, and a *little* shortness of breath—slight indications, possibly, of returning asthma. At dinner, got speaking of Cooper, started by an article on Cooper in the *North American,* written by Henry T. Tuckerman. Pronounced it a very fair, discriminating article. Thought Leatherstocking a creation. No one would care to meddle with that class of character after Cooper. In life, they judge a writer by his last production; after death, by what he has done best. Look at Shakspeare. You do not think of "—(naming some of Shakspeare's inferior plays)—"but of Macbeth, Hamlet, Othello. So it will be with Cooper."

October 10th.—Whist in the evening. Mr. Irving said, in the course of the game, "I do not like to be guilty of pretension, but I must say I'm the very worst player that ever was. I think, if I had Mrs. Sidesbottom here, I'd almost borrow her spectacles." (Mrs. S. was an inveterate card player of Liverpool, whose partner at whist he once was, and who pettishly offered

to lend him her spectacles when he mistook the card.)
He had played only in courtesy, to make up a hand.

October 11*th.*—On my return from the city, at a
quarter past seven P. M., found him rather nervous.
Asked at once if I had brought anything to read ;
whereupon I unfolded my stores—"Doctor Thorne,"
" Reginald Dalton," " Guy Livingstone." Rather inclined to condemn all without reading. Took up
" Doctor Thorne," and thought he would try it.

The next day was a very good one, and he seemed
quite like himself. Went to bed in good spirits, rejoiced that he had " Doctor Thorne " to read, in which
he had become quite interested.

Afterward read " Reginald Dalton." Relished the
pictures of Oxford college life. Had finished " Doctor
Thorne." Thought it very clever—out of the common
run. Went to bed not very " sanguin-ary," as he
termed it, of a good sleep.

October 23*d, Sunday.*—Feverish ; no appetite for
breakfast. I put on my coat, announcing my intention to take a good walk. " Better go to church," said
he ; " that would be a *good* walk." He was not able
to go himself.

October 30*th.*—After church, a call from Mrs.
S——, of Richmond, M—— and A—— H——.
They announce intention of John P. Kennedy to call
to-morrow, at twelve, on his way down from Idlewild,
the seat of N. P. Willis, the poet. On the morrow,
accordingly, Mr. Kennedy, Mr. Willis, and Mr. Wise,

author of Los Gringos, called. The latter had never met Mr. Irving before, and the others were to see him for the last time.

I quote from the *Home Journal* of November 19th, a portion of Mr. Willis's account of the visit:

During the ten minutes before Mr. Irving came in (for he was out upon his morning drive when we arrived), his nieces very kindly gratified our interest in the "workshop of genius," by taking us into the library—the little curtain-windowed sanctuary where his mind had found both its labor and its repose, though, by the open newspapers scattered carelessly over the large writing table in the centre, and the inviting readiness of the well-cushioned lounge in the recess, it now serves more the purpose of the repose more needed. It was a labyrinth of books, as it was a labyrinth of tender associations, in which, as the eye roved over its consecrated nooks and corners, the fancy, in all reverence, rambled lovingly!

I was looking admiringly, once more, at Jarvis's record of him at the Sketch-Book period of his life (the portrait with the fur collar, which all who have seen it will so well remember), when Mr. Irving came in from his drive. We had heard so much, recently, of his illness, that I was surprised to see with how lively and firm a step he entered; removing the slouched hat (a comfortable departure from the old-school covering, which I had never expected to see on so proper a head!) with as easy elegance as ever, sitting down with his gray shawl left carelessly over his shoulders, and entering upon kind inquiries and exchange of courtesies with no hindrance of debility that I could see. He is thinner, somewhat, in both form and features—owing to the asthma, which interferes somewhat with his repose when lying down; but the genial expression of his countenance is unchanged, and his eye as kindly and bright. As to sprightliness of attention and reply, I could see little difference from the Washington Irving of other days. The reports of his illness must have been exaggerated, I thought.

Conversation falling upon exercise, Mr. Irving remarked that he daily took his drive in the carriage—less from any desire to go abroad, than from finding, since he had given up habits of abor, that time hung heavy on his hands. If he walks out, it is only in the grounds. We spoke of horseback riding, and he gave us a most amusing account of his two last experiences in that way—a favorite horse called "Gentleman Dick" having thrown him over his head into a laurel bush, which kindly broke his fall; and another very handsome nag, having proved to be opinionative as to choice of road—particularly at a certain bridge, which it was very necessary to pass in every ride, but which the horse could not by any reasonable persuasion be got over. With the sending of this horse-dogmatist to town, to be sold to meaner service for his obstinacy, had ended the experiments in the saddle.

*   *   *   *   *   *

Attributable, perhaps, to a rallying of his animal spirits with cessation from work—I could not but wonder at the effortless play of "Diedrich-Knickerbocker" humor which ran through all his conversation—Washington Irving, in his best days, I am very sure, was never more socially "agreeable" than with us, for that brief visit. One little circumstance was mentioned in the course of this pleasant gossip. There was some passing discussion of the wearing of beards—his friend Mr. Kennedy having made that alteration in his physiognomy since they had met; and Mr. Irving closed a playful comment or two upon the habit, by saying that he could scarce afford the luxury himself, involving, as it would do, the loss of the most effectual quietus of his nerves. To get up and shave, when tired of lying awake, sure of going to sleep immediately after, had long been a habit of his. There was an amusing exchange of sorrows, also, between him and Mr. Kennedy, as to persecution by autograph hunters; though the ex-Secretary gave rather the strongest instance—mentioning an unknown man who had written to him when at the head of the Navy Department, requesting, as one of his constituents, to be furnished with autographs of all the Presidents, of himself and the rest of the Cabinet, and of any other distinguished men with whom he might be in correspondence!

But there was a *table* calling for us which was less agreeable than the one we were at—the "time table" of the railroad below—and our host's carriage was at the door. Mr. Kennedy was bound to the city, where Mr. Irving, as he gave us his farewell upon the porch, said he thought he might find him, in a day or two; and Wise and I, by the up train, were bound back to Idlewild. We were at home by seven, and, over our venison supper (the "Alleghany haunch" still bountiful), we exchanged our remembrances of the day, and our felicitations at having been privileged, thus delightfully, to see, in his home and in health, the still sovereign Story King of the Hudson. May God bless him! and may the clouds about his loved and honored head grow still brighter with the nearer setting of his sun. * * *

I draw again on my notes for the following memorandum, which records his last pilgrimage to his native city—made six days after the foregoing visit.

November 5th.—A good deal troubled with his cough. Visited New York. Lunched at Charles A. Davis's.

Two days after, Mr. Theodore Tilton, one of the editors of the New York *Independent*, spent a half hour at Sunnyside, of which he contributed to the columns of that print the following interesting account :

I had half an hour, one day last week, at Sunnyside, the residence of Washington Irving. Such a half hour ought to have been one of the pleasantest in one's life; and so it was. * * *

The morning had been rainy, and the afternoon showed only a few momentary openings of clear sky; so that I saw Sunnyside without the sun. But, under the heavy clouds, there was something awe-inspiring in the sombre view of those grand hills, with their many-colored forests, and of Hendrik Hudson's ancient river still flowing at the feet of the ancient palisades.

The mansion of Sunnyside has been standing for twenty-three years; but when first its sharp-angled roof wedged its way up among the branches of the old woods, the region was far more a solitunde than now; for at that time our busy author had secluded himself from almost everybody but one near neighbor; while he has since unwittingly gathered around him a little community, whose elegant country seats, opening into each other by mutual intertwining roads, form what looks like one vast and free estate, called on the time tables of the railroad by the honorary name of Irvington. But even within the growing circle of his many neighbors, the genial old Knickerbocker still lives in true retirement, entertaining his

guests within echo distance of Sleepy Hollow, without thought,
and almost without knowledge

————" how the great world
Is praising him far off."

Mr. Irving is not so old-looking as one would expect who
knew his age.   I fancied him as in the winter of life; I found
him only in its Indian summer.   He came down stairs, and
walked through the hall into the back parlor, with a firm and
lively step that might well have made one doubt whether he
had truly attained his seventy-seventh year!   He was suffering
from asthma, and was muffled against the damp air with a
Scotch shawl, wrapped like a great loose scarf around his
neck; but as he took his seat in the old armchair, and, despite
his hoarseness and troubled chest, began an unexpectedly viva-
cious conversation, he almost made me forget that I was the
guest of an old man long past his "threescore years and ten."

But what should one talk about who had only half an hour
with Washington Irving?   I ventured the question: "Now
that you have laid aside your pen, which of your books do you
look back upon with most pleasure?"

He immediately replied: "I scarcely look with full satisfaction upon any; for they do not seem what they might have
been.   I often wish that I could have twenty years more, to
take them down from the shelf one by one, and write them
over."

He spoke of his daily habits of writing, before he had
made the resolution to write no more.   His usual hours for literary work were from morning till noon.   But, although he had
generally found his mind most vigorous in the early part of the
day, he had always been subject to moods and caprices, and

could never tell, when he took up the pen, how many hours would pass before he would lay it down.

"But," said he, "these capricious periods of the heat and glow of composition, have been the happiest hours of my life. I have never found, in anything outside of the four walls of my study, any enjoyment equal to sitting at my writing desk, with a clean page, a new theme, and a mind wide awake."

His literary employments, he remarked, had always been more like entertainments than tasks.

"Some writers," said he, "appear to have been independent of moods. Sir Walter Scott, for instance, had great power of writing, and could work almost at any time. So could Crabbe; but with this difference—Scott always, and Crabbe seldom, wrote well. I remember," said he, "taking breakfast, one morning, with Rogers, Moore, and Crabbe. The conversation turned on Lord Byron's poetic moods. Crabbe said that, however it might be with Lord Byron, as for himself, he could write as well at one time as at another. But," said Irving, with a twinkle of humor at recalling the incident, "Crabbe has written a great deal that nobody can read."

He mentioned that, while living in Paris, he went a long period without being able to write. "I sat down repeatedly," said he, "with pen and ink, but could invent nothing worth putting on the paper. At length I told my friend Tom Moore, who dropped in one morning, that now, after long waiting, I had the mood, and would hold it, and work it out as long as it would last, until I had wrung my brain dry. So I began to write shortly after breakfast, and continued, without noticing how the time was passing, until Moore came in again at four in the afternoon—when I had completely covered the table with freshly written sheets. I kept the mood almost without interruption for six weeks."

I asked which of his books was the result of this frenzy. He replied, " Bracebridge Hall."

" None of your works," I remarked, " are more charming than the Biography of Goldsmith."

" Yet that was written," said he, " even more rapidly than the other." He then added : " When I have been engaged on a continuous work, I have often been obliged to rise in the middle of the night, light my lamp, and write an hour or two, to relieve my mind ; and, now that I write no more, I am sometimes compelled to get up in the same way to read."

Sometimes, also, as the last Idlewild letter mentions, he gets up to shave !

" When I was in Spain," he remarked, " searching the old chronicles, and engaged on the Life of Columbus, I often wrote fourteen or fifteen hours out of the twenty-four."

He said that, whenever he had forced his mind unwillingly to work, the product was worthless, and he invariably threw it away, and began again ; " for," as he observed, " an essay or chapter that has been only *hammered out*, is seldom good for anything. An author's right time to work is when his mind is aglow—when his imagination is kindled. These are his precious moments. Let him wait until they come ; but, when they have come, let him make the most of them."

I referred to his last and greatest work, The Life of Washington, and asked if he felt, on finishing it, any such sensation as Gibbon is said to have experienced over the last sheet of the Decline and Fall. He replied that the whole work had engrossed his mind to such a degree, that, before he was aware, he had written himself into feebleness of health; that he feared in the midst of his labor that it would break him down before he could end it; that when, at last, the final pages were written, he gave the manuscript to his nephew to be conducted through the press, and threw himself back upon his red-cushioned lounge with an indescribable feeling of relief. He added, that the great fatigue of mind, throughout the whole task, had resulted from the care and pains required in the construction and arrangement of materials, and not in the mere literary composition of the successive chapters.

On the parlor wall hung the engraving of Faed's picture of "Scott and his Contemporaries." I alluded to it as presenting a group of his former friends.

"Yes," said he; "I knew every man of them but three; and now they are all gone!"

"Are the portraits good?" I inquired.

"Scott's head," he replied, "is well drawn, though the expression lacks something of Scott's force. Campbell's is tolerable. Lockhart's is the worst. Lockhart," said he, "was a man of very delicate organization, but he had a more manly look than in the picture."

"You should write one more book," I hinted.

"What is that?"

"Your reminiscences of those literary friends."

"Ah," he exclaimed, "it is too late now! I shall never take the pen again. I have so entirely given up writing, that even my best friends' letters lie unanswered. I must have rest. No more books now!"

*   *   *   *   *   *

As I rose to go, he brought from a corner of the room a photograph of a little girl, exhibiting it with great enthusiasm.

It was a gift from a little child who had come to see him every day during his sickness. The picture was accompanied with a note, printed in large letters, with a lead pencil, by the little correspondent, who said she was too young to write. He spoke with great vivacity of his childish visitor. "Children," said the old man, "are great pets. I am very fond of the little creatures."

The author's study—into which I looked for a few moments before leaving—is a small room, almost entirely filled by the great writing table and the lounge behind it. The walls are laden with books and pictures, which evidently are re-arranged every day by some delicate hand; for none of the books were tumbled into a corner, and no papers were lying loose upon the table. The pen, too, was lying precisely parallel to the edge of the inkstand—a nicety which only a womanly housekeeper would persevere to maintain. Besides, there was not a speck of dust upon carpet or cushion.

I stood reverently in the little room, as if it were a sacred place. Its associations filled my mind with as much delight as if I had been breathing fragrance from hidden flowers. On leaving, I carried the picture of it vividly in my mind, and still carry it—the quiet, secluded, poetic haunt in which a great author wrote his greatest works.

As I came away, the old gentleman bundled his shawl about him, and stood a few moments on the steps. A momentary burst of sunshine fell on him through the breaking clouds. In that full light he looked still less like an old man than in the dark parlor by the shaded window. * * * I wish always to remember him as I saw him at that last moment.

I return once more to my notes :

November 10th.—His cough not so troublesome. Is evidently stronger than he was.

November 16th.—I returned to Sunnyside from an absence of two days in the city. Found Mr. Irving had been suffering from a renewal of his asthma, which had been distressing him for three or four days. A Mrs. ———— called just at twilight, to importune him for an autograph in her book. Mr. Irving being asleep, we tried to fight her off with an offer of a loose one ; but she was pertinacious, and we had to seize a moment of partial wakefulness to get him to write it in her book, which he did without seeing her.

November 20th, Sunday.—At breakfast, one of his nieces mentioned her dream of seeing a spirit ; her dread, and the nightmare consequent thereupon. "Did you question it?" was asked. "No; she did not want to have anything to do with spirits in this life;" and appealed for approval to Mr. Irving, who thought we were " better adapted to communion in the flesh." He then alluded again to the anecdote of Hall and himself, and their strange and solemn compact, which had no result.

Went to church.

November 22d, Tuesday.—A call from Mr. William G. Dix, seeking a personal acquaintance, and bringing a note from Rev. James Selden Spencer, assistant minister of Christ Church, Tarrytown. It was Mr. Irving's last interview with a stranger.

I happened to mention (says Mr. Dix, in a letter published after his death, recounting the interview) the name of Washington Allston. It set his soul all glowing with tender, affectionate enthusiasm. To hear the great painter so praised by the great writer, with a voice tremulous partly with infirmity but more with emotion, was something to keep, as surely as if every word had been engraven with the point of a diamond.

I drew my interview soon to a close, not wishing to make him weary ; and his cordial desire that I would call to see him again, and his expressions of goodwill, so much more hearty than I had any right to expect, will ever be cherished as a benediction. I seem to have received a parting blessing on my heart and soul. How little did I then think that it would prove the very last! * * *

When I was leaving Mr. Irving, I asked him to let me pluck some of the ivy leaves that adorn his house. He consented with a smile so full of kindness and tenderness, and with a tone so full of feeling, that I shall regard every leaf as more precious than gold.

November 27th, Sunday. — Attended church at Tarrytown. In the evening, it was remarked that we would have to contrive some religious game to prevent his falling asleep. " I shall have to get a dispensation from Dr. Creighton to allow me to play whist on Sunday evening," was his playful rejoinder. We kept him in conversation till nine o'clock, when sleep overtook him, though he still tried to struggle against it.

November 28th, Monday.—Mr. Irving seemed very comfortable. C——, S——, and myself, started for

the city in the morning train, leaving H—— and
M—— with the invalid. He walked out to the brook
lot about eleven, but did not drive out as usual, as he
feared a return of difficult breathing. He had come
back from his short walk with oppressed respiration,
and seemed more than usually depressed, but rallied
to a playful conversation with Mrs. H——, a lovely
neighbor, who was a great favorite with him.

On our return from the city, in the afternoon, we
found the family at dinner, with the addition of his
nephew, the Rev. Pierre P. Irving, who had come up
during our absence. The windows of the dining room
looked to the west and south, and the whole party
were lost in admiration of one of the most gorgeous
sunsets I have ever beheld. The whole western sky
was hung with clouds of the richest crimson, while the
scene had all the softness of our lingering Indian summer. Mr. Irving exclaimed again and again at the
beauty of the prospect. How little did any of us
dream it was to be his last sunset on earth !

He slept between dinner and tea. In the evening
seemed heavy, and a good deal depressed, as he had
been more than usual during the day, but was free
from nervousness, and would occasionally join in pleasant conversation.

On retiring for the night, at half past ten, his niece
Sarah, who always took charge of his medicines, went
into his room to place them, as usual, within easy
reach. " Well," he exclaimed, " I must arrange my

pillows for another weary night!" and then, as if half
to himself, "If this could only end!" or "When will
this end!" she could not tell which; for, at the instant, he gave a slight exclamation, as if of pain, pressing his hand on his left side, repeated the exclamation
and the pressure, caught at the footboard of the bed,
and fell backward to the floor.   The sound of his fall
and the screams of Sarah brought the whole family in
an instant to his room.   I raised his head in my arms.
Every means was resorted to to recall animation, and
continued until a physician—Dr. Caruthers, from a
distance of two miles—arrived, who pronounced life
entirely extinct.   He had passed away instantaneously.
The end for which he had just been sighing—the end,
which to him had no terrors—had come.   His departure
was sudden; but so he was willing it should be.   In
the fulness of years, with unclouded intellect, crowned
with the warmest affections of his countrymen, and
with an assured hope of a happy immortality, he had
gone down, according to his own pathetic aspiration,
" with all sail set."   Who that loved him would have
wished to recall him !

When his physician, Dr. Peters, arrived at the
house the next morning, he pronounced the immediate
cause of his death to be disease of the heart.   He had
informed me, eleven months before, that there was
enlargement of the heart, but he did not then express
serious apprehension from this cause.

His attention to his patient during a year of suffer-

ing was most unwearied, and, whatever skill could
accomplish, was faithfully done; but the difficulty lay
too deep for remedy. No skill could have averted or
delayed the catastrophe.

When the news of Mr. Irving's death was announced, the next morning, in his native city, the flags
on the shipping and the public buildings were instantly
hung at half mast; and the various public bodies
which had a session during the day, made allusion to
the event. The Common Council, also, at the instigation of the Mayor, passed resolutions to testify its
respect to his memory.

It is a remarkable incident in the obsequies of a
private individual, that the various courts of the city
adjourned on the day of the funeral, to afford opportunity to those who wished to attend it; and during the
hour when the last services were performing, miles distant, in the little rural church in which he had wor-
shipped, the bells of his native city were tolling a
mournful and responsive peal. On that day, also, the
shops and places of business of the village through
which the procession was to pass were closed. The
railroad depot at which passengers were to alight from
New York, the hotel, the public buildings, and many
of the private residences in the principal streets, were
draped in black, and mourning festoons were hung
across the road.

It was on the 1st of December that the mortal
remains of Washington Irving were conveyed to their

last resting place; but no breath of winter chilled the air. The Indian summer, which this season had lingered into the very winter, shed its soft and melancholy beauty over the scene, and nothing could have been more exquisite than the day, or more in keeping with the sad occasion. "It is one of his own days," was the remark of many present.

The carriages, with the officiating clergymen, his physician, the relatives of the deceased, and the pall-bearers, moved from Sunnyside at half past twelve o'clock. At the head of the lane which forms the entrance to the place, a long line of carriages, containing the residents of the immediate neighborhood, joined the procession. Upon its arrival at Christ Church, Tarrytown, where the services were to be held, it was met by a large concourse of the inhabitants of the neighboring country, and an array of men eminent in the various walks of literature and commerce, who had assembled from New York and other cities to pay the last tribute of respect to the honored dead.

At half past one, the clergy present entered the chancel, led by Bishop Potter. They were the Rev. Dr. Vinton, of St. Paul's, New York, Rev. Dr. Taylor, of Grace Church, Rev. Mr. Meade, Rev. Mr. Farmington, of Trinity, Rev. Dr. Morgan, of St. Thomas's, Rev. Dr. McVickar, Rev. Mr. Babbitt, and Rev. Mr. Moore. At the door of the church, the coffin was met by the rector, Rev. Dr. Creighton (pastor and friend of the deceased), and Rev. Mr. Spencer, his assistant, who preceded it up the aisle, the rector reading the opening sentences of the Episcopal burial service. The coffin was placed in front of the altar, when the choir joined in the solemn and beautiful anthem, "Lord, let me know my end."

When the impressive services were concluded, Dr. Creighton announced that, as had been requested, the lid of the coffin would be opened, to enable all who were so disposed to take a last look of the face of the deceased. Nearly a thousand persons, it is stated, who had been unable to gain entrance to the church, availed themselves of this mournful privilege, and passed in silent procession by the remains. The coffin was then returned to the hearse, and the procession of carriages, computed at one hundred and fifty, formed anew, and accompanied by a large concourse of pedestrians, proceeded to the cemetery. It was situated about a mile north of the church, on a beautiful hill, commanding on one side a noble view of the Hudson, and on the other a portion of the Sleepy Hollow valley. The route passed by the monument erected to the captors of Major André on the spot where he was taken, and across the bridge immortalized in the Legend of Sleepy Hollow, which was hung with emblems of mourning.

On reaching the place of interment, Dr. Creighton, according to the beautiful and impressive service of the Episcopal Church, consigned the body to the grave : " Earth to earth, ashes to ashes, dust to dust."

As he was laid down to take his last sleep among the scenes he had loved and celebrated, and by the side of his mother, as he had himself desired, the sun was declining ; and soon another gorgeous sunset, such as brightened his last evening in life, again lighted up the western sky. It was a glorious scene ; and few of the sad-hearted mourners who had stood around the grave, failed to associate that day's decline with the close of that pure and beautiful life.

My task is finished. I have traced the career of the author from its commencement to its close, as far as possible, through his own letters and words ; and if the reader has not imbibed a correct idea of his personal and literary character in this way, it would be idle to attempt a more formal delineation of his virtues as a man, or his genius as a writer.

I close with an extract from a beautiful and truthful portrait of him by a young author, which appeared among numerous other tributes after his decease. It is from the pen of George William Curtis :

With Irving, the man and the author were one. The same twinkling humor, untouched by personal venom ; the same sweetness, geniality, and grace ; * * * which endeared the writer to his readers, endeared the man to his

friends. Gifted with a happy temperament, with that cheerful balance of thought and feeling which begets the sympathy
which prevents bitter animosity, he lived through the sharpest
struggles of our politics, not without interest, but without bitterness, and with the tenderest respect of every party.

His tastes and talents and habits were all those of the literary man.   *   *   *   And it was given to him first of our
authors to invest the American landscape with the charm of
imagination and tradition.

*   *   *   *   *   *

When his death was known, there was no class of men
who more sincerely deplored him than those of his own voca-
tion.   The older authors felt that a friend, not a rival—the
younger, that a father had gone.   There is not a young literary
aspirant in the country, who, if he ever personally met Irving,
did not hear from him the kindest words of sympathy, regard,
and encouragement.   There is none of the older rank who,
knowing him, did not love him.   He belonged to no clique, no
party in his own profession, more than in any other of the
great interests of life; and that not by any wilful independence, or neutrality armed against all comers, but by the natural catholicity of his nature.

On the day of his burial, unable to reach Tarrytown in
time for the funeral, I came down the shore of the river he
loved.   As we darted and wound along, the Catskills were
draped in sober gray mist, not hiding them, but wreathing, and
folding, and lingering, as if the hills were hung with sympathetic, but not unrelieved gloom.   Yet far away toward the
south, the bank on which his home lay, was Sunnyside still, for
the sky was cloudless, and soft with serene sunshine.   I could

not but remember his last words to me, more than a year ago, when his book was finished, and his health was failing : "I am getting ready to go; I am shutting up my doors and windows." And I could not but feel that they were all open now, and bright with the light of eternal morning.

THE END.

APPENDIX.

APPENDIX.

(A.)—INTERPOLATED MATTER,

Referred to at Pages 213, 215, 220.

[The two chapters which follow, making seventy-nine pages, were inserted by the London publisher in my unfinished work at the close of the third volume, without my knowledge or supervision; a proceeding, I imagine, without precedent in the annals of literature. As I have been obliged to allude to the circumstance in the text, and as some of the English periodicals have also drawn attention to this " double editing," I place the whole before the American reader, not as a matter of choice, but of necessity.]

CHAPTER XXIII.

WASHINGTON IRVING—HIS INTRODUCTION TO THE FAMILY OF FOSTER, AND ITS HISTORY—THE LETTER—SECOND ATTACHMENT, AND "EMILY"—HER MAJESTY THE QUEEN OF SAXONY AND THE HALF CROWN—WASHINGTON IRVING AND THE METHODISTS ON THE HUDSON—ROYAL VISITORS AND GENERAL CANIKOF —THE POLES, ITALIANS, AND THE SPY—MR. IRVING RELATES ANECDOTES, AND RECALLS EVENTS AND FEELINGS OF HIS EARLY LIFE—ENGLISH ECCEN- TRICITIES AND IRVING'S ANGER—CANNON BALLS, AND THE HERO'S LEG—HIS- TORY OF HIS FIRST LOVE BROUGHT TO US AND RETURNED—IRVING'S SECOND ATTACHMENT—THE LITTLE PICTURE AND THE CONFIDANTE — DEPARTURE— LEIPZIG AND PONIATOWSKI—THE HARTZ AND THE AHNFRAU—DIE AHNFRAU —WASHINGTON IRVING, HIS RAMBLE AND HIS ROBBERS — HANOVER AND HESSE CASSEL.

[IN a letter of Washington Irving (who had recently re-visited England on public business) to Mrs. Dawson, in Febru-ary, 1846, he recalls his "delightful recollection of past times," of "moving accidents by flood and field," in the society of the family of the Fosters; and intimates his intention of paying her a visit as soon as he shall be able. He gives her an account of his mode of life in America, of his happy home at his lovely cottage at Sunnyside, and, after relating, as he says they do in story books, his own history, begs that she will give him hers in return. The letters and anecdotes of Washington Irving have been derived from Mrs. Dawson (Flora Foster) and Mrs. Fuller (Emily Foster), for the latter of whom this gifted writer entertained so warm an attachment. The reader will find evidence of this friendship in the second volume of this work.—E. P.*]

Our introduction (says Mrs. Dawson) to Washington Irving, at Dresden, was fraught with a peculiar interest to him from circumstances I will narrate hereafter. His mind was full of kindly sentiments toward us, long before he had seen us. The introduction itself was simple enough, and in the usual routine. Our opera box, engaged for the season, was the resort generally of our friends. *There* has been spent many a pleasant half hour with some, then young and happy as ourselves, who have since been distinguished in the world's history —young diplomats, now grown into powerful plenipotentiaries, who make treaties (and perhaps break them)—young English officers, whose names, as leaders of our splendid army in some of its most splendid achievements, have since "been famous in story." Whatever of beauty, or fashion, or wit, or rank, was assembled in Dresden, that classic little capital (the so-called Florence of Germany), found its way, sooner or later, into our roomy and comfortable opera box, to talk over the last Court ball, the last new work, or the enchanting music; for the old

---

* These original letters and anecdotes were received too late to be incorporated in their proper place in this work, but have been considered too interesting to be omitted. There has not been time to communicate with Mr. Pierre Irving, that he might insert them.—E. P.

King, who constantly attended the representations at the opera, made it almost an object for his council of state, that the most perfect singers should be secured both for the opera and his Chapelle Royale.

It was no matter of surprise to us, therefore, that Washington Irving should be brought to be presented to us between the acts of "La Gazza Ladra;" but it was a great matter of surprise to his friends, to see the sparkling eye and animated look with which Washington Irving addressed himself to his new acquaintances. It was not his wont to seek new friends, but rather to retire within himself the moment any new face presented itself; and yet here he had eagerly sought the introduction, and quietly remained at his post the rest of the evening, making rapid progress in our good graces, and enjoying, evidently, his seat beside us.

The circumstances which had thus attracted him toward us were certainly rather curious, but to some persons they would have been comparatively unimportant. On him the effect was different, and the seeds were thus first sown of a friendship that was to last for life.

It appears that, some time previously, my mother had written to her eldest daughter, in England, a full and affectionate letter. In it, as was her custom, she enlarged on the works she was then reading. These works happened to be Mr. Irving's. With all the warmth and enthusiasm of her nature she had commented on, and commended them, and finished her letter by transcribing a favorite passage from the "Sketch Book," at the bottom of which she wrote the author's name in full—*Washington Irving*—not leaving room for her own signature. This letter miscarried, and the police opened it. They found no name but Washington Irving's, and not pushing their inquiries farther, or not understanding English—if they did, they took this name as clear testimony that he was the writer of the letter—and knowing his whereabouts, returned it to him, as they supposed, in the usual course of business. Be it borne in mind, that this was not one of those tiny missives, on a glossy and scented page of "Queen's Size Ivory—Best," but an old-fashioned sheet of the largest dimensions, filled from end to end, every fold and corner written over, and every end and corner perused by his curious eye—feeling himself fully justified in doing what the police *ought* to have done before,.to find out some clue to the real owner, to whom he might restore it. He told us, afterward, that no praise had ever seemed to him so sweet, so genuine, as what he so unexpectedly found in those lines.

It should be perhaps remembered, that he was particularly sensitive to praise—not from vanity, but *modesty;* that is to say, he constantly needed the encouragement it afforded him, to keep his courage up to the proper height, or else he had not spirits to write.

Besides that, the letter, in its. affectionate details, was exactly "after his own heart;" and, as he himself expressed it, "this little peep behind the curtain at the domestic habits and feelings and events of our family circle, pleased and interested him beyond measure, and chimed in with his own tastes, occupations, and pursuits."

He had, at the time he received it (being in Vienna), little thought of meeting the writer, who evidently wrote from Dresden; but being arrived there, and becoming intimate with a cousin of ours, he soon put two and two together, sought an introduction, realized his suspicions, and eventually brought the letter, which we reread together with much amusement, and finally forwarded it to its original destination, with a few lines from Irving himself, adding the account of the new and charming friendship which that letter had originated, if not cemented.

To return to our opera box. Here a friendly footing was at once established by himself; for, only awaiting a moment when the box was rather clear of visitors, Mr. Irving, turning to my mother, with a bright smile, inquired :

"Have you lately heard from Miss Margaret ? "

Now was our turn to be puzzled ; for this was one of my sisters, far away, who had remained in England with my father in rather delicate health, and quite unknown to any present.

A rapid questioning on both sides followed. " Mr. Foster" (my father) "liked his journey to the north, I hope ? " continued Mr. Irving.

My mother looked more amazed. " And," continued Mr. Irving, with evident enjoyment, " and I hope poor Bessie " (my sister's favorite horse) " is better ? "

My mother broke in : " How did you know ?—how could you tell——"

" Ah," said Mr. Irving, " there's the mystery ! "

He then entered into the little detail which has been given in his letter, and here we were at once established friends.

SECOND ATTACHMENT, AND " EMILY."

Yes; and we *were* at once established friends. Here began that almost daily " intercourse with our family, which he remembered with lasting interest." * Our house did indeed become his home. His own letters bear witness to the intense pleasure with which he recalled " the many evenings of home-felt enjoyment I have passed among you. They are the sweetest moments I have passed in Dresden. I would not give one such evening, spent in varied, animated, intelligent, but unforced and unostentatious conversation, with now and then, but too rarely, a song, and now and then a recollection from some favorite author, or a choice morsel from a scrap book, given with beaming looks and beaming eyes—I would not give one such evening for all the routs and assemblies of the fashionable world."

Indeed, from the hour of that first introduction, few days passed that we were not together.

It requires not, surely, a very acute observer to detect, that not only the truest friendship united him to our family, but that a warmer and tenderer interest gradually sprang up.

* See " Life," Vol. II, chap. **xxxix.**

His first attachment was known to us, in all the details that since have been given to the world. An eminent writer has stated "it was his only love," but this is an error. The author of his "Life and Letters" makes no direct mention of it, possibly because the object of this second attachment still lives, and has herself thrown a veil over those *warmer* sentiments on the part of Mr. Irving which she appreciated but could not return. But as his first attachment has been given to the world, it seems but fair that those who wish to study the character of one of the most amiable of men, as well as one of the most celebrated of our writers, should not be misled by the idea that he passed in cold, bachelor serenity through the years of his prime. This idea seems incongruous with the character and disposition of Washington Irving, so eminently endowed with the perception of all that is lovable and attractive, and so formed to enjoy domestic life, of which he is the great painter.

Though locking in his heart the sacred relics of his young affection, and treasuring the sweet memory of that lovely girl who had been his first love, there was still a throbbing for domestic bliss. He himself recognized this in the letter to which I have referred. "I have strong domestic feelings and inclinations, and feel sometimes quite dreary and desolate when they get uppermost."

He was then in the pride and vigor of manhood, his whole soul full of the softest and most tender sensations; beyond description, tremblingly alive to the beauty of everything in nature, animate and inanimate. I have seen him watching the turning of a leaf to catch the sunshine glistening on its surface. With faith in all that was good, and enthusiasm for all that was lovely, how could he be, daily, by the side of a fair young girl, whose very name seemed music to his ear (see his letter), and which he only permitted himself to write, with this gentle excuse: "Emily—I hope she will excuse my apparent familiarity in using her beautiful name, instead of the more formal one of Miss Foster"—whose voice he longs to hear—"I would have given anything to have heard her in her own delightful way," &c.

"Emily," to whom he wrote those lovely verses, the only ones which appear in his "Life," and in which he describes her so exquisitely—could he be thus constantly with one so esteemed, so admired; sharing every taste, impression, and pursuit; meeting in gay and courtly halls, or by the quiet hearth; wandering among delicious groves, "when all things bloomed in lovely May," whiling away hours in "converse sweet," or watching the stars from the little balcony that overhung our garden, and listening to the rippling of its fountains——

This was the life he led for weeks—for months. His was not a nature to remain cold and insensible, to shut itself up in bachelor security. A thousand long-dormant hopes and visions arose. Every hope was not, could not be, buried in the tomb. His very love for Matilda H——, related with trembling and subdued voice in the dark shadows of twilight, and reawakening with all its force the visions of domestic bliss, all stirred within him hopes and aspirations which were—never to be realized!

Enough of this at present. I will recur to it at some future page.

HER MAJESTY THE QUEEN OF SAXONY AND THE HALF CROWN.

December 23*d*, 1822.—Mr. Irving came in with Barham Surás, to talk about plays, but soon got on the subject of his yesterday's adventures at the Schloss, where he had been presented to the old King by the English Minister, and been very well received. We compared notes about our presentations at this curious old Court. He was very much amused to hear that my mother, the evening she was presented, was invited, as the highest honor that could be shown her, to sit down to cards with the old King, the Queen, and Prince Antoine, to play whist for *half a crown* the rubber. Now, the flowered robe and velvet train of Mrs. Foster, rich as they were in ornament, had (forgive the confession, you matronly housekeepers!) *no* pockets. Money had not been provided, or thought of, in the evening's toilette! And my mother found herself indebted to the Queen of Saxony to the extent of two whole shillings and a sixpence.

Terrible dilemma! What was to be done? A whisper to the gilded chamberlain behind her chair brought no relief; he was in a similar predicament, and could offer her no silver, or gold either, but his golden key, insignia of his office!

The good old King read some hidden trouble in my mother's eye, and suggested payment in the morning. The hint was taken, and, accordingly, our trusty Gottlieb, the head servant in our household, with the due sum in silver, wrapped in silver paper and scented envelope, was safely delivered to her Majesty, who caused the messenger to be detained till her Majesty's commands were committed to writing by the lord in waiting, to my mother—pressing commands for Mrs. Foster's acceptance of an invitation to a state dinner to be given the next day. Mr. Irving relished this half-crown business exceedingly, as a sample of the curious mixture of simplicity with stately etiquette at this Court.

MR. IRVING AND THE METHODISTS ON THE HUDSON.

February 13th, 1823.—Mr. Irving came home with us after the opera, which is always over early, and stayed a long while talking as usual, before he wished "good night." He was exceedingly entertaining, and gave us a vivid description of the gatherings of the Methodists in America, which occur from time to time, and at one of which he was present. "These gatherings were generally on a spot particularly well suited to the occasion. Mr. Irving described it as a promontory or peninsula which spread itself out in an expansion of the Hudson, carpeted with verdure, and shaded by groves of splendid trees, while the whole is backed by mountain scenery of great beauty. Here thousands of persons are assembled from different parts of America, and remain encamped for three or four days."

As Mr. Irving approached the place, he said he saw "innumerable rows of carriages, wagons, &c., standing round; and the sound of female voices, singing in chorus, struck most pleasantly on his ear. Persons of this sect pay particular attention to their vocal music; and the psalms thus chanted in the open air, by voices of great power and sweetness, had a solemn and a thrilling effect. Some favorite preachers were surrounded by immense congregations, while others drew a smaller number of hearers round them; but many of them would suddenly stop, and launch into severe anathemas against any unfortunate strangers whose more elegant dress would show them to be mere spectators of the scene. In other parts of the grove, processions would be seen moving slowly and solemnly along—elders of the tribes leading their flocks to this holy place of meeting, and occasionally halting to offer up a short but fervent prayer. But the whole has such a striking effect, that many persons are converted at the moment—or fancy themselves so. The black population throng to these places as much as the white; and young girls would fall down senseless, and lay so for some time; for," says Mr. Irving, "it requires a great struggle to send the devil out of a negro; but when they are once turned Methodists, they are the most sturdy in their doctrine."

Irving said, "that he passed a group of negroes, an old white-headed man, and several old black women standing by him, who looked upon *him* with great contempt. The old man, casting a look over his shoulder, ejaculated: 'Ay' (here mentioning the name of our holy Saviour), 'ay, *He will carry the day!*' as if he were speaking of an election; and then added: 'If God Almighty were not too strong for the devil' (here another fierce and sidelong look at Mr. Irving), 'there would be no living in the 'arth!' We hope his faith was greater than his charity, and wished him an increase of the latter article."

The conversation then leading to religious topics, he read us some passages from the Prayer Book of the Church of England, commenting on its excellence. He read the collect for Advent Sunday, a favorite one with him, expatiating on the beauty of the language. Our house, he said, now seems to him *his home.* But let only one of the many visitors who frequent our house come in, he immediately buttons himself up, retires to *his recess,* sheltered by curtains and book stands, and there stays, silent and uninterested, till we are again alone, when his animation returns, his countenance, pale and languid, lights up, and he becomes again the most lively and interesting companion. He often asks us to give him subjects for a poem. This evening he was describing to us the *storms in America :* we gave him this as a subject for his verses. The poem was never made ; or, if made, did not satisfy his fastidious taste, and found its way into the fire, with many other similar attempts, which he destroyed in a similar manner. It would have been his pleasure to have written much more for himself, and less for the public ; as he says in one of his letters : " Could I afford it, I should like to write, and lay my writings aside when finished. There is an independent delight in study, and in the creative exercise of the pen." And yet, at this time, his pen was almost idle. The poem which was to describe storms in America never appeared. We little dreamed, at that time, that experience would show us, soon after, as we travelled toward the haunted mountain of the Hartz, a storm, which Irving himself, bewildered and terrified by its effects on our small party, owned was equal in grandeur, and also in its awful ravages, to those of his own country.

ROYAL VISITORS AND GENERAL CANIKOF.

February, 1823.—Mr. Irving was describing with admirable humor, to the three philosophers, the scene at General Canikof's last night.

The old General (he is Russian Minister here) has often been taxed by the young ladies in Dresden with want of gallantry, in not giving a ball. "Yet," said Mr. Irving, "the old General adores the young ladies; and lately, at a *bal masqué*, came out with silver wings, and blue-and-silver tunic, in the character of 'Papillon.'" The old General had the reputation of being *tant soit peu avare;* but let that pass. The visit of the two young princes of Prussia to the court of Dresden, formed an admirable pretext. Society called on the General for a ball, and the General determined to do the thing well. His magnificent saloons were thrown open. A gorgeous scene presented itself. Nobles in all the gay uniforms of foreign courts, and the princes of our own; Prince Frederic, with his pale and intelligent countenance, the heir of the throne, though destined to enjoy it but a brief period—his reign and his life subsequently being cut short by a melancholy accident, which plunged his country into tears and mourning; Prince John, the youngest and perhaps the handsomest of his family; the present sovereign, then a young and happy bridegroom, whose nuptials with the lovely Princess Amelia of Bavaria had so recently been celebrated; and last, though not least, *the* visitors of the day, the two princes of Prussia.

Irving and we tried to make out the future politicians in the gay young princes, whose whole being, soul and body, seemed absorbed in the ins and outs of the dance. One of these young men is now the King of Prussia. Their father never visited the Saxon Court since the events well known to historians, which he felt must have made his presence so obnoxious in this country; but the young men came, and a right courtly welcome they had, and right well did they appear to enjoy it.

Well, as Mr. Irving rightly described it, gay and magnificent indeed were the state reception rooms of the old General. Sea-green satin, of the richest material and most tender hue, formed the curtains, the draped recesses, and, above all, covered the large centre ottomans, on which had, as yet, only reposed ladies of high rank and magnates of the land, on rare and state occasions. We have already stated, that the worthy old General was, to speak in the mildest form, a *little* particular. With what horror, then, did he gaze around him, as he beheld advancing the animated procession of the *Grandpère* (the concluding dance of the evening), headed by the young Prince of Prussia, the present much-canvassed king of that country, leading the van, hand in hand with the lovely Countess Palfy, and followed by an emulous train of dancers of courtly rank. When he beheld the Prince of Prussia and his partner, after threading, at a flying pace, room after room of his suite of apartments, and in the fashion of the dance, a sort of "Sir Roger de Coverley," enacting a follow-my-leader chase between chairs stiff with gold, and buhl tables loaded with exquisite china; finally, by a fresh whim of the young prince, return to the grand saloon, and trip their way across the whole extent on to the wide and massive chimney place beyond—this was cruel enough; but when, with a slip and a bound, prince, and count, and lady fair, following their joyous leaders, sprang on the devoted ottoman, and traversed its full length of sea-green cushions with their many "trampling feet," poor Canikof looked, and shook, and trembled, and almost cried!

Irving laughed tears as he remembered his dismay, and, with his constitutional humor, described to us, as he imagined it, the scene of the following morning: the old General, his shambling figure, and small, wizened face, bowed down with anxious scrutiny over his beloved and desecrated ottoman, counting the footprints left on its glossy surface—the footprints of future monarchs, it is true; that was some consolation to the sorrowing diplomatist. Perhaps, among all the troubles his faithful but independent subjects cause him, his present Majesty of Prussia, then the gayest of the youthful band of princes present that evening at this eventful ball, and leader of the inroad of that gay train over and among the old General's sea-green satins, and over his hitherto immaculate ottoman, if his thoughts ever wander back so far, would still find a smile for the memory of that youthful folly. May all his follies prove as innocent!

THE POLES, ITALIANS, AND THE SPY.

There are few musical amateurs of some few years' standing, who were not familiar with a beautiful melody known by the name of "Oginski's Polonaise." It was full of tender and melancholy symphonies. The composer was a Russian Pole—oh, conjunction hateful to the Polish ear! It excited unusual interest in English circles, as coming accompanied with the story—a true one—that it was composed by him a few hours before his anticipated death; as tyranny and persecution had driven him to the determination to put a period to his life with his own hands, at the early age of twenty-four. Indeed, he shortly afterward shot himself with a pistol he had loaded for the purpose, and was found bathed in his blood, and supposed to be dead; but the wound was not mortal. Under the care of his friends, and his medical adviser, he recovered eventually, and we were this evening introduced to a noble-looking veteran, with gray hair floating round a countenance of great vigor and intelligence: this was Oginski. Mr. Irving, whose dislike to strangers does not include the Poles (*happily* for our house, the home of an *English* family is the only place where they feel they can speak with freedom of their friends, and of that country so dear to their hearts)—Mr. Irving, I was saying, entered gladly into conversation with him, especially when he, too, found this was Oginski, the author of the celebrated "Polonaise," whose touching notes had often brought tears into the eyes of many a romantic young maiden, as she hung over her pianoforte, and wept his untimely death.

His career was not, however, yet over, and his age was yet to afford fresh matter for tears to the sentimental, and for deep, brooding vengeance to his countrymen and countrywomen. He was arrested for some light words spoken against the Russian Government in a private *salon*. Yet how shall we explain it to English ears? In this polished and refined *société*—this brotherhood, as Mr. Irving termed it—there was always *one* well-known individual, an *attaché*—no, a hanger-on of

those imperial governments who thought fit to attach such a
blot on the blazonry of their splendid escutcheon : in every
circle, however intimate, in every clique, in every coterie, was
placed, by one of these imperial governments, *a spy*. No matter that a titled name, an elegant exterior, clothed *the thing ;*
it existed, *it* moved softly on silken carpets, *it* smiled blandly
and complacently at the passing joke, the little *jeu d'esprit* that
whiled away an hour.   The modest rhymes of the *bouts rimés*,
that favorite resource of lively and witty brains, were not too
insignificant for *its* searching eye ; *its* ear caught every obser-
vation, nay, every intonation, and Government measures of the
most stringent nature were suddenly taken against individuals
who were utterly unconscious of offence, and who had no wish
to break any laws, human or divine.   Some such fate overtook
Oginski, if we are rightly informed ; and the cruelty of Russian laws made wretched and miserable the remnant of this old
man's life, who had been saved almost by a miracle from the
suicidal act of his own hand, forty years before.   To the shame
of that Government be it spoken, that not only was he sen-
tenced to be transferred to Siberia, but mutilation of that noble
countenance was resorted to, to add to the sufferings of an old
man of sixty-four.

Several other similar instances fell under our immediate
knowledge, and our personal friends were victims of a tyranny
comprehensive and malicious beyond the imagination of an
Englishman.

A friend of ours, of a noble Venetian family, a Count
C—— (but even yet the name of one against whom the Aus-
trian Government has put its mark must not be given at length
till that unhappy country be free)—well, a Count C—— was
anxious to return for a few months to Venice, to see his father,
who was ill, and even, as he feared, dying. His father had
published a work on the arts, of great celebrity, splendidly
illustrated, many of the drawings being by his son (our friend),
who, like his father, though he entertained liberal sentiments,
was totally devoid of political intrigue, and only desirous of

spending his life in studying the arts, and in peaceful enjoyment of the society of affectionate and intellectual friends.

The intended journey was named but to a few, considered safe and true friends, and only a brief interval was to elapse before he started; but, brief as it was, it was long enough for the spy to inform his Government, and a mandate was on its way forbidding him to leave Dresden under any pretext whatever. But where spies are, there are counter spies, and a friendly hint reached Count C——. A few hours remained before the mandate could arrive. These were well employed; and the Venetian, at the instigation of friends more deeply versed in political resources than himself, provided himself instantly with a permit from the Pope's Nuncio, superseding all other hindrances, started off at once, and succeeded thus in eluding all the traps and snares with which he was to be encompassed, and reached his sea-girt home in time to receive the last blessing and the last breath of his father; after which he returned among us. No words can paint the rage of the disappointed officials, who had wished to punish both father and son by a separation as cruel as it was unnecessary.

MR. IRVING RELATES ANECDOTES, AND RECALLS EVENTS AND FEELINGS OF HIS EARLY LIFE.

The following remarks, put down at the time, are interesting, as being word for word what Irving said:

Mr. Irving came to us early, and brought letters of Moore's and Walter Scott, to himself, which interested us. He spoke of his favorite authors; *most warmly* of Goldsmith's "Citizen of the World." "Poor Goldsmith!" added Mr. Irving. "Johnson himself knew and fully appreciated his talents; but the satellites that crowded round that pompous star, looked down upon poor Goldsmith, who certainly was very inferior in conversation; for it was his foible to wish to excel in everything, and, by trying to imitate Johnson's way of talking, he got now and then quite out of his depth. So far went his folly, that he was quite chagrined at a man's excelling him even in *tumbling*. He went once to Holland to teach English, forgetting it was necessary to know Dutch; and walked over France with a flute, which he played abominably."

Irving then described Moore's manner of composing his poems. He said: " Moore will walk up and down his garden backward and forward for hours, conning over one small verse, polishing it, turning it about, substituting one word for another, working at it with indescribable patience and perseverance, till he had worked it up to the exact point at which *he was satisfied;* then he thought he had accomplished enough for the day, and came in cheerful, contented, and thoroughly disposed to enjoy himself."

Irving spoke of his own childhood. He said he was considered *slow* at school, but that, if he could get away *with a book*, he was happy, particularly if it were voyages and travels. He would sit down with it on the roadside, or resort to a little country inn, where the old landlord, a simple-hearted man, would sit down beside him, and to him he would read aloud for hours.

He told us he was for some time Military Secretary to the Governor of New York. Many excursions had he to make in the country. The recollection of one of these seemed particularly pleasant to him, where he inhabited, with his brother, a little inn on the banks of the Lake Ontario, busily engaged in reading novels; and afterward, having to embark in a sloop on the lake, they lost patience at not making way. They landed in a boat to try and get forward in wagons, but could not push forward, and were obliged to make the best of their way back to the sloop, to be well laughed at by the companions they had left. The joke against them was particularly enjoyed by one of the party, a small but robust man, who appeared something of a wag, and had kept them alive by his good humor and his jollity.

It was only on their arrival at their destination that it transpired among a few of the party, that their jolly friend was a Catholic priest, going on a mission to the interior; but the good man, in the slyness or simplicity of his heart, had thought best to keep this little fact back, and thereby joined without scandal in much of *the merriment* of the party; indeed, might be said to have been the great promoter of it. He told us many more anecdotes of his childhood and his youth.

Irving is an admirable *relater*. His countenance varies with his mood. His smile is one of the sweetest I know; but he can look very, very sad. He looks sometimes so lively, one would think he had never had a melancholy moment; at other times so *abattu*, that he might never have had a gay one. He judges *himself* with the utmost severity, feeling a deep depression at what he fancies are his shortcomings, while he kindles into enthusiasm at what is kind or generous in those he loves: withal, when not oppressed with morbid feelings, he rouses himself with a happy facility, a genial glow lights his eye and colors his cheek, and his conversation soon sparkles again with wit and humor. Some persons, in looking upon life, view it as they would view a picture, with a stern and criticizing eye. He also looks on life as a picture, but to catch *its beauties, its lights*—*not* its defects and its shadows. On the former he loves to dwell. He has a wonderful knack at shutting his eye to the sinister side of anything. Never beat a more kindly heart than his—alive to the sorrows, but not to the faults of his friends, but doubly alive to their virtues and their goodness. Indeed, people seemed to grow more good with one so unselfish and so gentle.

Once only do I remember seeing him thoroughly worried into anger, positive anger; and it sat so ill upon him, he could not make it out. We could not, at first; and yet it was down-right disgust and indignation.

Perhaps the cause may not seem to justify it, in an American, but still I will relate it. At least, it will testify how thoroughly, after his own country, his sympathies were with the English; how he identified himself with them—with their glory, their fame—and shrank, like a true son of the English race, from anything that could throw discredit on the name of

Englishman. To explain these remarks, I refer to the following anecdote:

ENGLISH ECCENTRICITIES AND IRVING'S ANGER.

There was a curious passion among the English travellers of the male sex at that time. It was their delight to indulge in what they called "humbugging the natives." It will hardly be believed to what singular excesses it drove them; and Mr. Irving's patience was sorely tried, even to breaking down, at what he saw.

Some noble youths—or who *should*, at least, have been noble, by their birthright—some officers of our army (who had not all youth for their excuse, since one among them had attained the rank of major)—men of fashion, evinced their ingenuity, if not their taste, in a variety of attempts on the patience and endurance of the good old King himself. Did I not record facts well known to all the society, namely, all the *corps diplomatique* and *élite* of Dresden, it might not be believed that these young men stationed themselves first in the King's box, at the opera, prior to his arrival, lounging about in every attitude that suited them best; that it was some time before they were prevailed upon to withdraw by the most polite but urgent representation of the officials, and not till Mr. Irving had himself stepped from our box, where he could see the whole proceeding, and added a stringent recommendation to the same effect. But even then they only removed to a short distance, stationing themselves in the passage, where they greedily seized, from the hands of the petrified pages, successive glasses of ices and refreshments, which it was the custom to carry, between the acts of the performances, into the royal box, for his Majesty the old King, or such members of his family as might be present.

This was only one instance out of many in which their zeal to display their own and their country's independence demonstrated itself, to the shame and annoyance of other less ambitious members of the English society then at Dresden. I need only mention one more instance, in which their active endeavors to surprise and upset the nerves of his Majesty were decidedly successful.

Whether from the particular respect in which he was held from his station, his mild and benevolent character, or whether from knowledge of his only weakness—an amazing reverence for the courtly etiquettes of his race—they seemed to take especial pride in making him their butt. Being attacked on all hands for not having, in their late exploit, shown him sufficient "honor," either as a king or a gentleman, they declared, "Well, we will honor him with a vengeance." This was supposed to be an empty boast. But a few days afterward, the King retired to his country palace, where the windows of his bedroom opened toward the river, behind the old-fashioned carvings of which his Majesty often remained seated, viewing the tranquil river below, and solacing his mind from the fatigues of ruling his little kingdom—be it noticed, *en passant,* one of the best ruled and happiest kingdoms in Germany. An early riser, he also retired early to rest. By eleven o'clock the palace was still. Silence reigned around; and particular care was taken never, if possible, to disturb the slumbers of the monarch. Eleven o'clock, then, was tolled out by the huge old bell of the palace. The king slept—all slept, or appeared to do so. The very river seemed to sleep, as it glided on noiselessly under the silvery moonshine which reposed upon its surface; when, suddenly, a loud and unearthly sound was heard— the clash of cymbals, the trumpet's bray, the roll of drums, mixed with wild voices in uproarious merriment. Such a clamor had never awoke the echoes of the dark woods. It woke more than the echoes of the dark woods—it woke the old King, *as was intended,* in terrible alarm, from his first slumber. A rush was made by all the inmates of the palace to the windows, but nothing could be seen; nothing but the ruffled track that a boat leaves upon the water, and, far away, a dark speck which some pronounced to be the boat that had floated there, close under the royal windows. Some whispered it was a horrid water demon! Who manned the boat, who plied the swift oars, who made the unearthly and unseemly clamor to startle and affright the sleeping King, might have remained a mystery, had not the perpetrators enjoyed too much their joke and their triumph.

Need I say this was a little *passe temps* of the young Englishmen of fashion I have already spoken of? But the joke and the triumph did not last long. The old King, whose "nerves had been upset," was seriously indisposed, some said in consequence of this "serenade." All the society was in arms against our countrymen. Irving cut every one of them dead wherever he met them, and they thought proper to retire before the storm. They fixed a day for their departure, ordered post horses to their large landau, in which they contemplated moving off all together to some other city; asked for their bill, in which the landlord included a pretty heavy sum for a door they had completely riddled, having made it a mark for some airguns they had been experimenting upon. This charge for the door they pronounced excessive—as much, indeed, as for a new door. The landlord vowed he must have a new door. "Well, then, we will have the old one," they exclaimed; "we pay for it;" and, dislocating the door from its hinges, they mounted it on the top of their landau, and then drove away from Dresden, where, if it was any satisfaction to them, their feats were long the theme of comment and conversation.

We need not say whether the remarks were flattering; but certainly, if they had not succeeded in "humbugging," they *did* succeed in *astonishing the natives*. All this was a source of great annoyance to Mr. Irving, who, as I have said, identified himself so much with the English, and was extremely sensitive on the subject. Far from joining in the French view of the subject of the battle of Waterloo, he entered most warmly into the different accounts, then the subject of much conversation, so many military men being at Dresden. As we were young girls, not nineteen, and not much versed in military tactics, a little ignorance in the arrangements of that day may be forgiven us.   Washington Irving enlightened us, and gave us, in his vivid and picturesque manner, a history of that battle. He might have stood in the serried ranks of the squares, or joined in the triumphant charge of the Guards; and, as usual, he had thrilling incidents to tell, not found in general records.*

"One officer told me," said Irving, " that he had been riding with several others, and particularly one very fine young man, who turned round, smiling, and then saying, ' What a hit I had there ! ' supposing a ball had merely grazed him; but, in a moment or two, he turned pale, and fell from his horse.   The ball had passed through his body, and in ten minutes he died."

Speaking of the love of country, Irving referred to the different amount of love of country manifested by moun-taineers, or the dwellers upon plains and flat lands.   He gave, as a reason, that the features of one were strongly marked, and easily impressed themselves on the memory; while the outlines of a plain life, an unmeaning face, were hard to remember; the strong-marked features take one, as it were, by the nose.

He brought us his scrap book to write in, while he copied out, also, many favorite pieces into ours.   I wrote for him, at his request, " O Primavera," and Wallenstein's touching ejacu-lation :

> " Könnt ich dem Augenblicke sagen
> O Bleibe doch, du bist so schön," &c.

Evening after evening is spent in happy converse.   Why is it that, at times, a deep shade gathers on his brow?   Yes-terday, a large party were here—De Rumignys, the French Minister, the young Countess Loos and her *fiancé* Baron Kleist, the favorite of the King of Prussia, Prince Schomburg, Campusano, the Spanish Minister, pretty Madame De Bergh, the wife of the Danish Minister, who cannot be presented at Court for some court punctilio, but consoles herself with sing-ing the sweetest of Danish melodies and Swedish songs; in short, all good, kind-hearted people Irving has learned to like,

* For general account, see " Journal of Flora Foster," Dresden, 1823.

to some extent at least.   He was languid, pale, depressed beyond measure, and hardly spoke ; yet he did not leave us till
all the world was gone, nor, indeed, till long after.   He said
he would write in the morning.

He has written.   He has confessed to my mother, as to a
true and dear friend, his love for E——, and his conviction of
its utter hopelessness.   He feels himself unable to combat it.
He thinks he must try, by absence, to bring more peace to his
mind.   Yet he cannot bear to give up our friendship—an intercourse become so dear to him, and so necessary to his daily
happiness.   Poor Irving !

Irving has sent lovely verses to " Emily," on her birthday.

He has almost resolved to make a tour in Silesia, which
will keep him absent for a few weeks.

My mother encourages him to do so, and leads him to hope
that, on his return, he will feel more cheerful and contented.
He sometimes thinks he had better *never* return.

That would be too sad.

Irving went with us (will it be our last ramble together ?)
on a half-driving, half-walking expedition into the country.

CANNON BALLS, AND THE HERO'S LEG.

As we passed along, Mr. Irving was much struck with the
care with which the inhabitants (whose houses had suffered in
the battles fought near Dresden, on the return of the unfortunate French armies from Russia) had picked up the cannon
balls which had destroyed their houses and laid bare their
hearths, and built them in conspicuous places into the façades
of their new houses.   The smallest cottage was scarcely without its cannon ball, protruding half its black round surface from
the white plastering of the wall ; while many small tenements
or farmhouses had nine or ten.

Mr. Irving, not then a proficient in German, got us to copy
out for him a simple inscription under one of these memorials,
and over the entrance door of a pretty little village dairy farmhouse.

The house itself seemed almost buried in its orchard trees, on which were clusters of the snowy flowers of the pear, and pink-and-white blossoms of the apple. A tiny stream of clear water washed its way over a few large stones into a narrow water course, over which hung the quivering leaves of many a water plant, under which peeped out the yellow primrose and the gay daffodil. The rustic garden was spread out along one bank of the little rivulet, and the pale honeysuckle flaunted about its long branches, and scented the morning breeze with its sweetest of perfumes. There was something delightful in this little scene, which for a moment quite riveted the author of the "Sketch Book" to the spot.

The following was the inscription above alluded to, which Mr. Irving afterward copied into his album, after making an ineffectual attempt to translate into English verse its simple pathos :

INSCRIPTION.

Gott sey gedankt für seine Gnade
Der diesen Bau ohn allen Schade
Anfangen lassen und vollenden
Er wolle ferne hin abwenden
Krieg, Hünger, Feuer und Wasser's Noth
Auch Pestilenz und schnellen Todt.

SAMUEL GUNTHER.

Amen.

I believe that not one of our little party turned from the spot without offering a momentary prayer, that this pretty and peaceful homestead might indeed be spared from fresh ravages of war, or any of the sad list of calamities against which it thus, with simple earnestness, seems to invoke the protection of Heaven.

The inscription was enshrined in a bordering of quaint and curious devices of many colors, which caught the eye at once.

We continued our way to the old castle of Wesenstein, of which we had heard so much ; but were much disappointed to

find it a large mass of whitewashed buildings, destitute of ornament or beauty. The site, however, was admirably chósen,
and romantic in the extreme, for it was built *in* and on to some
tall, almost perpendicular rocks, in every crevice of which the
birch and the mountain ash had found a footing, while the
glossy dark leaves of the ivy, and tiny bunches of violets, dot-
ted the face of the gray rock; and round the base of the rock
grew in profusion the lily of the valley.

Mr. Irving stooped down, and gathered a handful of the
flowers, distributed them among us, under the promise that we
would conform to his own habit. " On very pleasant days like
this," he said, "he would gather a flower, dry it, and keep it in
an album with a date, and the names of each of the party."
In this way he had collected many memorials of happy hours.
On our return, he showed us his book, in which were many
flowers of many lands, the dates, the names—that was all;
but, in turning over its pages, what memories did it recall?
Some had been gathered on the Alps—the modest gentian,
close to the eternal snows; some under the wild tamarind tree,
in an American forest, with—one much loved; some were from
Italy, under the summer skies of that country he so much admired : in speaking of it, he quoted the lines:

> " There blossoms, fruit, and flowers together rise,
> And all the year in gay confusion lies."

One more little anecdote of this pleasant day. We had
often seen, on a bare and sunburnt slope pointing toward Dresden, a solitary monument. It was a plain block of granite.
On it was sculptured, in brass, a helmet; and a broken sword
of the same metal lay across the stone. This had long been
pointed out to us as *Moreau's Monument.* We were very anxious to take Mr. Irving to a spot so interesting, for there, we
told him, reposed the ashes of a hero, though history still
doubts whether to call him a patriot or a traitor. Accordingly,
we made a great effort to urge our tired steps that way. Mr.

Irving rather smiled at our ciceroneship, when he pointed to the words engraved on the monument, and rather wickedly enjoyed our disappointment, when we read that there reposed alone the hero's leg, he having been transported, by the care of Alexander, to die at ———. However, he rather rallied at the concluding line, which announced that here he fell; and the spot was remarkable for something, after all.

HISTORY OF HIS FIRST LOVE BROUGHT TO US, AND RETURNED.

Mr. Irving had not been to us for a day or two, but this morning he came. He had with him some sheets, many of which he had been writing. He has long wished us to know every detail of his first affection, but it has been too painful a theme to him ever to dwell on long. Still the desire was strong within him to communicate all to the friends he loved so well. And though others could hardly have torn from his lips one word on the subject, he felt as if it would be some consolation to past, and perhaps to present sorrows, to lay before us the history of his first love.

It was left with us under a sacred promise that it should be returned to him; that no copy should be taken; and that no other eyes but ours should ever rest upon it. The promise was faithfully kept, though great was the temptation to keep this history of his early love. Nothing he has ever written was so beautiful, so touching.

There were from sixteen to twenty pages, touching on many incidents of his youth, which led him into that deep and intense attachment which was returned to his heart's desire by that sweet girl. Their first, their last interview, all was there; even some faint description of his broken-hearted loneliness when that sweet dream was over.

Every word seems still before me, though years have passed since I last saw those pages. Were it not a breach of confidence, of that compact made between those, of whom two have been called away into a better and brighter world, I could even now recall the whole, in nearly his own words.

That he subsequently destroyed this memorial of the past, is evident. His faithful biographer puzzles himself to find for whom it was written, and when; only finding the first and last sheet, which enabled him to judge it was written to a lady, and that she was married.*

IRVING'S SECOND ATTACHMENT; THE LITTLE PICTURE AND THE CONFIDANTE.

Soon after this, Mr. Irving, who had again for long felt " the tenderest interest warm his bosom, and finally enthral his whole soul," made one vigorous and valiant effort to free himself from a hopeless and consuming attachment. My mother counselled him, I believe, for the best, and he left Dresden on an expedition of several weeks into a country he had long wished to see, though, in the main, it disappointed him; and he started with young Colbourne (son of General Colbourne) as his companion. Some of his letters on this journey are before the public; and in the agitation and eagerness he there described, on receiving and opening letters from us, and the tenderness in his replies—the longing to be once more in the

---

* *Note by the Biographer.*—The reader will find a reference to this " memorial of the past " at pages 213 to 220. The impression of Mrs. Dawson that it was " destroyed," is incorrect. The biographer mentions sixteen pages preserved, instead of " only the first and last sheet," as she supposes. This fragment is numbered from page 3 to page 18, the first and second pages and the last being missing. It commences in the middle of a sentence at page 3, and ends in the same way at page 18. It gives, as it stands, a sketch of the author's life from his entering the law office of Mr. Hoffman, in 1802, to his making the acquaintance of the Fosters at Dresden, at the close of 1822. It was written after that acquaintance had ripened into the most familiar friendship, and, from its tone and tenor, was evidently drawn forth by inquiries which only the most cordial and unreserved intimacy would warrant. Some of the paragraphs begin: " You have more than once spoken to me about my family."—" You want to know some of the *fancies* that distress me."—" You wonder why I am not married."—" I have now talked to you on subjects that I recur to with excessive pain, and on which I am apt to be silent."

little Pavilion, to which we had moved in the beginning of the summer—the letters (though carefully guarded by the delicacy of her who entrusted them to the editor, and alone retained among many more calculated to lay bare his true feelings), even fragmentary as they are, point out the truth.

Here is the key to the journey to Silesia, the return to Dresden, and, finally, to the journey from Dresden to Rotter· dam in our company, first planned so as to part at Cassel, where Mr. Irving had intended to leave us and go down the Rhine, but subsequently could not find in his heart to part. Hence, after a night of pale and speechless melancholy, the gay, animated, happy countenance with which he sprang to our coach box to take his old seat on it, and accompany us to Rotterdam. There even could he not part, but joined us in the steamboat ; and, after bearing us company as far as a boat could follow us, at last tore himself away, to bury himself in Paris, and try to work.

The author of his " Life " bears witness to the deep depression which weighed upon his mind, though he apparently does not know or does not reveal the real cause. He quotes from Mr. Irving's memorandum book : " A strange horror dwelt upon his mind ; a dread of future evil ; a fear of failure even in his literary career ; a confession, which he even at last makes to his brother, of being wretchedly out of spirits." Again he says : " I feel like a sailor who has once more to put to sea." And no doubt his career, after leaving us, appeared to him, for a long time, dreary enough.*

---

* While the editor does not question Mr. Irving's great enjoyment of his intercourse with the Fosters, or his deep regret at parting from them, he is too familiar with his occasional fits of depression to have drawn from their recurrence on his return to Paris any such inference as that to which the lady alludes. Indeed, his " memorandum book " and letters show him to have had, at this time, sources of anxiety of quite a different nature. The allusion to his having " to put once more to sea," evidently refers to his anxiety on returning to his literary pursuits, after a season of entire idleness.—P. M. I.

It was fortunate, perhaps, that this affection was returned by the *warmest friendship* only, since it was destined that the accomplishment of his wishes was impossible, for many obstacles which lay in his way. And it is with pleasure I can truly say, that in time he schooled himself to view, also with friendship only, one who for some time past has been the wife of another.

Though he exclaimed, at one time, "Oh, Dresden, Dresden! with what a mixture of pain, pleasure, fondness, and impatience I look back upon it!" he learned, I think, to banish all these feelings but pleasure; or, if any regrets did sometimes occur, the only confidante must have been *the little picture* suspended from the walls of Sunnyside, and of which it is seen that he himself, in a letter to "Emily," says: "I treasure it as a precious memorial of those pleasant days." This was a gift to him from herself—a little miniature copy of a painting in the Dresden Gallery painted by herself.*

I pass over many happy days spent together, many occurrences, though a volume might be filled with them; accounts written at the time of the boar hunt, the private theatricals at our house, the tableaux on his birthday, &c.; some as too closely resembling the account he has given himself, and some too long to be inserted here.

Some pages are missing from my journal at the time of his return from Silesia; but I remember the meeting was a joyous one on all sides. His old habits were resumed; his footstep was heard as evening closed in, and his pale and intellectual countenance was seen at the half-open door, saying, as plain as words, "Can I come in?—am I welcome?" some little parcel always in his hand, an old book to look over together, a new

* This miniature was received by Mr. Irving at Paris, four or five months after his parting with the family, at the close of July, 1823, on their return to England. One of the records of his diary at Paris, under date of December 15, 1823, is as follows: "Return home, and find parcel from Mrs. Foster, with German books, and miniature painted by Emily."— P. M. I.

one to read, and, more seldom, but still at short intervals, some unpublished manuscript of his own. On these occasions, strict orders were given that no visitor should be admitted till the last word had been read, and the whole praised or criticised, as the case may be. Of criticism, however, we were very spare, as a slight word would put him out of conceit with a whole work.

One of the best things he has published was thrown aside unfinished for years, because the friend to whom he read it, happening, unfortunately, not to be well, and sleepy, did not seem to take the interest in it he expected. This anecdote he repeated to us himself. Too easily discouraged, it was not till the latter part of his career that he ever appreciated himself as an author. One condemning whisper sounded louder in his ear than the plaudits of thousands.

DEPARTURE.

I will now pass on to our final departure from Dresden, Mr. Irving accompanying us on our journey. He had been very fidgetty for some time previously, as this honor or pleasure had been warmly solicited by Captain M——, the warmhearted and lively brother of our English Minister. He belonged to our *corps dramatique* as well as to the *corps diplomatique*, and his friendship had led him to make us the confidants of many dis- .tresses, of which the worthy young sailor would often come to bemoan himself over, and go away laughing and in high spir- its, with an elasticity belonging to his profession.

Well, the day of our departure at last drew nigh. Adieus were multiplied, visits paid and received; many a parting bless- ing from kindhearted Germans, many flowery compliments from our French acquaintances, many a hearty shake of the hand from our English friends, cheered our last few days at Dresden.

But at last all was ready—trunks packed, the horses to, a weeping band of affectionate waiting maids pressing around us to catch the last glimpse, the last smile, and we mounted into our carriages; one, a light English barouche, in which were my mother, my sister, and myself, with Washington Irving on the coach box, on which exalted seat he was often joined by one or other of the ladies; and the other a German travelling carriage, in which were the three philosophers, as Irving always termed them—my two little brothers, namely, and their excellent and clever German tutor.

An escort of friends, mounted on horses, gave our first start a gay and holiday appearance.

These took leave of us at the end of the first stage, and we bade them and the pretty domes and towers of Dresden a long adieu. On we went rattling over the *chaussée*, still bearing in our hands beautiful bouquets brought to us by Monsieur le Comte de Rumigny, French Minister, who, with his wife, had always been our staunch friends, and who, having a large garden resplendent with flowers, had for some time set apart more than a rood of it for us whenever we liked to go in and gather bouquets, or sit there and read amid the gay parterre. Washington Irving was full of spirits. He sang songs with "Emily" —a new accomplishment, or an old one new revived, which he had kept back for occasions like the present. I am ashamed to say that, fatigued with the day's packing, I fell asleep to the soothing melody.

About eleven o'clock, I was startled out of a confused dream by a loud blast of a horn. It was our postilion. Before I had time to recollect where we were, I heard Washington Irving's voice crying out, "Look! look there!" We all looked, and, standing up in the carriage, all gazed on the scene before us. The night was lovely, clear, and starry; the red crescent of the moon was just risen behind the dark outlines of an old tower; the whole country lay dim and still before us, and the beautiful and silvery Muldau reflected the moon in a long ray upon its rippled surface. We had time to admire the whole, which harmonizes so well together; it invited the eyes to look upon it, while the ferry boat took us across.

We stopped to take a little supper on some provisions we had brought with us, having dismounted while our horses were being changed at a neat roadside inn, and where the look of the host took Mr. Irving's fancy.

The lusty landlord looked down upon his own bulky shape with great complacency, while he regarded Mr. Irving's more slender figure with great contempt, as he watched him making some ineffectual attempts to shut our carriage door. "Ach!" said he, "Sie haben nicht viel courage! Sie essen nicht genug rind-fleisch!"

Mr. Irving laughed heartily. He said he knew "that man was a character;" and on we drove again, and reached our halting place at half past twelve. Our postilion sounded a most knightly blast on his horn, which gained us admittance after some delay, as the warders were taking a comfortable doze; and we then proceeded to the inn recommended to us by our good Tropaneger, the Philosopher-in-chief, *i. e.*, tutor to our young brothers.

Mr. Irving declared he had noticed that our postilion prided himself not a little on the melody of his horn. Moreover, that he seemed to pay particular honor to a pretty white cottage he had passed; and Mr. Irving almost fancied he saw a pretty little maiden timidly raise a chintz curtain, and *look out*. We were amused at the *chintz* curtain, whose pattern he discovered by no light but the moon, and the pretty little maiden, who some vowed was no other than a bearded old man in his night-cap. But Irving was staunch to his story, and would never throw the pretty maiden or the chintz curtain overboard.

LEIPZIC AND PONIATOWSKI.

The next morning, Mr. Irving, who had been already up to the observatory, would have us all go also. It was a tall tower, mounted by an extraordinary staircase, that wound up and up the wall, seeming to grow out of it without support; still he pressed us to go forward and contemplate the view from the top. Indeed, it was most interesting. It embraced an immense tract of country, but it was not that. Below us, at our feet, was the spot where was fought the battle of Leipzic, so fatal to Napoleon; and in that muddy stream, just where the bank rises steep and high, the gallant Poniatowski met his fate. Devotedly attached to Napoleon, he had fought his way through opposing ranks, to rejoin him in the last bloody contest, to be near his person. He was warned back again and again by his friends, even by his *enemies*, by whom he was held in reverence and esteem, though so young, for his generous and noble conduct. He saw Napoleon but a short distance ahead, flushed, struggling with his own officers, who were entreating him to fly. Napoleon defeated—in danger. He made one more effort, leaped his horse into the stream that separated them, swam him across the stream, and urged him on to the bank at that spot. The horse sprang up it, but the rider, wounded, bleeding, exhausted, fell backward from his saddle, the muddy waters of the Elsler closing over him; and so he died! The only time Napoleon wept on a field of battle was that day, when some one brought him news of that sad loss. Napoleon himself indeed suffered dreadfully under the different events that passed rapidly on the scene, now so peaceful, which lay before us.

During the first day's fighting, all seemed in his favor, and he sent word to have *Te Deums* sung in all the churches. This order was not obeyed; the burghers of Leipzic saw from their walls what he did not—that the other divisions of his army, which were fighting round Leipzic, were all repulsed; and, in fact, lest he should make his retreat through Leipzic, which lay direct between him and the main army, and in fear lest the French should set that town on fire, as they did the villages around, to cover their retreat, they closed their gates against the French.

On Sunday, Napoleon rested. Monday was the final defeat. Mr. Irving pointed down close under us to a spot where there had been a hot dispute between Napoleon and his generals. He wished to take the field again, even when driven back upon Leipzic. He went with his drawn sword among the soldiers, but they threw away their muskets, and refused to fight. He tried to enter at two gates of the town, and had to ride half round before he got in.

So great were the crowds retreating on all sides, that two guards had to take hold of his horse's head, and strike right and left to make way for him. The King of Saxony was watching this terrible scene from this very spot. Napoleon sent messengers to him to acquaint him that the Saxon troops had gone over to the Russians, and offered to take him on to Paris with himself; but the King sent word that he would remain, and yield to his fate.

The events of those days are recorded in history, but there was something in the interest with which Washington Irving pointed all out to us, that gave them a double interest to us.

After dinner, we walked with Irving to see the tomb of Poniatowski—white marble, on a green sward near the Elsler —one immense and beautiful weeping willow shading it, while others surround it at a short distance.

THE HARTZ AND THE AHNFRAU.

Here again I miss much. Old chateaus visited, all of which had some legends connected with them more or less curious, recorded by Musæus, whose work in many volumes was our evening study, when stopping for the night. It was in German, but Mr. Irving would get us to translate it to him.

DIE AHNFRAU.

One particular character we went far out of our way to see. It was the "locale" of the celebrated "Ahnfrau," a piece which he had seen acted at Vienna, and which had laid a strong hold upon his imagination. The "Ahnfrau" was represented in the piece by an alarming spectre, frightful to behold, to the terror of a fair young girl and her lover. Here we were close to the abode of the "Ahnfrau," the very real and true site of the drama; and here Mr. Irving had ascertained her picture was preserved by her descendants.

VOL. IV.—16*   (24)

The castle was reached; the family were out. Indeed, the castle had long been uninhabited, save by the old porter and his family. Here, then, was a real chateau à la Radcliffe. Mr. Irving rubbed his hands as the old man walked before us, rattling his bunch of keys.

He was for showing us the chapel, and the hall, and the clipped yews of the garden; but Mr. Irving asked for the picture gallery, the portraits, the family portraits. We hardly liked to name the Ahnfrau in these her own familiar precincts. We gathered up our courage, however. The cold, damp passages inspired a chill. We kept together. Who knew what ghastly head might peep over the shoulders of the last comer? Mr. Irving was all attention and expectation. At last we reached the picture gallery. The old porter would fain have lingered over the picture of his late master, a mild-looking gentleman in a bob wig, or his ladies in powdered hair and blue satin bodice. Still Mr. Irving urged him on, for, at the farther end of the gallery, he had discovered a high, narrow, curtained recess. He pointed to it, and eagerly named the awful name, "Die Ahnfrau." "Go," said the old man, peevishly, who did not seem inclined to move further than his master's picture. Well, we went, Irving leading the van. His hand was on the curtain. He drew it aside. Ah! what did we behold—a spectre? What loveliness is that? So fair, so sweet, so charming a face never before was designed upon canvas, surely. *This* the Ahnfrau? Impossible! Those blue, cerulean blue eyes that follow us wherever we go, instead of the sightless orbits we expected; the delicate features, the oval face, the full, rich lips—this is a deception; it cannot be! But our looks stray to her dress. All is there; all is correct—the black robe, the black mantle on the golden and floating hair, the jewelled coronet of the Countess of B——— in her hands. We looked with an inward thrill. "You know the superstition," said Irving, "of course? If on her hand appears a white glove, she betokens a marriage to her descendants; if on her hand a black glove, it is death to the beholder."

What was on her hand? Well, it was bare; but a casket by her side, on which was carved some ancient scroll, indicated thereby the mystic emblems of fate. We strained our eyes, but not a tip of a finger for good or evil could we see through the half-open lid.

But oh! that was a great comfort. The little dog at her feet, her constant companion when she appears, was white. We decided to take that for a happy omen. We gazed again on that sweet face, drew the curtain, and retired. The old porter had hobbled away, but the bright sunshine and the smell of flowers in the little garden were very welcome, although the dreaded Ahnfrau had looked so sweet upon us.

WASHINGTON IRVING, HIS RAMBLE AND HIS ROBBERS.

I pass on rapidly, more rapidly than we did, through this wild and romantic scenery.

The storm has already been described. The few days spent in Alexis Bad, to recruit, I believe, are also described in some papers of my sister's.

I doubt, however, whether Mr. Irving's evening ramble up the dell is related; so I will briefly record it here.

When, after the *tremendous* storm and our *tremendous* up-set was over, we advanced into the very heart of the Hartz Gebirge, to rest awhile under the shadow of the witch-haunted old Brocken itself, we had come with surprise (in the midst of those regions of almost impenetrable wood, and among the gray rocks and deep dells where the eagle flapped his wing above our heads, and the wild deer bounded across our path) on as gay a court as ever assembled at the court of Rubezahl himself, the hoary old mountain king, who is said to sleep his sleep under the Hartz Gebirge, ready to wake up a young and handsome prince at the end of that time, a male "beauty" without his beast. Some say his beard has grown three times round the base of the mountain all but some few yards; when these last yards are completed, the mountain will split open with a tremendous crash, and the handsomest prince that ever was seen will step forth and rule over all United Germany, which is then to reach its pinnacle of glory and prosperity.

Mr. Irving, who had contemplated writing several stories founded on these Hartz legends, of which there are an innumerable store, was very anxious to explore the country, and we were traversing it in new and unhackneyed traces, when our fate and our mountain guides led us to Alexis Bad, where, suddenly turning the angle of a huge rock (round which our road wound over a track marked merely by a few wheel marks on the green sod), we beheld with amazement a large and elegant building, open columns supporting a portico, while a broad flight of stone steps led to a green parterre, surrounded by other halls, and ornamented with statues and fountains. Among these, a bevy of fair ladies and their lords, in all the elegance of Paris costume, were wandering about, or lounging on benches, or seated in groups, enjoying the golden sunset. A few of these fair ladies came forward, and a mutual recognition took place, and explanations followed. The Duke of Anhalt Bernburg, sovereign of this country, and the Duke of Anhalt Cothen, with his Duchess, a fine, tall woman, natural daughter to the King of Prussia, were here to drink the waters and while away a few weeks, after the fashion of German princes. Their establishment of *dames d'honneur*, chamberlains, and *aides-de-camp*, and all the paraphernalia of a court, followed them, together with some visitors from Dresden and Berlin; among the latter, some friends of ours.

How several days were spent here, I refer to other papers, already, I believe, in the possession of the editor. But Mr. Irving, in his rambling mood, ran himself into a danger far greater than he supposed. Being not like us, who were amused and pleased with this brief renewal of former gayeties, he became rather disgusted with this unexpected rencontre with this small court. He said he had hoped to find no chamberlains or gold sticks at the foot of the Brocken; he came to look for other objects; and, while the dance and the music were merrily going forward, he strolled away up the glen we named the

Eagle's Glen, from having there seen the most magnificent birds of the species I ever beheld alive. On and on he went, " rapt in sweet and bitter fancies." Where, indeed, he did fancy himself, I do not know; but one thing was clear: where he really was, he did not know—which was unfortunate, as night began to close in, and no habitation seemed near. Nothing but trees and rocks, and rocks and trees, everywhere. He trusted to meet a miner, for they are generally, night and day, at work in different parts of the forest; but he was disappointed.

A grand procession of miners had that evening taken place, and all were gone to Alexis Bad to join, who could shoulder a pickaxe or don the black velvet uniform, affected by their body on state occasions. Here was a dilemma. He saw an eminence before him, from which he hoped, at least, to get a peep of the stars, from which he was shut out in the narrow path he was pursuing, by overhanging branches which closed overhead. Besides, he hoped to catch a glimpse of the lights of Alexis Bad. He climbed the eminence not without difficulty. Clinging to the roots of the trees, and scrambling along as he best might, he reached the top; but hardly had he done so, when he saw a light, evidently the ruddy glow of a fire, throwing a red glare around. He made at once toward it, not doubting that where there was a fire there were men; but he had no sooner come in front of it, than he repented of his haste. Four men lay around it, with swarthy faces and outlandish garments; and their countenances, lit up by the fitful blaze of the fire, looked ominously bad. They started forward at his approach; and one wild-looking, brawny fellow, fixed his eyes with a covetous stare on Mr. Irving's gold chain which dangled from his watch pocket. Irving was certainly not pleased with the company he had fallen into; but his self-possession did not desert him even for a moment, and, if he did not feel pleasure, he still thought it best to affect it.

" Good evening to you, my friends," said he, using the few words of German he could command. " I saw your fire from

below, and am come to ask one of you to show me the way to
Alexis Bad." With that he came still more forward, and
stood familiarly by them.

The men turned round and consulted for a moment together; then the oldest, apparently, among them, spoke:

"We cannot go with you to Alexis Bad, but thither lies
your way."

They pointed to the intricacies of the forest, and Mr. Irving
gave a nod. "It is well," he said; but, having given one look
to the stars, the friendly stars above him, one thought to the
direction in which he had been walking, he was sure the men
had directed him wrong—purposely wrong, since no inhabitant
of those forests could be ignorant of the situation of Alexis
Bad. However, with admirable coolness, he stood to warm
himself a few minutes by the fire, then wished them all again
"Gute nacht;" then, following the route they had pointed out,
which led diametrically opposite to the right one, he commenced quietly walking onward. No sooner, however, did he
find himself beyond the ruddy glare of the fire, than he threw
himself down into a small hollow of the rock where the grass
grew thick and high, and lying perdue and motionless, though
with ear and eye stretched to the utmost, he beheld exactly
what he expected—the four ruffians stealing on after him in the
track they supposed he had followed at their instigation. Indeed, he heard a muttered oath of the fellow who had eyed his
watch chain, at the folly which had let him pass on. They had
barely cleared the spot where he lay, passing, indeed, within a
few yards of him, when, with a stealthy movement, as of one
who had before then seen an Indian creep through the bushes
in the hunting fields of his own America, he crept from tree to
tree till he was convinced he had the right point of the compass before him.

He still fancied that he could hear the distant voices of the
men growling that they had not yet come up with him, and
beating about the bushes in the track he had so wisely left.
He felt he had no time to lose—now was the time, or never.

Rising to his feet, he bounded off as fast as his feet would bear him, over moss, rock, and hollow—down away, right among trees and branches and roots and briars—now stumbling, now up and away again, now starting off with still fiercer speed; for a loud halloo—another and another—told him his pursuers had discovered their mistake, and were hot on his track.

Never, never had he run such a chase. It was, he felt, for his life; for these fellows, now they knew he had detected their real character (or why should he thus fly from them?), would not have let him escape alive. He had not liked the courtly gatherings below, but never man flew faster through the dark woods and their dark denizens than he did that night. It was too much for his strength; he felt it was ebbing from him. More falls—less power to rise and fly again—his pursuers gaining on him. One look over his shoulder told him the large brawny fellow was within twenty paces of him. For a moment he thought all was up with him, when one more bound, one more determined effort, and he cleared the wooded bank, sprang down on the sward below, and found himself directly opposite the open door of a little hut, where a woodsman's wife, her eldest son, and several other workmen stood chatting together over the gay doings up at the Bad. Here was relief, help, safety, protection, and in right good time too; for Irving stood for some instants speechless and breathless from his run, but not a little thankful to be delivered from his four pursuers, who had perceived the hut even before himself, and retreated, no doubt not in the best of tempers, to their lair. The young woodsman and his friend walked back with Irving, and he was not sorry to be safe among us once more. We were very severe on his imprudence, and would not be satisfied till we had exacted a promise that he would never so risk himself again.

HANOVER AND HESSE CASSEL.

I pass over this part of our journey, and the days of delay at Cassel before parting, and the parting that was no parting. Then the journey through Nimmegen and Dusseldorf to Rot-

terdam.   There I find *our last evening* before our real parting
described as follows, headed by an outline from the original of
a bunch of Dutch currants—so do trifles mix themselves up
with the tide of human passions, crushing griefs, and deep
despair.

Mr. Irving, like a man expected to be his own executioner,
had been out to take our berths in the steam vessel.   We had
taken a dismal walk along the slimy canals of Rotterdam,
though something neat and old-fashioned in the Dutchmen's
houses for a brief moment took up Mr. Irving's attention.   We
had dined ; the dessert was still on the table ; there followed a
sorting of our separate property in sketch books, memorandum
ditto, umbrellas, boxes, and all the small paraphernalia that
accumulate on such a journey as ours, and with two carriages to
offer room and shelter for many an odd volume or writing case,
or " trap " of one sort or another.   Irving was in terrible spirits.   He gave mamma a beautiful little copy of Cowper's
poems, and to each of us some favorite book.   Our tea and
evening were as melancholy as our approaching separation.
Very little was said ; little good was achieved by moving
Irving to the sofa.   We sat round, looking silently upon one
another.   Little did I expect we should come home to merry
England with such heavy hearts.

Well, the next day we parted, as has been told again, and
once again.   The ship was dancing on the bright waves, the
wind blowing fresh, and all eyes and thoughts turned toward
England.   People did not quite return to England with the
enthusiasm of Scott :

> " Is there a man, with soul so dead,
> Who ne'er to himself has said,
> This is my own, my native land ? "

Whose heart has ne'er——   *Well*, indeed, I say as before—
and it was well with us—we were returning to a happy home ;
to my father, loved and honored by rich and poor ; to a happy
home, where the Gothic windows shone with the traces of

many-colored lamps to welcome our arrival; and illuminations by night and congratulations by day made our return a cheerful one. But Irving, lonely and depressed in his crowded steamboat, the deepest despondency hung upon his spirits, and long benumbed his faculties, and checked his pen. The mist, however, cleared away, the kindly heart gladdened once more. Literary fame and honors, and hosts of friends and admirers, gradually encompassed him about. His brief share in politics was hailed as an epoch, when England and America shook hands, and for that brief period almost learned to recognize each other's worth. His genial spirit shone on all, and smoothed the lion's ruffled mane without debasing the stripes and stars.

We met again *often*. Not only did he visit us at our own home, but during the time he was Secretary to the American Mission; and when, courted by the noble and the wealthy, he had to share in all the engagements of the *corps diplomatique*, and even sometimes attend four *reunions* in one day, he still found many an hour to visit us in our old-fashioned house near Cavendish Square. There did he love to assume the habits of other days, though with more chastened feelings, yet spirits buoyant as in the first months of our Dresden intimacy. There did he pour out many a glowing description of his *bellissima Granada*, and fill in with many an anecdote his history of his life in Spain. The changes and chances of married life occupied too much of my time to keep up even this valued friendship by a continuous correspondence; but, amid joys and sorrows, he had never been forgotten, and never did forget.

In the words of a poet, who appreciated Irving almost as much as we did ourselves, though not so united by the ties of so intimate a friendship :

> " Let Fate do her worst, there are relics of joy,
> Bright dreams of the past which she cannot destroy,
> Which come in the night-time of sorrow and care,
> And bring back the features that joy used to wear :
> Long, long be my heart with such memories stored."

I stop, for this melancholy tone ill suits the cheerful character of Irving's mind toward the latter part of his life. Surrounded by a loved and loving family, he found in them a dear,
domestic circle. His friends, well chosen, were steady and
true; his country, admiring and grateful. Let us hope that
gentle heart was satisfied; and his soul, at peace with all, at
the last passed without pain or sorrow, let us humbly trust, into
the regions of eternal bliss.

FLORA DAWSON.

May, 1863.

CHAPTER XXIV.

LETTERS, ETC., OF WASHINGTON IRVING * — JOURNAL BETWEEN DRESDEN AND
ROTTERDAM, JULY, 1823.

MR. IRVING dined with us. We walked to the Grossen
Garten. Such a lovely sunset! All the west was glowing
like living amber, fleecy crimson clouds sailing like little islands
in a sea of splendor. It looked as if the region of fairyland
were opened, and all its treasures scattered about. All the
Dresden cockneys were out to take, as Mr. Irving said, "the
smoke and air." Londoners of that class contrive to get out
of their smoke; the Dresdeners like to carry it with them.
Irving says "that the pipe is the feature of a German face,
like the proboscis of an elephant's."

I do not think I ever saw Mr. Irving so happy as during
our day at Tharandt. We walked in what Gesner calls "Die
heilige Hallen"—tall beech woods, the ground enamelled with
violet and yellow pansies. We have all preserved some of
them in our books.

---

* The following narrative, and the letters of Washington Irving, have
been derived from Mrs. Fuller, the Emily Foster referred to in the second
volume.

We have been dreadfully gay all the time Mr. Irving has been at Prague; but this evening we took one of our favorite walks to an old square farmhouse on the top of a hill, that seems a fit scene for some foul deed. Its wooden shutters are usually closed, and it is separated from the road by a deep, low pond, overhung with coarse, rank, treacherous-looking grass and rushes, the brown stagnant water covered with slimy weeds, looking like poisonous verdigris on rusty copper. We peeped in, almost expecting to see some horrible sign of crime and murder; but, instead of that, there was to-day a pretty little wild duck, popping, and prying, and paddling about with its scarlet beak, starting its tail, and looking much more aristocratic than its farmyard kindred.

After the walk, I was sitting in the dusk of twilight, when some one rushed in, and I was delighted before I quite recognized Irving, looking very handsome, in a pair of fine black mustaches, grown during his travels.

Adieu to Dresden! Irving accompanies us. *We* all go in the large English carriage; the boys and the tutor follow in a German one.

The night before we arrived at Leipzic was very interesting. In the dark we traversed an almost bare plain, with only a few shaggy trees, a dull, graystone, half-ruined tower, and two tall, gaunt wooden crosses; then a black wood with the stags belling. All on a sudden there is a loud blast of the postilion's horn. The river Muldau lay rippling before us, under a pale, clear crescent moon, delicately fretted, and embossed like a sheet of dead silver; enclosed on all sides by dark, bushy banks. It looked, indeed, "like the calm, unknown lake." As we stopped at a little wayside inn for a cup of coffee, all at once a band of music struck up some of our favorite waltz tunes, to which we had all danced so often in Dresden. It was a wild farewell to Dresden gayeties.

After the fearful storm,* or rather waterspout, and our up-set, we had to travel three days shawlless and bonnetless, as we gave all our things away to that beautiful dark girl at the inn.

Between showers and sunbeams, we reached the Hartz Mountains; more like American scenery, Mr. Irving said, than anything he had seen in Europe. Hill over hill, richly mantled with forests of vigorous growth, pale poplars, thick beeches, tufted limes, ancient oaks, graceful birches, the elegant *land* weeping willow, green lawns, deep valleys, blue vistas and crags, and rocks interspersed. We all arrived in high spirits at Alexis Bad, and have to squeeze into the smallest compass we can, for this is the great fifty years' anniversary among the miners.

Irving is quite in his element, reading to us endless country legends, full of water nymphs and gnomes. No wonder this is the fairyland of Germany. We walked through a rocky glen to the Mäyde Sprung (Maiden's Leap), and beyond to a most romantic spot, where are the iron foundries. I thought of poor Fridolin. We met the three sovereign dukes of these parts, who most politely asked us to a ball, which we willingly accepted. Irving is pleased with the fine race of people here. He was particularly struck with a miner, with whom he con-versed; his features were noble, and his manners dignified and benevolent. Irving called him one of "Nature's gentle-men."

In the evening, we walked to a lovely little valley, its steep, green banks fringed with birches. A tall, handsome shepherd was guiding a flock of sheep with tinkling bells over the high, smooth downs. His costume, richly ornamented with embroidered leather trappings, brass, and chains, and an inlaid crook under his arm, attracted our notice. When Mr. Irving asked what they were for, he answered, with the utmost sim-plicity, " Ein bisschen Staat " (a little bit of state).

---

* Described in the second volume, p. 128. [In the American, p. 160.]

There were tableaux for the Duchess in the evening. She is a Prussian princess, tall, dignified, and kind, and, though no longer young, still handsome.

Wednesday.—At the ball, the stupid chamberlain, one of the old-fashioned, ignorant, German-court tribe, neglected to present Mr. Irving, who very properly walked off; and no message or entreaty could recall him. In vain the poor stupid old chamberlain scudded away in search of him. The Grand Dukes sent flattering messages, mamma and we sent coaxing ones—no Irving appeared. This caused quite a hubbub among the Hof-Gesindel. The fact was, as we afterward found, he sallied forth on a long, and, as it proved, dangerous ramble, among the endless forests far away, while we were dancing, and receiving compliments, many of them on his account; for the Grand Dukes, and the Duchess more especially, expressed their raptures at his books. After a grand supper, we all went on the balcony to see the fireworks. I know not how to describe the magic effect of them among these forests, rocks, and glens. As far as the eye could reach, fountains of light in every form, and of every hue, spouted from the dark sides of the mountains; balls of fire, blue, ruby, and golden, shot up and illumined the trees with shadowy glances, while nearer were seen a few dark, spirit-like forms moving about. Exactly facing our balcony, a narrow valley ran out, and pierced far into the mountains. Its entrance was guarded by two high, projecting, precipitous rocks, resembling gigantic portals, and from the top of these an unceasing volley of rockets from each side arched over the chasm beneath, and, mingling at an immense height, spangled the sky with sparks.

In the mean time, Mr. Irving had his adventures, which I will try to relate as much as I can in his own words.

He set out, pleased, no doubt, to give his hard-worked imagination a cooling holiday among the midnight woods, that with their *tête-à-tête*, and silent repose, invested a retrospect— of town, and lights, and balls, of home recollections, and all the sea of life and action, even the nearest events, with a dis-

tance that gives to all a soft charm; or perhaps he only looked
on the black and fantastic tree trunks in a sort of mental doze.
Whatever were his thoughts, they were suddenly brought home
with a start. He was not so far from human company as he
fancied, for he caught sight of the shadowy figures of two men
closely following him—now stealthily slinking across the moonlight, now lost again in the darkness of the trees; but at length,
by quick walking, he left behind, as he thought, these unwel-
come, would-be companions; and again his mind· wandered
over the tracks of the past, or watched the moon, so high and
far in the skies of deep-stained blue, that glided in and out the
netted traceries of the boughs overhead, throwing softly shadows of the silent trees upon the ground—— But what was
that ? A shadow of a different nature crossed his path; and,
as he looked up, he again, and now distinctly, saw those unpleasant, inquisitive persons, who were still closely following
him, evidently with no good design, and who were now so near
upon him that he heard the crush of the leaves under their feet.
What would have been the end of this adventure there is no
knowing, had he not at that moment espied an opening among
the trees, and the welcome sight of the lights of the town, for
which he made in all haste. Although he seemed rather
pleased than otherwise when relating to us this adventure, still
such things must be more pleasant in the telling than in the
reality. He did not arrive home till the ball was nearly over,
about three in the morning.

We set off the next day at nine o'clock, and did not get
out of the carriage till we arrived at the Ross Trapp (horse
trap). The whole of the road seemed a Ross Trapp to me.
Fine piles of rocks were mingled with noble oaks, and a considerable river foamed beneath. Stags stare at you, shy and
wild; hawks sail along on their broad wings from crag to
crag; and we saw one eagle that Mr. Irving discovered, and
pointed out to us.

Blankenburg is an old, gray, unpaved town. In the morning we all went up to the celebrated castle, the most ancient

dwelling mansion I have seen. It was built in 1100, and is full of the traces of everyday life in old times. There is a richly-carved spinning wheel, and numerous portraits of one of the pretty spinsters—fair, prim, and quaint. There were also some English beauties, and those three lovely Countesses Königsmark, whose vestiges were scattered all over the castle. King August der Starcke admired one of them. I suppose he liked an Amazonian expression; for she is generally in the position of Raphael in his own portraits of himself, looking over her shoulder, with a pair of bright *espiègle* eyes; a quiver on her back, a long, slight waist, and satin skirt in rich, full folds. Still more curious, though less charming, was the famed white lady, the heroine of the tragedy of the Ahnfrau (the ancestress), who haunts so many castles. She is all in white, with a long white veil, which will not be changed till the Day of Judgment; only when she announces a misfortune, which appears to be chiefly her lot, she wears black gloves, and her little white spaniel is then a black one. We also saw the beautiful ivory crucifix by Michael Angelo. We afterward went down Baumann's Höhle—a grand cavern; but we would not wear the horrid miners' dresses, they were too frightful.

We arrived at Stolberg by infamous roads, the moonlight trembling through the superb forests of beech, pine, and spruce fir. The next day rain and cloud, and distant gleams of sun. Flora and Mr. Irving capped verses as they sat on the box. These are not so bad:

> " Dark lies the vale and ruined tower,
> But bright the distant scene;
> So Hope still gilds the future hour,
> Though Sorrow lies between."

Late at night we stopped at Bleicherd. There was a marriage, and every little inn was taken up, much to Irving's vexation on our account. We had the pleasure of standing in the rain, and seeing them dance, through the lighted windows. At last, as we were famishing, we sat down on the doorstep of a

pothouse, and had some bread and beer soup, which Irving induced some peasant girl to bring, all breathless from the dance.
We had endured such fear and shaking from the bad roads,
that Irving persuaded us to put ourselves in the Post Wagen
—a wagon indeed. We all got under the awning, and laid
down in the straw; jumbling over ditches, rocks, and seas of
mud; Mr. Troppeneger following alone in the carriage, till we
reached Heiligenstadt, where, after baths and a good breakfast,
we got reinstated in our due honors.

The country is lovely; woody valleys widening here and
there into sloping meadows and striped cornfields, or enclosing
pretty farmhouses, painted and barred like Swiss cottages; or
little churches, nestling among the most emerald-green foliage.
The sky is the purest azure. Irving prepared us a charming
surprise, by having our dinner laid out of doors, on the crown
of a hill, under a lime tree, round which green bowers are built
up for the cherry gathering, of which we all partook. Irving
said we enjoyed our cherries more than any *bon vivant* could
enjoy his turtle soup. It was a good-natured evening; heaven
and earth seemed to smile a reconciliation after the storm. We
arrived at Cassel by a brilliant full moon. The next day we
went to a fine gallery of paintings, which Denon called a set
of jewels; so he took them to Paris.

We saw Wilhelmshöhe, where, among many paintings, one
charmed us, and Irving quite fell in love with it. It was a
little princess, half woman and half child. She was kneeling,
with one arm reposing on a huge nosegay. Her dress was
white satin, with a broad band of turquoise blue down the front,
and a full cap of blue-and-white, which had the effect of a gar-
land; but it was the easy, playful grace; the sweet, regular,
oval face; the animated air of childish *naiveté*, and the faintest
touch of highbred pride, that enchanted us all. She was feeding a lamb—she looked like a dear little lamb herself. The
gardens and fountains are beautiful. In the evening we went
to the opera. I suppose Irving will leave us to-morrow. He
read us his MSS.

Good Irving gives up his route, and goes with us to Rotterdam.

We proceeded through the Sauerland and Arolsee. Ever since we entered Hesse, the country seems to grow richer and more populous; and all the simple luxuries of a well-cultivated land (ham, butter, and bread) improve. We travelled through the night, halting at a deserted convent, hid in a romantic nook, where we comforted ourselves with hot wine soup, and silk handkerchiefs, the night being stormy. At the next town, after our toilette, at a neat inn, we walked on, and Mr. Irving remarked, "How much this country puts one in mind of England!—field gates, hedges, cottage gardens, roses, and broad beans." About Eberfeld one sees a manufacturing appearance, and the rich soil is quite petted into profusion.

We had rain at Dusseldorf.

Rees, where the people speak Dutch, is the first place in our journeyings where we do not understand the language.

The evening cleared for our arrival at Nimmegen. The carpeted stairs, tea urn, and sugar tongs, looked quite English; not so the enormous whole cheese, overgrown sausages, &c., which appeared at tea. The ,noble Rhine divides us from the pretty little town, where Mr. Irving and we took a delightful evening stroll round the ramparts. Its walls show signs of many a siege of ancient and modern date. It combines a veteran, warlike air with the peculiar national Dutch *bien-être*. The streets are paved with a mosaic pattern of small bricks; the houses, built of the same, present notched and carved gable ends, with immensely tall windows. Swarms of Sunday beauties were sitting on their chequered steps, with a complete harness of gold ornaments about the head. We hurried from the view of the majestic Rhine, glowing under an evening sun, summoned by the bell of the flying bridge.

I like to pass at once into such a characteristic place as this. The roads are not so alarming as they were the day before. We were perched on high dikes, the greatest elevation within sight; so narrow, that on one side the carriage wheels were often over the edge; so that, in spite of heat and fatigue, we walked great part of the way. The enormous joints of meat seem to proclaim more of good living than good taste. Irving says they do well to make the best of in-doors, as out-of-doors is so deficient. He is delighted and diverted with the number of "Lust hausen"—summer houses—hung over the canals, like little round cages, each holding its stout mynheer, who sits there with his pipe in dreamy content.

The solemn, republican-looking storks march pompously over the swampy fields, or, seated in enormous nests on the tops of barns and stacks, look like the lords of the land, and are certainly the most gentlemanlike animals on two legs we have seen in this dull country. We reached Rotterdam about midnight, its broad, straight canals shining in the starlight. They are edged with trees, and filled with heavy Dutch luggers; their wings on each side give them the appearance of great heady nightmoths, sleeping on the canals. In the morning, this amphibious town—this awkward parody on Venice— did not please us so well, with its heat, its glare, its stagnant water and vile smell of pitch and tar, putting us in mind of our woes to-morrow; nor did the humdrum buzz of business cheer us. Irving truly says, in this place it is not the people that have grown to the soil, but the soil that has grown to the people; each has to build himself up a hive like the bees. Mr. Irving is sadly out of spirits. We are going to home and friends; but he, to wander about the wide world alone.

Wednesday.—After bathing, we were hurried *pêle-mêle* into the steamboat. Mr. Irving accompanied us down the river, quite into the sea, when he was put down into the little open boat to return to the shore. I shall never, however long I may live, forget his last farewell, as he looked up to us, so pale and melancholy. It was a very painful moment to us all. We have not often felt so grieved at parting with a dear friend.

————

He afterward came to see us at our house in Bedfordshire;

but, owing to various circumstances, it was not so cheerful a visit as we could have wished.

Then again I met him in London, some years later. Every spare evening he had he spent at our house. He was still the same ; time changed him very little. His conversation was as interesting as ever; his dark-gray eyes still full of varying feeling; his smile half playful, half melancholy, but ever kind. All that was mean, or envious, or harsh, he seemed to turn from so completely, that, when with him, it seemed that such things were not. All gentle and tender affections, Nature in her sweetest or grandest moods, pervaded his whole imagination, and left no place for low or evil thoughts ; and, when in good spirits, his humor, his droll descriptions, and his fun, would make the gravest or the saddest laugh.

LETTERS OF WASHINGTON IRVING.

[*To Miss Emily Foster.*]

Mr. —— arrived here two or three days since, with his two sons. How often I have recollected your anecdotes of the embarrassments and cross purposes of the —— family last summer ! They have had nothing but a tissue of *anlegenheit* since they have been here. At one time they lost their portmanteau; then they lost part of their clothes at the laundress's, which they have not as yet recovered ; and so they go on from one petty scrape to another, and always manage to be too late for everything.

I scribble this in a great hurry, for I am busy making arrangements for breaking up our encampment. You will complain of this letter, no doubt. Take it, however, for what it is, as good as I can at this moment write ; and however brief I write, and however little it may appear to come " from the heart," as you hint in one of your letters, believe me, my sentiments toward you all do not shift with my style, nor depend upon the tone and turn of a period.

If you knew what I felt at the idea of once more seeing you all, you would not require any rhetoric in the matter.

At Toplitz I expect to hear when you go to Schandrau, or whether the unsettled state of the weather does not deter you from making the excursion. And now, God bless you all!

Yours truly,

WASHINGTON IRVING.

[*Washington Irving to Mrs. Foster.*]

I thank you, my dear Mrs. Foster, for your kind attention in sending me the plan for my route, as likewise for your kind note accompanying it. You talk of my coming back—I am ashamed to say it, I am almost wishing myself back already. I ought to be off like your birds, but I feel I shall not be able to keep clear of the cage. God bless you all! I wish I liked you all only half as much as I do.

Yours ever,

WASHINGTON IRVING.

Mr. Irving says he is suffering much from violent pain in the head:

[*Washington Irving to Mrs. Foster.*]

Perhaps a good deal of mountain scrambling to-morrow may drive it off, or may overpower the feeling of pain, by mental excitement. I love mountains; the soul seems lifted up by them, as well as the body, and one breathes a purer and freer atmosphere. The evening is now coming on. You are all seated, I suppose, in the little Pavilion. I shall lie down on the sofa, and drive away this pain by picturing you all at your occupations, and recalling the many evenings of homefelt enjoyment I have passed among you. They were the sweetest moments that I have passed in Dresden, though I fear I often trespassed on the patience of others. We fancy others feel the sunshine that is only in our own bosoms, and, while full of good humor and good will, the idea never enters one's mind that even one's good humor may be irksome.

I shall never forget poor Miss W., who, wrapped up in ecstasy with her own music, did not perceive that all the company were either yawning, or laughing at her.

Still those were sweet moments, for they made me know and prize you all. I would not give up one such evening for all the fashionable parties we were at together. Perhaps there is some selfishness in this. I felt of some consequence in those little domestic scenes; but when we entered the great maze of fashion, I was like the poor duck * in the Grossen Garten,† and was fain to draw off to a corner. But I always liked such domestic scenes and full-flowing conversations the best. When I consider how I have trifled with my time, suffered painful vicissitudes of feeling, which for a time damaged both mind and body—when I consider all this, I reproach myself that I did not listen to the first impulse of my mind, and abandon Dresden long since. And yet I think of returning! Why should I come back to Dresden? The very inclination that draws me thither should furnish reasons for my staying away.

---

* "In a neglected part of the Grossen Garten was a lonely little lake, near a deserted palace. The only vestige left of the gayety once there, was a melancholy swan, pining alone, until a wild duck took pity on its forlorn estate, and kept it company. There, cheered by his gay little friend, they used to sport and play, until, in an evil hour, three more swans were brought to the place. When the little wild duck came, as usual, to seek his old companion, ungrateful as he was, he turned against him, and, puffing out with pride, joined his new acquaintances to drive off his former friend, who still hung about in corners, and tried to follow, with love stronger than life. But if he dared approach, they all united to attack him, till at last, with blows from their beaks, they killed him, faithful to the last." This is the duck Mr. Irving refers to.

† Mr. Irving was in this, as in some other modest fancies, quite mistaken; he was a great deal too much sought after to be suffered to remain in a corner. Besides that, when he was in spirits, and when a few of the friends he valued were with him, he was lively and brilliant even in general society; although, no doubt, a little jar against his feelings threw him back into reserve.

Well, well, I must leave off scribbling, for I am writing at random. Good-night.

[*Washington Irving to Mrs. Foster.*]

May 28, 1823.

I ought to say something of Herrnhuth, which is one of the great objects of curiosity in this part of the world. We passed three or four hours there, and went through the institutions, churchyard, &c. It is all very excellent in its way, but I would rather live in a wilderness than there. I have no relish for this *triste* simplicity, that consists in negatives. It seems the study of these worthy people to divest life and nature of everything that Heaven intended should embellish this short existence. I am not, it is true, the one to judge impartially in this instance, having been accustomed to dress everything too much with the illusions of the fancy; but surely we were not gifted with the delightful powers of the imagination thus to combat with them and quench them. Nature is simple herself, but then she is varied and beautiful in her simplicity. If the Herrnhuthers were right in their notions, the world would have been laid out in squares and angles and right lines, and everything would have been white, and black, and snuff-color, as they have been clipped by these merciless retrenchers of beauty and enjoyment. And then their dormitories—think of between one and two hundred of these simple gentlemen cooped up at night in one great chamber! What a concert of barrel-organs in this great resounding saloon! And then their plan of marriage! The very birds of the air choose their mates from preference and inclination—but this detestable system of *lot!* The sentiment of love may be, and is, in a great measure, a fostered growth of poetry and romance, and balderdashed with false sentiment; but, with all its vitiations, it is the beauty and the charm, the flavor and the fragrance of all intercourse between man and woman; it is the rosy cloud in the morning of life; and if it does too often resolve itself into the shower, yet, to my mind, it only makes our nature

more fruitful in what is excellent and amiable. But I forget—
you sent me to bless, and not to curse the Herrnhuthers, and I
will not curse them. May they be blessed here and hereafter!
but, in the mean time, preserve me from their heaven upon
earth. I know nothing more dismal, more quenching to heart
and mind, than this sterile, monotonous simplicity. The quaint
German song says :

> " Ich habe viel gelitten
> In dieser schöner Welt ; "

but give me the world, the " naughty world," with all its cares
and crosses, but with all its natural charms, its innocent pleasures, and the fantastic embellishments that poetry has thrown
about it, in preference to the regular, right-angled, whitewashed
world of a Herrnhuther——
And so, good-night!

HORSCHBERG, May 23.

We arrived here late last evening, after a very rugged journey across the country by roads only fit for country wagons.
We passed through most beautiful scenery, and the Riesengebirge were in sight, though mantled in clouds. In the afternoon, the wind and the weather changed, and we had an occasional shower. Still, the mountains looked grand in their dark
covering of mist, and, as the clouds detached themselves and
rolled off in great piles into the blue sky, they were finely lit
up by the sunshine.

On entering Horschberg, we found the public square and
some of the streets partially illuminated, and mine host of the
" White Horse," where we put up, ushered us into rooms bril-
liantly lit up by half a-dozen tallow candles in each window.
He informed us that it was the *Pfingster fest*, when the townsmen shot at the target, and that the procession would soon
come by, escorting home the King of the Year. The grand
pageant passed shortly after, with full band playing the jäger
chorus from the " Freischütz," and all the burgerschaft in mili-

tary array, with the king of sharpshooters in the midst of them : the tag, rag, and bobtail of the place shout in the rear. Mine host of the " White Horse," a jolly round fellow, had stuffed himself in an old hussar jacket on this occasion, informing us that, in his younger days, he had belonged to one of the volunteer corps. He kindled up like a veteran warrior at the military parade of his townsmen, and pointed out the uniform, of each company that passed by, telling us the name, character, achievements, and craft of every leader.

This is an overcast, rainy morning, and we are confined to the house. My companion is making an excellent sketch, from the window, of the public square which lies before our hotel. After an early dinner we start for Schmiedeberg. I ought to have mentioned, that Horschberg is the scene of my friend Rübezahl's gambols, which gave it an interest to me.

Schmiedeberg, afternoon.—We arrived here about four o'clock, after passing through some beautiful valley scenery. We are now at the foot of the Riesengebirge, and the weather promises to be fair to-morrow, so that we shall be able to explore some of the scenery. The mountains do not equal my expectations ; but that is the case with everything in this world of which we hear a good deal beforehand. The valley in which Schmiedeberg is situated is soft and verdant, and, when it is seen with the advantage of sunshine, must be lovely.

My fellow traveller is already in the field, landscape hunting ; but I am obliged to keep to the house. I have unluckily taken cold on the sudden change of weather yesterday, and am threatened with a pain in one side of my head. I hope I may escape any serious attack.

PRAGUE, Wednesday, May 28, 1823.

MY DEAR MRS. FOSTER :

We arrived here late last evening, and I received your letter early this morning. The one which you sent to Herrnhuth, I never received, as I never thought of inquiring for a letter there. Should it be returned to you, remember I claim it as my property. I sent you a long, rambling letter from Schmie-deberg, written at various times and places, and finished in a very feverish mood, and, I apprehend, in a very feverish style, for I am suffering from a violent pain in my face and throat. My indisposition continued for two or three days, accompanied by great pain and fever. I was really afraid, at one time, that I should be laid up among the mountains; but, luckily, I kept clear of the doctors, and, through the good nursing of a kind-hearted chambermaid, I was once more enabled to put my head out of doors. Should Livius have another attack of his com-plaint, I advise him to send forthwith to Schmiedeberg for my *Stube-mädchen*, who is worth all his doctors and apothecaries put together. As soon as I could bear travelling, we set off, and crossed a part of the Riesengebirge, to Lanschut, and so on to Koniggratz and to this place, where I am scrawling this letter, under a tree in a garden of some Bohemian prince, while my companion is at his usual work of sketching.

Your letter of Sunday only makes me regret that I did not get your other, which you say contained your journal up to Friday; but how in Heaven's name could you suppose it would find me at Herrnhuth? Did you suppose I could linger among those meagre-souled people? I am quite annoyed at the idea that the letter should lie in the office of that joyless commu-nity.

I write my letters at haphazard moments, which will ac-count for those written sometimes with pen, sometimes with pencil, as either is at hand. We had a tedious, irksome jour-ney after entering Bohemia. I was not perfectly recovered, and such roads, and such delays, and such impassive phlegm, and absolute stupidity! Yesterday we were in constant exer-tion to get on, from four o'clock in the morning till eleven at night, and only accomplished what in England would have been half a day's journey. Really it requires all the *menschliche tugend* and *Empfindsamkeit* of a German to bear with these people. Bohemia is a tedious, monotonous country; yet I am glad to have seen it at this favorable season—to it the most favorable.　Last November, when I passed through, it was all brown; the fields newly ploughed and sown, partly wrapped in fog, destitute of foliage or herbage, and altogether dreary.　At present it is covered with verdure, the wide fields waving with grain, like the green billows of a lake; the houses surrounded by orchards in full leaf and blossom; and, though the country is still monotonous from its want of hills, yet it has a look of fertility and abundance that is always gratifying.　When the summer is advanced, and the crops are gathered, it will again be arid and dismal.

I have not been able to enjoy the Riesengebirge so much as I expected.　My unlucky indisposition deterred me from venturing to these snowy summits, or lingering long among these uncertain valleys.　Even now I feel myself languid and almost good for nothing, after so severe an attack of pain and fever, and such a rough course of travelling as succeeded it.

Mr. Cockburn is delighted with Prague, and is determined to fill his sketch book from it.　He certainly possesses a most happy talent for taking sketches, either of landscape, street, or groups, quite masterly, I think.　Indeed, he is a young man of peculiar and strong traits of character and indications of talent, though encrusted, if I may use the word, with almost unconquerable diffidence, as it respects society.　I have been more and more pleased with him the more I have seen and known of him; though I fancy he is a man *you* would know much longer before he would give you an opportunity of knowing what he is worth, he is so diffident among ladies.　I always like to meet with these naturally gifted men, of natural good sense and natural good feeling; and I prize them the more from being very much *amused* by the polished, and passable, and universally current men of society.

I must finish this letter, and send it to the post; and yet, what a letter!　Still it may procure me a reply, and for that purpose I let it go.　I am, in truth, quite spiritless and listless. My mind has been in a restless state of strife and indecision, and has sunk into almost apathy, from its exhaustion.　I hope to hear from you again. I do not know when I shall leave this. I have fifty plans of what I ought to do, and only one of what I should really like to do. My ideas have been flying to all points of the compass; and what I shall do in the end, whether go north, south, east, or west, stay where I am, or tamely go back to Dresden, is what perplexes me. It is very ridiculous to talk in this way, and I feel that it is so; yet how can I write frankly, and not speak from what is uppermost in my mind? If I come back to Dresden, I ought to be ready to start at once with Lutzerode; and if I start with him, I only come back to take a farewell that would be a more uncomfortable one than I will choose to acknowledge. I am now away, and have, in a manner, cheated myself into a parting; for, when I bade you all adieu, I thought I should certainly see you all again in twelve days or a fortnight. Why, then, not keep away, now I am here?

I like Prague; there are bold, proud features about it. I like these old, war-worn warrior towns; and the vast, silent, deserted palaces of the Bohemian nobility that one meets with, frowning in heavy magnificence, give a poetical character to the place. Thank Heaven, I know nobody here, and, during the short stay I have to make, I am not obliged to go to evening parties, or to pay formal visits. I feel as if I could be for a long time without any desire to see another evening gathering. I want to be either quite alone, with my mind in full exercise, or quite in motion, with my imagination kept in excitement by the rapid change of objects. A partial pause at this moment throws me into a state of inquietude, and suffers a thousand fruitless and uncomfortable feelings to come thronging upon one. I must conclude this scrawl, for I see the time is nearly expired within which I can throw it into the post. I hope to hear from you to-morrow or next day, and will write to you again. It is a good-for-nothing scrawl, but it must go.

Give my remembrances to the young ladies and to the boys. I think of them all continually; and if they really think and care for me half as much, they do twice as much as I hope for. Yours ever, most truly,

WASHINGTON IRVING.

PRAGUE, June 1, 1823.

I thank you a thousand times, my dear Mrs. Foster, for your letter of Wednesday. I cannot tell you how interesting it was to me, placing the dear little circle of the Pavilion so completely before my eyes. I was so impatient to read it, that I would not wait till I got to my lodgings, which are distant from the post office ; yet I would not read it in the bustle and confusion of the street. I tried to get admitted to Wallenstein's garden. It was closed ; so I scrambled up the grassy ramparts, and read it in quiet, with old Prague and the Muldau at my feet. I have since read it over half a dozen times ; for, whenever I read it, it seems to bring me among you all again.

I am scribbling in poor Cockburn's room, who is quite ill with a fever and sore throat. It happens to be a bilious attack brought on by a cold. We have called in a physician, who appears to be one of the *langsams*. He has prescribed a variety of doses and applications ; but I trust nature will fight her own battle against both the disease and the doctor.

All Prague is in an uproar with a religious *fête*. The great street below my window is swarming with crowds of priests, burgerschaft in regimentals, the different trades, crafts, and mysteries, with banners and garlands of flowers, and peasant men and women, in every variety of color and costume, until the whole street looks like a great moving flower bed. Just opposite the hotel is a temporary altar erected, to which there is a grand procession, and the air resounds with music from a variety of bands attending the different corps, which, mingling with the ringing of bells and the chanting of priests and school children, makes the oddest confusion of sounds you can imagine.

A few days since we had a grand ceremony of the kind, in which all the artillery assisted ; and there was a procession on the fine bridge which bestrides the Wolga. It had a noble effect, and looked like a conquering army entering old Prague.

There is something very striking and interesting to me about this old city. It has more of a continental look than Dresden. The latter, in fact, seems to have been altered, and repaired, and pulled down, and built up, until it has become quite a decent, good-looking, commonplace town; like a disbanded soldier, tamed down into a sober, respectable citizen. But old Prague still keeps up its warrior look, and swaggers about with its rusty corslet and helm, though both sadly battered. There seems to me to be an air of style and fashion about the first people of Prague, and a good deal of beauty in the fashionable circle. This, perhaps, is owing to my contemplating it from a distance, and my imagination lending it tints occasionally. Both actors and audience, contemplated from the pit of a theatre, look better than when seen in the boxes and behind the scenes. I like to contemplate society in this way occasionally, and to dress it up, by the help of fancy, to my own taste. When I get in the midst of it, it is too apt to lose its charm, and then there is the trouble and *ennui* of being obliged to take an active part in the farce; but to be a mere spectator is amusing. I am glad, therefore, that I brought no letters to Prague. I shall leave it with a favorable idea of its society and manners, from knowing nothing accurate of either; and with a firm belief that every pretty woman I have seen is an angel; as I am apt to think every pretty woman, until I have found her out.

Monday, 2d.—I have passed the night on a sofa in Cockburn's room. He has had a very restless night, with a high fever, and complains of his throat this morning.

The physician has just been here, and pronounces Cockburn's malady to be the scarlet fever; and, indeed, it appears to be so from the color of his skin. Leeches are to be applied to his throat, which is much inflamed. You need not tell his mother the nature of his malady, as they might write home, and make his family uneasy. I have a better opinion of the doctor than I had at first. The people of the house are very attentive. There is an excellent Stubemädchen, who nurses him with a true woman's kindness; and for my own part, I shall do my best; so I hope, among us all, we shall set him up again before long. This has been an unlucky journey for us both, and both have paid the penalty for invading Rübezahl's dominions.

I wish you would have the kindness to send to Mr. Morier's, and inquire whether any letters have arrived for me, and, if so, send them here by return of post; also, if there are any letters for me or for Mr. Cockburn at the post office. Should little Montucci ever call or send his artist about my likeness, tell him not to wait for my return, but to do what he pleases, so that he does not caricature me. I am very indifferent about it, and am sorry I referred him to you; but at the time I thought of having impressions struck for America—it was a mere transient thought, and not worth the trouble.

You charge me with tormenting myself almost into a nervous fever, because I cannot write. Do you really think me so anxious about literary reputation, or so nervous about the fleeting popularity of a day? I have not been able to write, it is true, because I have been harassed in mind.

———

I was delighted to see the two boys once more before I set out. The dear little fellows! In some respects they put me so much in mind of their two sisters. You can't think how much I was gratified by the goodwill shown by the little rogues at parting. I like to be liked by children, for there is no stuff nor hollowness in their manifestations of attachment.

———

The trees are dressed out in their young leaves and gay blossoms, the birds are in full song; neither have yet entered upon the cares of the year. The former, as yet, have not begun to bear fruit, nor the latter to lay eggs.

I am very much pleased with my travelling companion. He is full of feeling for his profession, and for his favorite amusement of drawing. An old fortress, a field of battle, or a fine landscape, puts him into an ecstasy. Such is just the companion to have in travelling through these old campaigning countries, and among beautiful scenery. He had made a military plan of the battle of Bautzen, and, from a tower of the town, he explained the whole very clearly, as I thought, even to my inexperienced apprehension. This morning our road lay through the scenes of the severest fighting; and as Cockburn was fighting the battle over again with the enthusiasm of a young soldier, and placing the same vividly before my imagination, I could not but contrast it with the scene actually before my eyes. The quiet beauty and serenity of the landscape, the fields all in verdure, enamelled with pansies, the *heart's-ease* and *forget-me-not* springing, as if purposely sown, from the turf under which so many brave fellows lie buried, and thousands of larks hovering in the air, and filling it with melody. What demi-devils we are to mar such scenes of quiet and loveliness with our passions!

Shakspeare, I think it is, says, if mortals had the power of Jove, we should have continued thunder—*nothing but* thunder. As it is, how infinitely more mischief and misery does man inflict with his pigmy imitations, than the Deity with all his tremendous power of lightning and thunderbolt! What is the amount of all the evil inflicted by lightning, tempest, earthquake, and volcano, to the overwhelming and widespreading miseries of war!

I do not recollect whether you mentioned having been at the ruined convent where I am scribbling this; though, as you are all such explorers of glens and visitors of ruins, you can hardly have missed it. The whole way from Zittau hither is full of fine scenery. We came through it after five o'clock. I don't know when I have been more delighted, except, perhaps, at Tharand; but then I had such companions to help me enjoy it. The valley which leads up to the ruin puts me in mind of English scenery, as, indeed, many of the places in this part of Saxony do; the cottages are so surrounded by gardens and grassplats, so buried in trees, and the moss-covered roofs almost mingling and blending with the surrounding vegetation. The whole landscape is completely rustic. The orchards were all in bloom, and, as the day was very warm, the good people were seated in the shade of the trees, spinning, near the rills of water that trickled along the greensward.

But I must stop scribbling, for I see Cockburn is finishing his sketching. He has made a couple of very pretty sketches; one of a part of this noble old ruin, another, a peep from it, between the rocky defiles of the valley to the open plain that stretches beyond, sprinkled with cottages, with Zittau glittering in the centre.

Zittau.—We have had a lovely walk from Oëwien. We stopped so long on the way, for Cockburn to sketch a cottage scene and a group of peasant girls, that the moon was out in all her splendor before we reached Zittau.

I think your idea for the picture by Arnold is very good. Let Emily, for instance, have a book, and be looking up to Flora and pointing out a passage, while Flora is leaning on her and looking down at the book. I do not think Flora has a *down look*, but I think some of her *looks down* are very becoming; and if Emily, while sitting to Arnold, could but cast up her eyes, in the act of recollecting, and repeating some favorite passage of poetry, I think the painter could not well conceive anything better. Take care, however, that he does not infuse any German *Empfindsamkeit* and *gefühl* in the picture. Let it be as unaffected and natural as the beings it represents. Perhaps, when you think more on the subject, or they come to sit to the painter, some other or better attitude may suggest itself. I have merely given my idea with respect to the one you suggested.

Do not, I beg of you, give yourself any more trouble about

Montucci and the sketch. It is really, really of no importance to me, particularly as I do not intend to have it engraved for America. At first I did feel a little solicitous, and I wished it to supplant the likeness already engraved for my country, in which I am made to look like such a noodle, that, if I really thought I looked so, I would kick myself out of doors. But I am quite well satisfied with the sketch of the young, so let Montucci do as he pleases about it.

I can give you nothing in return for the interesting little pictures you draw in your letters of your family circle. Do let me have as many of them as you can; and yet they only (play the fool with me) make me wish myself back, and—well—well—well!

I wish to heaven I could get these wandering thoughts of mine to settle down on paper! I think, if I could get my mind fully employed upon some work, it would be a wonderful relief to me; at present I am all discomposed.

I must finish this letter, that I may be in time for the post. Mr. Cockburn desires me to thank you most heartily for your kindness in sending him the letters, and for your attention to his brothers.

Give my warmest remembrance to your little family circle.

Yours truly,

WASHINGTON IRVING.

P. S.—The continued illness of Cockburn puts the journey with Lutzerode out of the question. I never made any fixed engagement to go with him, and hope he is not calculating upon it. Have you heard whether he is or no? I can say nothing about my future movements, for, as yet, my mind is in confusion on the subject, and I do not like to confess all the wild ideas and impulses that flit across it.

PRAGUE, Saturday, June 13, 1823.

I have just got your letter of Tuesday, my dear Mrs. Foster. Your kindness really overpowers me. How stupid I was, not to have written earlier last week! and how intolerable are those tedious Germans with their post horses and post offices, that letters, when they are written, are so slow in coming to hand! Really I grow heartily weary of this *langsam* country. Your letter, which I have just received, I ought to have received yesterday morning; and I began to wonder at your silence, and to conjecture whether the measles had really got into the family.

I thank you a thousand and a thousand times for the kind, the very kind solicitude you express about me—you, who have so many dear, delightful things at home to occupy heart and soul, to trouble yourself about a wanderer like me! I am happy to be able to give you a good account both of my companion and myself. Mr. Cockburn is entirely free from fever; nothing ails him now but weakness, and he is daily gaining strength. He sits up the greater part of the day, in defiance of the doctor's advice, and finds both strength and spirits recruited by it, both of which had been in a very languid state while lying in bed.

As to myself, I believe I may consider myself as out of all danger of contagion; my health is as usual, and, now that my companion can sit up and amuse himself, I go out a good deal in the open air. There are really delightful walks in the vicinity of this place. I often wish for you all here, that I might show you some charming strolls. There are several islands in the Muldau that are laid out in walks; one that particularly delights me is called, I think, *der Grosser Venedig.* It is covered with trees, and has the most beautiful shady avenues and rambling footpaths, that wind among groves and thickets along the banks of the Muldau. I spend hours there in the morning, before the Germans come to poison the air with themselves and their tobacco pipes; as the pure air is too insipid for a German. Indeed, he knows as little what pure air is, as a drunkard does of pure water: they both must qualify the element to their palates I don't know a better punishment for German delinquents, than to deprive them of their pipes, and banish them to

Buenos Ayres—they'd die of the purity of the air. But enough of the Germans—how came I to talk of them?

I am delighted to hear such good accounts of Troppeneger. Those dear little boys!—I am glad they have got a worthy fellow to take care of them, who feels the value and importance of the trust confided to him. I like his schemes, and projects, and theories, and enterprises; they show zeal and interest in what he is about, and bespeak a simplicity of heart which, when it is combined with good mental qualities, is, I think, invaluable. I like a man of sense, who, now and then, in the fulness of his heart, does things to make one smile. He is worth a dozen of those coolheaded, wary fellows, who never do a foolish thing; they as seldom do a kind one.

I must finish this letter to get it to the post office (which is nearly a mile off), before a gathering storm of rain and thunder cuts off all communication. Will you tell Emily and Flora that their kind wishes are more gratifying to me than I can express? Good heavens! what would I give to be with you all this evening, at the strawberry supper you speak of!

Mr. Cockburn desires me to express to you his very great sense of your kindness to his mother and to himself.

God bless you all!

Yours truly,

WASHINGTON IRVING.

Will you remember me kindly to the Rumignys, and tell them I thank them heartily for their inquiries?

BORDEAUX, Jan. 9, 1826.

MY DEAR MRS. FOSTER:

Your letter, without a date, has been forwarded to me from Paris, and stares me in the face with silent reproach of my long procrastination. I have, as usual, intended and reintended to write to you, but the mood and spirit have failed me, and I have kept on deferring from day to day, without reflecting that days and days imperceptibly make up months. I have indeed been full of anxiety and uneasiness. I came down into this part of France with my brother, last summer, to pass the vintage at the chateau of a friend, in the midst of the vineyards of Medoc. While there, I first heard of the storm that was breaking upon the busy world. I of course felt uneasy for my friends and connections who were subject to its injuries, when, shortly after, I received the distressing account of the failure of my excellent friend Mr. Williams. For a time I was completely confounded by this intelligence. Independent of the grief I felt for the ruin of a man who had always exerted such a paternal kindness toward his countrymen, and particularly toward myself, I did not know how far the interests of my immediate connections and of myself might be involved in his misfortunes. In fact, I remained here for some time in doubt whether we were not all ruined.

To divert my mind from brooding over mere surmises and apprehensions during the long interval of uncertainty that must necessarily take place, I determined to apply myself closely to a course of study and of literary occupations. I had an excellent library of a friend at command; so, pitching my tent for the winter, I went doggedly to work to drive my mind, in spite of itself, into a channel of thought, and to shut out resolutely the cares that were thronging upon me. In a little while I succeeded; and when I look back on all that I have read, and noted, and extracted during the time, and the original manuscripts I have written, I am surprised at myself. A great deal of my reading has been in Italian literature, of which I had a very good collection at hand. I have not been writing with any view to speedy publication, but rather as an exercise for my mind, which likes to travel upon paper. The good effects of this literary occupation have been, not merely to relieve my mind from the immediate anxiety which pressed upon it, but also to lift it out of a kind of slough of apathy and almost melancholy into which it had sunk, and which, at times, made life a burden to me. While thus employed, the aspect of affairs has gradually improved. I have had time to receive letters from my friends, which allay the apprehensions I had entertained on their account, and give me reason to expect that, after the confusion of the moneyed world has subsided, everything will go on again smoothly and prosperously. And thus I have given you another chapter of my humdrum history.

I shall remain here until spring. I can live quietly here, being but little disturbed by visits or invitations, and having my time to myself for reading, and writing, and thinking; whereas, in Paris, I was continually subject to interruptions and distractions. I envy you the perfect quiet of the country : there is nothing I should more delight in, had I a library at hand, and a family circle to resort to when tired of all solitude. I enjoyed this while down in Medoc, where I could be all day by myself, if I pleased, in one wing of a great French chateau, or galloping at random about those vast heaths called *The Landes*, which had something grand in their space and silence. After having lived for some time in a capital where one's time and mind are cut up into mere bits, there is something delightful in the long tracts of quiet and thought which one enjoys in the country. Your minds must by this time be crowded even to the top shelves, being such indefatigable readers. I should like to have seen you all when the Count Einsiedler made his appearance among you. He must have felt astonished at finding himself in such a little world.

By the by, I met Prince Frederick of Dresden in Paris last spring, who laid aside all court stateliness, and was extremely cordial and sociable. He asked after you all very kindly. I have had two or three messages from the old Queen, through different channels, during my stay in Paris.

Give my affectionate remembrances to your family.

Farewell! and believe me, under all changes of time, place, and fortune, Very truly your friend,

WASHINGTON IRVING.

The following poem Mr. Irving wrote in my scrap book when he was in London in 1832. He declared it was impossible for him to be less in a writing mood :

ECHO AND SILENCE.

In eddying course when leaves began to fly,
And Autumn in her lap the stores to strew,
As 'mid wild scenes I chanced the Muse to woo
Through glens untrod, and woods that frown'd on high,
Two sleeping nymphs with wonder mute I spy:
And lo! she's gone—in robe of dark-green hue:
'Twas Echo, from her sister Silence flew,
For quick the hunter's horn resounded to the sky.

In shade affrighted Silence melts away;
Not so her sister. Hark! For onward still
With far-heard step she takes her listening way,
Bounding from rock to rock, and hill to hill:
Ah! mark the merry maid in mockful play,
With thousand mimic tones, the laughing forests fill.

[The following letter of Mr. Irving to Mrs. Flora Dawson, and the few lines which preface it, as if from the editor, were also inserted, without my knowledge, in the English edition of my third volume, where they will be found in Chapter XXI, at page 314, corresponding to page 382 of the American.]

ON the 5th of February, he wrote the following letter, recalling some of the incidents of his life since they met, and describing his mode of life at Sunnyside, to Mrs. Dawson (Flora Foster):*

38 HARLEY STREET, LONDON, Feb. 5, 1846.
MY DEAR MRS. DAWSON:

Your letter (which I did not receive until after my return to town) has indeed called up delightful recollections of past times, of "moving accidents by flood and field," and of those valued friends who shared them with me. I would at once accept your kind invitation, and come to Flitwick to talk over

* See Vol. II.

old times, but at present I am not my own master. I have come unexpectedly to England to transact some business with the American Minister at this Court; and as soon as I can despatch it—which I trust will be in the course of three or four days—I have to hasten back to the Continent. I expect, however, to visit England again in the course of the spring or summer, when I will be more at leisure, and will then avail myself of your invitation. I have long been desirous of hav-ing intelligence of you all. I received a letter, a few years since, from one of your brothers resident in Jamaica, intro-ducing a friend, and, in my reply, made inquiries about the family. As he never answered my letter, I fear he did not receive it. It is a hazardous thing to make inquiries about friends after such a lapse of years, but I wish you would give me such particulars of family news as would be pleasant to give and to receive.

As to myself, on my return to America I built me a pretty little cottage on the banks of the Hudson, in a beautiful coun-try, and not far from my old haunts of Sleepy Hollow. Here I passed several years most happily; my cottage well stocked with nieces, and enlivened by visits from friends and connec-tions, having generally what is called in Scotland a houseful—that is to say, a circle more than it will hold. This state of things was too happy to last. I was unexpectedly called from it, by being appointed Minister to Madrid. It was a hard struggle for me to part from my cottage and my nieces, but I put all under charge of my brother, and promised to return at the end of three years. I have overstayed my time; nearly four years have elapsed. I understand my cottage is nearly buried among the trees I set out, and overrun with roses and honeysuckles and ivy from Melrose Abbey; and my nieces implore me to come back and save them from being buried alive in foliage. I have accordingly sent in my resignation to Government, and am now going back to Madrid to await the arrival of my successor. When relieved from the duties and restraints of office, I shall make farewell visits to my friends in

England and elsewhere; then ship myself for America, and hasten back to my cottage, where everything is ready for my reception, and where I have but to walk in, hang up my hat, kiss my nieces, and take my seat in my elbow chair for the remainder of my life.

I have thus, my dear Mrs. Dawson, given you my own history, as they do in story books, in the expectation that you will give me your own in return. In the mean time, believe me, with the kindest and warmest sentiments of regard,

Most truly, your friend,

WASHINGTON IRVING.

(B.)—PROVISIONS OF THE WILL.

THE following is an abstract of Mr. Irving's Will, which was drawn up by himself. It bears date on the 3d day of December, 1858, not quite a year before his death. He declares his general intention to be, to dispose of all his estate so that it may be, as far as possible, kept together as a maintenance for his brother Ebenezer and his daughters, who have been accustomed to reside with him, to enable them to live with the same degree of comfort and in the same respectable style they have been accustomed to under his roof.

He gives to his nephew, Pierre Munro Irving, the copyright of his Life of Washington, with the stereotype and electrotype plates which have been executed for the same, and the plates engraved for its illustration, together with the printed copies of the work which may have been stricken off, leaving him to do with the copyright, types, &c., what he may think proper for his pecuniary benefit. He bequeaths to him, also, all his letters and unpublished manuscripts.

All the rest of his personal estate he gives to his brother Ebenezer for his life; and, on his death, to his daughters, then surviving him and unmarried. The Will then proceeds:

Second, I give and devise my land and dwelling house in Westchester County, which I have called Sunnyside, to my brother, Ebenezer Irving, for his life. On his death, I give the same in fee to his daughters or daughter surviving him, and unmarried; trusting they will endeavor, as I have endeavored, to make this homestead a rallying point, where the various branches of the family connection may always be sure of a cordial welcome.

I trust, also, they will never sell nor devise this particular property out of the family—though circumstances may render it expedient or necessary for them to rent it out or lease it for a term; but it is my wish that the last survivor of those to whom I thus bequeath my estate will, in turn, bequeath it entire to some meritorious member of the family bearing the family name, so that Sunnyside may continue to be, as long as possible, an *Irving homestead.*

I give all the residue of my estate, real and personal, to accompany the devise of Sunnyside to the same persons, for the like interests, and subject to the like contingencies and power.

Third, I authorize my executors to make sale of, or otherwise convert into money or productive funds, all other lands and tenements I may own, wheresoever situated.

Last, I appoint my brother, Ebenezer Irving, and my nephew, Pierre M. Irving, executors of this my will. I revoke all other and former wills.

(C.)—LITERARY STATISTICS.

Sums realized by Mr. Irving for his Copyrights in England.

Sketch Book,	Murray, Publisher,	£467 10s.
Bracebridge Hall,	"	1,050 00
Tales of a Traveller,	"	1,575 00
Life of Columbus,	"	3,150 00
Companions of Columbus,	"	525 00
Conquest of Granada,	"	2,100 00
Tour on the Prairies,	"	400 00
Abbotsford and Newstead,	"	400 00
Legends of Spain,	"	100 00
Alhambra,	Bentley, Publisher,	1,050 00
Astoria,	"	500 00
Bonneville's Adventures,	"	900 00
	Total,	£12,217 10s.

Sums realized in the United States, where there was no absolute sale of the Copyright, as in England.

Life of Columbus, 1st edition, ...	$3,000 00
" " and Abridgment, 2d edition,	6,000 00
Conquest of Granada (for five years), . .	4,750 00
Companions of Columbus (3,000 copies), . .	1,500 00
Alhambra, ...	3,000 00
Tour on the Prairies, ...	2,400 00
Abbotsford and Newstead, ...	2,100 00
Legends of the Conquest of Spain, . . .	1,500 00
Astoria, ...	4,000 00
Bonneville's Adventures, ...	3,000 00
Lease of Copyright, from 1828 to 1835, of Knickerbocker's New York, Sketch Book, Bracebridge Hall, and Tales of a Traveller,	4,200 00

Lease of Copyright of the same works, and Life
of Columbus, Conquest of Granada, Companions of Columbus, and Alhambra, from 1835
to 1842, ... $8,050 00
Estimated receipts, prior to 1828, on History of
New York, Sketch Book, Bracebridge Hall,
and Tales of a Traveller, . . . 19,500 00

Making a total on the American Copyrights of the
above enumerated works, prior to 1843, of $63,000 00

Hiatus from 1842 to 1848, in which the author's
writings were out of print.
In the latter year, Mr. George P. Putnam became
his Publisher.

Total of receipts from Mr. Putnam, from July,
1848, to Mr. Irving's decease, November 28,
1859, (besides stereotype and steel plates,
amounting to about $17,000.) $88,143 08
Payments made for Irving's Works by Mr. Putnam, from the author's decease to September
30, 1863, showing the continued demand, . 34,237 03

$122,380 11

Whole amount realized on his Works during his
life, ... $205,383 34
Since his death to September 30, 1863, . 34,237 03

$239,620 37

ANALYTICAL INDEX

TO THE

LIFE AND LETTERS OF WASHINGTON IRVING.